The

Affirmative Action Debate

Edited by Steven M. Cahn

Second
Edition

Routledge   New York and London

Published in 2002 by
Routledge
29 West 35th Street
New York, NY 10001

Published in Great Britain by
Routledge
11 New Fetter Lane
London EC4P 4EE

10 9 8 7 6 5 4 3 2 1

Cataloging-in-Publication Data is available from the Library of Congress.

ISBN 0-415-93866-X (hb)
ISBN 0-415-93867-8 (pb)

To the memory of
Geoffrey Marshall (1938–2000)

Contents

Contents

Acknowledgments

I am grateful to Damon Zucca, my editor at Routledge, for urging me to prepare this second edition and offering wise counsel regarding the new materials it incorporates.

The impetus for the book came from a conversation with Adrian Driscoll, and I remain grateful for his initial encouragement. I also appreciate the help I received originally from Daniel Kaufman, now assistant professor of philosophy at Southwest Missouri State University. Maureen Eckert, my research assistant at the Graduate Center of the City University of New York, generously helped prepare the manuscript for publication.

Minor alterations in some selections have been made for the sake of uniformity and accessibility.

Introduction

Steven M. Cahn

In March 1961, less than two months after assuming office, President John F. Kennedy issued Executive Order 10925, which established the President's Committee on Equal Employment Opportunity. Its mission was to end discrimination in employment by the government and its contractors. The order required every federal contract to include the pledge that "The Contractor will not discriminate against any employe[e] or applicant for employment because of race, creed, color, or national origin. The Contractor will take affirmative action, to ensure that applicants are employed, and that employe[e]s are treated during employment, without regard to their race, creed, color, or national origin."

Here, for the first time in the context of civil rights, the government called for "affirmative action." The term meant taking appropriate steps to eradicate the then widespread practices of racial, religious, and ethnic discrimination. The goal, as the president stated, was "equal opportunity in employment."

In other words, procedural affirmative action, as I shall call it, was instituted to ensure that applicants for jobs would be judged without any consideration of their race, religion, or national origin. These criteria were declared irrelevant. Taking them into account was forbidden.

The Civil Rights Act of 1964 restated and broadened the application of this principle. Title VI declared that "No person in the United States shall, on the ground of race, color or national origin, be excluded from participation in, be denied the benefits of, or be subjected to discrimination under any program or activity receiving Federal financial assistance."

But before one year had passed, President Lyndon B. Johnson argued that fairness required more than a commitment to such procedural affirmative action. In his 1965 commencement address at Howard University, he said:

> You do not take a person who for years has been hobbled by chains and liberate him, bring him up to the starting line of a race and then say, "You're free to compete with all the others," and still justly believe that you have been completely fair.
>
> Thus it is not enough just to open the gates of opportunity. All our citizens must have the ability to walk through those gates. . . .
>
> We seek not . . . just equality as a right and a theory but equality as a fact and equality as a result.

And so several months later President Johnson issued Executive Order 11246, which stated, "It is the policy of the Government of the United States to provide equal opportunity in Federal employment for all qualified persons, to prohibit discrimination in employment because of race, creed, color or national origin, and to promote the full realization of equal employment opportunity through a positive, continuing program in each department and agency." Two years later the order was amended to prohibit discrimination on the basis of sex.

While the aim of President Johnson's order was stated in language similar to that of President Kennedy's, President Johnson's abolished the Committee on Equal Employment Opportunity, transferred its responsibilities to the secretary of labor, and authorized the secretary to "adopt such rules and regulations and issue such orders as he deems necessary and appropriate to achieve the purposes thereof."

Acting on the basis of this mandate, the Department of Labor issued in December 1971, during the administration of President Richard M. Nixon, Revised Order No. 4, requiring all contractors to develop "an acceptable affirmative action program," including "an analysis of areas within which the contractor is deficient in the utilization of minority groups and women, and further, goals and timetables to which the contractor's good faith efforts must be directed to correct the deficiencies." Contractors were instructed to take the term "minority groups" to refer to "Negroes, American Indians, Orientals, and Spanish Surnamed Americans." The concept of "underutilization" meant "having fewer minorities or women in a particular job classification than would reasonably be expected by their availability." "Goals" were not to be "rigid and inflexible quotas" but "targets reasonably attainable by means of applying every good faith effort to make all aspects of the entire affirmative action program work."

Such *preferential* affirmative action, as I shall call it, requires that attention be paid to the same criteria of race, sex, and ethnicity that procedural affirmative action deems irrelevant. Is such use of these criteria morally justifiable?

That is the key question in a debate that has continued for more than three decades. This collection of scholarly articles presents the major lines of argument within the controversy.

The authors agree that injustices have occurred, that their victims deserve recompense, and that strenuous efforts should be made to try to prevent any further wrongdoing while striving to achieve a more enlightened society. The disagreements arise in specifying who has suffered injustice, what is due them, and which steps should be taken to promote equity and amity.

In seeking to disentangle the complications involved, note that preferential affirmative action has been defended on three grounds: (1) to offset past discrimination; (2) to counteract present unfairness; and (3) to achieve future equality. The first is often referred to as "compensation," the second "a level playing field," and the third "diversity." Each of these considerations could be defended independently of the others. Compensation for past wrongs might be owed, even though at present the playing field is level and future diversity is not sought. Or the playing field at present might not be level, even though compensation for past wrongs is not owed and future diversity is not sought. Or future diversity might be sought, although compensation for past wrongs is not owed and at present the playing field is level.

Of course, all three factors might be relevant, but each requires a different justification and may call for a different remedy. For example, past wrongs would be offset when suitable compensation had been made; present wrongs would be corrected when the playing field became level; future equality might require continuing attention to ensure that appropriate diversity, once achieved, is never lost.

The concept of preference itself is ambiguous. Does affirmative action imply only (1) showing preference among equally qualified candidates (the "tiebreaking" model), or (2) preferring a strong candidate to an even stronger one (the "plus factor" model), or (3) preferring a merely qualified candidate to a strongly qualified candidate (the "trumping" model), or (4) canceling a search unless a qualified candidate of the preferred sort is available (the "quota" model)? Defending any of these policies does not imply support for a higher-numbered one. And lack of agreement regarding which policy is at issue leads to confusion.

A further distinction should be drawn between affirmative action in school admissions and affirmative action in employment. Preferences for members of certain groups might be defensible in awarding educational opportunities, even if those preferences were not appropriate in filling demanding positions. After all, colleges traditionally take account of an applicant's athletic skills or home state; employers normally do not consider such factors.

Preferential affirmative action has been a divisive issue in the United States. And with recent attempts by referendum, legislation, and judicial action to change current policies, emotions have intensified. What is most needed is not increased passion but greater attention to recognizing and analyzing the subject's complexities. That is the aim of this volume.

In his classic work *On Liberty,* John Stuart Mill wrote, "He who knows only his own side of the case, knows little of that." Readers may not change their minds after studying the material contained here. They will, however, became more aware of challenging considerations that have been offered by opposing advocates. And that awareness is a crucial step toward deepened understanding.

Individuals, Groups, and Discrimination

Discrimination and Morally Relevant Characteristics

James W. Nickel

Suppose that a characteristic which should be morally irrelevant (e.g., race, creed, or sex) has been treated as if it were morally relevant over a period of years, and that injustices have resulted from this. When such a mistake has been recognized and condemned, when the morally irrevelant characteristic has been seen to be irrelevant, can this characteristic *then* properly be used as a relevant consideration in the distribution of reparations to those who have suffered injustices? If we answer this question in the affirmative, we will have the strange consequence that a morally irrelevant characteristic can become morally relevant if its use results in injustices.

The context in which this difficulty is likely to arise is one in which a group has been discriminated against on the basis of morally irrelevant properties, but in which this discrimination has been recognized and at least partly come to an end; and the question at hand concerns how the members of this group should now be treated. Should they now be treated like everyone else, ignoring their history, or should they be given special advantages because of past discrimination and injustices? There are a variety of considerations which are pertinent in answering this question, and I will deal with only one of these, the "reverse discrimination argument." This argument claims that to extend special considerations to a formerly oppressed group will be to persist in the mistake of treating a morally irrelevant characteristic as if it were relevant. For if we take a morally irrelevant characteristic (namely the characteristic which was the basis for the

Reprinted from *Analysis* 32 (1972) by permission of the author.

original discrimination) and use it as the basis for granting special considerations or reparations, we will be treating the morally irrelevant as if it were relevant and still engaging in discrimination, albeit reverse discrimination. And hence, it is argued, the only proper stance toward groups who have suffered discrimination is one of strict impartiality.

To state the argument in a slightly different way, one might say that if a group was discriminated against on the basis of a morally irrelevant characteristic of theirs, then to award extra benefits now to the members of this group because they have this characteristic is simply to continue to treat a morally irrelevant characteristic as if it were relevant. Instead of the original discrimination *against* these people, we now have discrimination *for* them, but in either case we have discrimination since it treats the irrelevant as relevant. Hence, to avoid discrimination we must now completely ignore this characteristic and extend no special considerations whatsoever.

The objection which I want to make to this argument pertains to its assumption that the characteristic which was the basis for the original discrimination is the same as the one which is used as the basis for extending extra considerations now. I want to suggest that this is only apparently so. For if compensation in the form of extra opportunities is extended to a black man on the basis of past discrimination[1] against blacks, the basis for this compensation is not that he is a black man, but that he was previously subject to unfair treatment because he was black. The former characteristic was and is morally irrelevant, but the latter characteristic is very relevant if it is assumed that it is desirable or obligatory to make compensation for past injustices. Hence, to extend special considerations to those who have suffered from discrimination need not involve continuing to treat a morally irrelevant characteristic as if it were relevant. In such a case the characteristic which was the basis for the original discrimination (e.g., being a black person) will be different from the characteristic which is the basis for the distribution of special considerations (e.g., being a person who was discriminated against because he was black).

My conclusion is that this version of the "reverse discrimination argument" has a false premise, since it assumes that the characteristic which was the basis for the original discrimination is the same as that which is the basis for the granting of special considerations. And since the argument has a false premise, it does not succeed in showing that to avoid reverse discrimination we must extend no special considerations whatsoever.

Note

1. I do not mean to imply that we are in this situation, where discrimination against blacks is a thing of the past. We are not.

Inverse Discrimination

J. L. Cowan

The justice or injustice of "inverse discrimination" is a question of pressing social importance. On the one hand it is argued that when a morally irrelevant characteristic such as race, creed, or sex has been treated as morally relevant and injustices have resulted, it is then proper to treat that characteristic as morally relevant in order to make reparations. On the other hand it is argued that if the characteristic in question is morally irrelevant, its use even in this manner would still constitute discrimination, discrimination now in favor of those possessing the characteristic and against those not, but unjust discrimination still.

Public discussion of this issue all too rarely goes far beyond the level of the arguments as given. Yet the logic of these arguments is murky, to say the least. It is therefore to be hoped that the analytical skills supposedly characteristic of philosophers might here play a valuable social role, and we are indebted to J. W. Nickel for beginning such a clarification. I should like here to try to continue it.

Nickel maintains that the argument against inverse discrimination given above goes wide of the mark since the characteristic which is now operative is not actually the original morally irrelevant one. "For if compensation in the form of extra opportunities is extended to a black man on the basis of past discrimination against blacks, the basis for this compensation is not that he is a black man, but that he was previously subject to unfair treatment because he was black. . . . In such a case the characteristic which was the basis for the original discrimination (e.g., being a black person) will be different from the characteristic which is the basis for the distribution of special considerations

Reprinted from *Analysis* 32 (1972) by permission of the author.

(e.g., being a person who was discriminated against because he was black)" (chap. 1, p. 4).

The problem is that Nickel does not make it entirely clear just what he is about here. He may simply be pointing out that if a person has suffered injustice through morally unjustified discrimination, then reparation to that person will be appropriate. But surely it was not against this relatively uncontroversial point that the original argument was directed. And Nickel's formulation leaves open the possibility that he is actually trying to support the far more questionable claim which was the original target of that argument.

"Being discriminated against because he was black" is clearly a complex predicate. What I would like to suggest is that the portion of it which was morally irrelevant in independence remains so within the complex and is thus mere excess baggage. The reason why he was discriminated against is not what should now ground reparation, but rather simply the fact that, and the extent to which, he was unjustly discriminated against for whatever reason. Thus, assuming that the discrimination is otherwise the same, we would presumably not wish to say that Jones, who has been discriminated against as a black, should now be favored over Smith, who has been equally discriminated against as a woman or a Jew or whatever. We are therefore left without a moral relevance for blackness, and thus without a moral basis for inverse discrimination based on blackness as opposed to discriminatory injustice per se.

Nickel's reasoning thus does not really, as it might be taken to do, provide any support at all for the kind of self-contradictory thinking the original argument was surely intended to rebut. This is the reasoning that since blacks, to retain this example, have suffered unjust discrimination we should now give them special treatment to make it up to them. Once again there is no problem insofar as this simply means that where individual blacks have suffered injustice it should, as with anyone else, insofar as possible be made up to those individuals who have so suffered. The fallacy arises when rather than individuals it is the group which is intended, and individuals are regarded merely as members of that group rather than in their individuality. This creates a contradiction, since the original premise of the moral irrelevance of blackness on the basis of which the original attribution of unjust discrimination rests implies that there is and can be no morally relevant group which could have suffered or to which retribution could now be made. Thus those who would argue that since "we" brutally kidnapped "the" blacks out of Africa and subjected "them" to the abominations of slavery, or that since "we" have exploited and degraded "women" since Eve, "we" therefore now owe retribution to our neighbor who happens to be black or a woman, are involved in inextricable self-contradiction. Except to the extent that he or she as an individual has unjustly suffered or will unjustly suffer from this history while we as individuals have unjustly profited or will unjustly profit, there can be no such obligation.

Nickel's original formulation is thus ambiguous. "The context in which this difficulty is likely to arise is one in which a group has been discriminated against on the basis of morally irrelevant properties, but in which this discrimination has been recognized and at least partly come to an end; and the question at hand concerns how the members of this group should now be treated. Should they now be treated like everyone else, ignoring their history, or should they be given special advantages because of past discrimination and injustices?" (chap. 1, p. 3) Once the question is disambiguated the answer is clear. They should most certainly be treated like everyone else. But this does not mean "their" individual histories should be ignored. As with anyone else, injustices done "them" as individuals should be prevented or rectified insofar as possible. But past or future discrimination and injustice done "them" as a group and special advantages to them as a group are both out of the question, since in the moral context there is no such group.

Reparations to Wronged Groups

Michael D. Bayles

If a group of people (blacks, women) has been wronged by its members' being discriminated against on the basis of a morally irrelevant characteristic, is it morally permissible to use that characteristic as a basis for providing special considerations or benefits as reparations? It is frequently argued that since the characteristic is morally irrelevant, its use as a basis for providing reparations must also constitute wrongful discrimination.

James W. Nickel contends that such reparations are not wrong because they are not based on the morally irrelevant characteristic. Being black, for example, is a morally irrelevant characteristic for discriminating against or for a person. However, Nickel claims that if a black man receives special consideration as reparation for past discrimination the basis is not the morally irrelevant characteristic of his being black. Instead, it is the morally relevant one of his having been "subject to unfair treatment because he was black" (chap. 1, p. 4).

J. L. Cowan criticizes Nickel for even including the morally irrelevant characteristic as part of the complex predicate on the basis of which reparations are given. It is not a man's having been subject to unfair treatment because he was black which is the basis of reparation, Cowan contends, "but rather simply the fact that, and the extent to which, he was unjustly discriminated against for whatever reason" (chap. 2, p. 6). We would not, Cowan points out, wish to favor a person who has been discriminated against for being black over another who has been discriminated against for being Jewish. He further claims that the problem of using a morally irrelevant characteristic as the basis for reparation

Reprinted from *Analysis* 33 (1973) by permission of Marjorie Bayles.

arises when rather than individuals it is the group which is intended, and individuals are regarded merely as members of that group rather than in their individuality. This creates a contradiction, since the original premise of the moral irrelevance of blackness on the basis of which the original attribution of unjust discrimination rests implies that there is and can be no morally relevant group which could have suffered or to which retribution could now be made. (chap. 2, p. 6)

The solution of the problem proposed by Nickel and Cowan, that the reparation is based on a characteristic other than the morally irrelevant one, is spurious. By parallel reasoning it can be argued that the original discrimination was not on the basis of a morally irrelevant characteristic. Racists do not discriminate against blacks simply because they are black. Rather, they claim that blacks as a class are inferior in certain relevant respects, e.g., they lack certain abilities and virtues such as industriousness, reliability, and cleanliness. Thus, reasoning similarly to Nickel and Cowan, racists could contend that they do not discriminate on the basis of a morally irrelevant characteristic, but the morally relevant ones which are thought to be associated with being black. Further, a reformed racist could contend that he was mistaken to believe blacks lacked such abilities and virtues. But, since it was a mistaken belief which was the basis of his discrimination, he was not responsible and owes no reparations. In short, if being black is not the basis for reparations, it was not the basis for the original discrimination.

However, there need be no contradiction involved in claiming that being black is both morally irrelevant for discriminating against people and morally relevant in discriminating in favor of people to provide reparations. One may simply hold that there is no justifiable moral rule which, when correctly applied, supports discriminating against blacks, but there is one which supports discriminating in favor of them. One may hold that people have an obligation to give reparations to groups they have wronged. By using the characteristic of being black as an identifying characteristic to discriminate against people, a person has wronged the group, blacks. He thus has an obligation to make reparations to the group. Since the obligation is to the group, no specific individual has a right to reparation. However, since the group is not an organized one like a state, church, or corporation, the only way to provide reparations to the group is to provide them to members of the group.

Being black can, thus, become morally relevant in distinguishing between those individuals who are members of the group to whom reparations are owed and those who are not. But being black is only derivatively morally relevant. It is not mentioned as a morally relevant characteristic in the rule requiring one to provide reparations to groups one has wronged. Instead, it becomes relevant by being the identifying characteristic of the group wronged. The way in which it is an identifying characteristic here differs from the way in which it is an identifying characteristic for the racist. Being black is an identifying characteristic for the racist only because he thinks it is contingently connected with other characteristics. But being black is not contingently connected with the group one has wronged. Rather, it is logically connected as the defining characteristic of members of the group.

Cowan has failed to distinguish the relevance of being black as applied to groups and individuals. One may hold that one owes reparations to the group, blacks, not because the group is the group of blacks, but because the group has been wronged. But with respect to individuals, one may, as reparation, discriminate in their favor on the basis of their being black. One discriminates in favor of individuals because they are black, but one owes reparations to the group, blacks, because it has been wronged. Nor does such a position commit one to favoring individual blacks over individuals who belong to another wronged group, e.g., women. One has a morally relevant reason to favor members of each group on the basis of their being black or female, respectively. It does not follow that either should be preferred over the other.

Nothing has been said to support accepting any moral rules or principles applying to groups. (As a matter of fact, most people appear to accept one such rule, namely, that genocide is wrong.) Nor has anything been said to support accepting the rule that one has an obligation to provide reparations to groups one has wronged. These remarks have only indicated how being black can derivatively be a morally relevant characteristic for discriminating in favor of individuals if such a rule is accepted.

Reverse Discrimination and Compensatory Justice

Paul W. Taylor

Two articles have recently appeared in *Analysis* concerning the apparent contradiction between (1) at time t_1 members of group G have been discriminated against on the basis of a *morally irrelevant* characteristic C and (2) At time t_2 characteristic C is a *morally relevant* ground for making reparation to members of group G.

In the first article ("Discrimination and Morally Relevant Characteristics" [chapter 1 in this volume]), J. W. Nickel presents what he calls the "reverse discrimination argument" and offers a counterargument to it. The "reverse discrimination argument" is that, if we grant as a matter of compensatory justice special advantages or benefits to persons who have been unjustly treated on the basis of a morally irrelevant characteristic (such as being a woman, being black, being a Jew, etc.), we are in effect using a morally irrelevant characteristic as if it were morally relevant and thus still engaging in an unjust treatment of persons. Hence if we are to be just we must avoid reverse discrimination. Nickel's counterargument is that the special treatment given to persons having characteristic C at time t_2 is not grounded on the (morally irrelevant) characteristic C, but on the (morally relevant) characteristic C', namely, being a person who has been discriminated against because he was C.

In an article by J. L. Cowan ("Inverse Discrimination" [chapter 2]), Nickel is criticized for failing to realize that characteristic C' is actually a complex predicate made up of a conjunction of two characteristics—C'', namely, having been discriminated against (for whatever reason), and the characteristic C itself.

Reprinted from *Analysis* 33 (1973) by permission of the author.

Cowan's point is that C'' is a morally relevant characteristic in matters of compensatory justice but that C remains morally irrelevant. He holds that reverse discrimination is wrong, since it involves giving people favorable treatment *because they are* C and hence using a morally irrelevant characteristic as a justifying ground for special treatment. Nevertheless, he concludes, special treatment should be extended to any *individual* who has been discriminated against (for whatever reason) in the past, that is, anyone who has characteristic C''. For it is a requirement of compensatory justice that reparation be made to those who have been dealt with unjustly (for whatever reason).

In this article I want to defend three views, all of which are inconsistent with the claims made by Nickel and Cowan. (I) With respect to the principle of compensatory justice, characteristic C has been *made* a morally relevant characteristic by those who engaged in a social practice which discriminated against persons because they were C. (II) Since C is a morally relevant characteristic at time t_2 with respect to the principle of compensatory justice, that principle requires reverse discrimination. (III) The reverse discrimination in question is aimed at correcting an injustice perpetrated at time t_1 by a social practice of discriminating against C-persons because they were C. Given this aim, the reverse discrimination must be directed toward the class of C-persons as such. Furthermore, the obligation to compensate for the past injustice does not fall upon any particular individual but upon the society as a whole. The society is obligated to establish a social practice of reverse discrimination in favor of C-persons. (It is assumed, of course, that this practice will be consistent with all other principles of justice that may apply to the action types which are involved in carrying it out.) I offer the following considerations in support of these views.

I

Suppose there is a socially established practice at time t_1 of unjustly treating any person who has characteristic C, such treatment being either permitted or required on the ground that the person is C. For the purposes of this account I hold that the treatment in question is unjust because characteristic C would not be mutually acknowledged as a proper ground for such treatment by all who understood the practice and took an impartial view of it (in accordance with John Rawls's *A Theory of Justice*).

When a social practice of this kind is engaged in, the members of the class of C-persons are discriminated against because they are C. By reference to the rules of this practice, having C is a relevant reason or ground for performing a certain kind of action which is in fact unjust (though not recognized to be so by the practice itself). In this context the characteristic C is not accidentally or contingently associated with the unjust treatment, but is essentially tied to it. For the injustices done to a person are based on the fact that he has characteristic C. His being C is, other things being equal, a sufficient condition for the permissibility of treating him in the given manner. Within the framework of the social practice at t_1, that someone is C is a ground for acting in a certain way toward him. Therefore C is a relevant characteristic of a person.

But is it *morally* relevant? The answer to this question, it seems to me, is that at time t_1 characteristic C is not morally relevant, but, if we accept the principle of compensatory justice, at time t_2 it is. The principle of compensatory justice is that, in order to restore the balance of justice when an injustice has been committed to a group of persons, some form of compensation or reparation must be made to that group. Thus if there has been an established social practice (as distinct from an individual's action) of treating any member of a certain class of persons in a certain way on the ground that they have characteristic C and if this practice has involved the doing of an injustice to C-persons, then the principle of compensatory justice requires that C-persons as such be compensated in some way. Characteristic C, in other words, has become at time t_2 a characteristic whose *moral* relevance is entailed by the principle of compensatory justice. In this kind of situation, to ignore the fact that a person is C would be to ignore the fact that there had been a social practice in which unjust actions were directed toward C-persons as such.

II

Given that characteristic C is morally relevant to how C-persons are to be treated if compensatory justice is to be done to them, it follows that reverse discrimination is justified. For this is simply the policy of extending special benefits, opportunities, or advantages to the class of C-persons as such. Contrary to what Nickel affirms, this is not selecting C-persons for special treatment on the basis of the complex characteristic C', namely: being a person who was discriminated against because he was C. For even if the individual C-person who now enjoys the favorable compensatory treatment was not himself one of those who suffered injustice as a result of the past social practice, he nevertheless has a right (based on his being a member of the class of C-persons) to receive the benefits extended to all C-persons as such. This follows from our premise that the policy of reverse discrimination, directed toward anyone who is C because he is C, is justified by the principle of compensatory justice.

Cowan claims that compensatory justice does not require a policy of treating all C-persons favorably (other things being equal) because they are C. His argument is that, if the original unjust treatment of C-persons was unjust precisely because their being C was morally irrelevant, then "there is and can be no morally relevant group which could have suffered or to which retribution could now be made" (chap. 2, p. 6). My reply to this argument is that the moral relevance or irrelevance of a characteristic is not something that can be determined outside the framework of a set of moral principles. It is true that the principles of *distributive* justice were transgressed by the past treatment of C-persons precisely because, according to those principles, characteristic C is morally irrelevant as a ground for treating persons in a certain way. Nevertheless, according to the principle of *compensatory* justice (which applies only where a violation of other forms of justice has taken place), the fact that systematic injustice was directed toward a class of persons as being C-persons establishes characteristic C as morally relevant, as far as making restitution is concerned. For the same reason, it may be noted, characteristic C will become again morally irrelevant the moment all the requirements of compensatory justice with respect to the treatment of C-persons have been fulfilled. Thus justified reverse discrimination is limited in its scope, being restricted to the righting of specific wrongs within a given range of application. Once the balance of justice with regard to C-persons has been restored, they are to be treated like anyone else. The appropriate test for the restoration of the balance of justice (that is, fulfillment of the requirements of compensatory justice) is determined by the set of criteria for just compensation that would be mutually acceptable to all who understand the unjust practice and who view the matter disinterestedly (following Rawls, as before).

III

Does the foregoing view entail that, in the given society, *each individual* who is not a C-person has a duty to make reparation to *every* C-person he happens to be able to benefit in some way? This would seem to be unfair, since the individual who is claimed to have such a duty might not himself have intentionally or knowingly participated in the discriminatory social practice, and might even have done what he could to oppose it. It also seems unfair to C-persons, who would then be compensated only under the contingency that particular non-C individuals happen to be in a position of being able to benefit them. We must here face the questions: To whom is owed the compensatory treatment, that is, who has the right to reparation? And upon whom does the obligation corresponding to that right fall?

If we consider such compensatory policies as affirmative action and the Equal Opportunity Program to be appropriate ways of restoring the balance of justice, a possible answer to our questions becomes apparent. For such programs are, within the framework of democratic institutions, social policies carried out by organized agencies of a central government representing the whole people. They are not directed toward any "assignable" individual (to use Bentham's apt phrase), but rather are directed toward any member of an "assignable" group (the class of C-persons) who wishes to take advantage of, or to qualify for, the compensatory benefits offered to the group as a whole. The obligation to offer such benefits to the group as a whole is an obligation that falls on society in general, not on any particular person. For it is the society in general that, through its established social practice, brought upon itself the obligation.

To bring out the moral significance of this, consider the case in which an individual has himself treated a particular C-person unjustly. By so acting, the individual in question has brought upon himself a special obligation which he owes to that particular C-person. This obligation is above and beyond the duty he has—along with everyone else—to support and comply with the social policy of reverse discrimination being carried out by his government. For everyone in the society (if it is just) contributes his fair share to the total cost of that policy, whether or not he has, personally, done an injustice to a C-person. So the individual who commits such an injustice himself has a special duty, and his victim has a special right, in contrast to the general duty of everyone to do his share (by obeying laws, paying taxes, etc.) in supporting the policy of reverse discrimination directed toward the class of C-persons as a whole, and in contrast to the general right on the part of any C-person to benefit from such a policy if he wishes to take advantage of its provisions.

The issue of the justifiability of reverse discrimination does not have to do with an individual's making up for his own acts of injustice done to this or that person. It has to do with righting the wrongs committed as an integral part of an organized social practice whose very essence was discrimination against C-persons as such. In this sense the perpetrator of the original injustice was the whole society (other than the class of C-persons). The victim was the class of C-persons as a group, since they were the *collective target* of an institutionalized practice of unjust treatment. It is for this reason that Cowan's concluding remarks do not stand up. At the end of his article he makes the following statements regarding the present members of a group which has been discriminated against in the past:

They should most certainly be treated like everyone else. But this does not mean "their" individual histories should be ignored. As with anyone else, injustices done "them" as individuals should be prevented or rectified insofar as possible. But past or future discrimination and injustice done "them" as a group and special advantages to them as a group are both out of the question, since in the moral context there is no such group (chap 2, p. 6).

But there is such a group. It is the group that was, as it were, *created* by the original unjust practice. To deny the existence of the group is to deny a social reality—a reality which cannot morally be ignored as long as the wrongs that created it are not corrected.

Cowan's position assumes that compensatory justice applies to the relations of one individual to another, but not to organized social practices and whole classes of persons with respect to whom the goals and methods of the practices are identified and pursued. This assumption, however, completely disregards what, morally speaking, is the most hideous aspect of the injustices of human history: those carried out systematically and directed toward whole groups of men and women *as groups*.

My conclusion is that society is morally at fault if it ignores the group which it has discriminated against. Even if it provides for compensation to each member of the group, not *qua* member of the group but *qua* person who has been unjustly treated (for whatever reason), it is leaving justice undone. For it is denying the specific obligation it owes to, and the specific right it has created in, the group as such. This obligation and this right follow from the society's past use of a certain characteristic or set of characteristics as the criterion for identification of the group, membership in which was taken as a ground for unjust treatment. Whatever duties of justice are owed by individuals to other individuals, institutionalized injustice demands institutionalized compensation.

Reverse Discrimination

William A. Nunn III

In his recent article supporting the policy of reverse discrimination, Paul W. Taylor ("Reverse Discrimination and Compensatory Justice" [chapter 4]) argued, roughly, that when a certain group of persons within a given society is discriminated against because of some nonmoral characteristic (e.g., skin color), and such discrimination is essentially tied to a pervasive social practice, the characteristic upon which the discrimination is based takes on a moral quality; consequently it becomes the moral duty of the society to make reparation to that group. Although I find it difficult to disagree with the allegation that in some sense institutionalized injustice demands institutionalized compensation, I think that Taylor's argument contains two fundamental flaws. First, he has not concerned himself with the task of making reasonably clear some of the essential terms he employs—among them "institutionalized injustice" and "institutionalized compensation." Second, a consistent application of his thesis to a given society is more likely to perpetuate than eliminate the injustices of discrimination.

I

There are a good many different kinds of organized social practices in every society, most of which in one way or another are discriminatory. Certain religious groups, for example, either forbid or actively discourage intermarriage between their members and those of other religious groups. Although I think it

Reprinted from *Analysis* 34 (1974) by permission of the author.

unlikely that this sort of discriminatory practice could be justified by disinterested observers who understood it, it is on quite a different level from, say, a governmental prohibition against interracial marriage in the form of an antimiscegenation statute. Both of these social practices embody a form of discrimination which is both institutionalized and unjust. Yet it is arguable that no society has the right to interfere with the former, whereas the latter ought not to be tolerated by any society. Again, the policy of not a few social and professional organizations excluding certain persons from membership solely on the basis of race, sex, or other nonmoral criteria is clearly not on all fours with an overt or covert sanction of discrimination by a government on the same grounds. The difficulty, then, is to determine which discriminatory social practices fall under Taylor's concept of institutionalized injustice and which do not. Once that problem is resolved, we may turn our attention to the nature and scope of the required compensation—a subject he dismisses with a vague reference to the "restoration of the balance of justice" (chap. 4, p. 14). Clearly a democratic government, in its capacity of representing all the people, has a duty to rectify discriminatory legislation and enforcement of the law. It may also have a duty to abolish certain forms of private discrimination in which it has a compelling interest. It is not clear that private organizations have a duty to abolish and make reparation for their discriminatory practices. Nor is it clear that in every case of unjust discrimination some form of compensation is either desirable or possible. The appropriate compensation for an unjust tax might include a refund with interest; or for the unjust taking of private property a restitution of the property itself or, that not being possible, an award of damages for its value. But it is doubtful whether the concept of compensation is at all meaningful in the case of an antimiscegenation statute. The appropriate remedy for the last form of discrimination is repeal—not an award of damages (how would damages be measured?) or the enactment of a statute requiring that henceforth all marriages be interracial.

Taylor has not offered a clue as to whether he thinks all unjust social practices must be abolished or, if not all, how to differentiate between those that should and those that need not be abolished. Nor has he demonstrated the necessity or even possibility of compensation in such cases. The vagueness of his use of these important terms gives rise to a suspicion that the phrase "institutionalized injustice demands institutionalized compensation" may be little more than a high-sounding but vacuous slogan.

II

Assuming *arguendo* that the meaning of the above-discussed terms is reasonably clear and that there are no logical difficulties involved in their application, compensation for past discrimination is nevertheless unjustifiable if it incorporates reverse discrimination. By "reverse discrimination" I refer to a policy of according favored treatment to a group of persons unjustly discriminated against in the past because of some nonmoral characteristic C possessed by each member of the group (hereafter the C-group), and corresponding unfavored treatment to a group of persons no member of which possesses the characteristic C (hereafter the C'-group). As Taylor correctly argues, individual moral desert is not relevant to the application of such a policy. It is both justifiable and necessary, he believes, even though it is possible (indeed probable) that not every C-person suffered and there are C'-persons who neither caused, condoned, practiced, nor benefited from the initial discrimination. The reason it is justifiable, he explains, is that the original discrimination created the C-group's right to reparation—not as individuals, but as a class—and the existence of that right entails reverse discrimination. In short, the C-group must be compensated at the expense of the C'-group.

In applying the policy, it seems to me that whatever good is accomplished by compensating members of the C-group for past wrongs is vitiated by the corresponding denial of benefits to the C'-group. Where before the entire C-group was victimized for the benefit of individual C'-persons, now the entire C'-group has been substituted as a victim for the benefit of individual C-persons. The criterion for discrimination is no longer C but C'. Thus while certain C-persons are compensated for the wrongs done them or other members of the C-group, the C'-group is unjustly discriminated against as a class. It follows that a right to reparation is created within the C'-group—not as individuals, but as a class—and the existence of this right entails what we might call reverse reverse discrimination. It is not difficult to see where this path leads.

The theory of compensatory justice, as explained by Taylor, will not do insofar as it incorporates reverse discrimination. The best way of avoiding the injustices of discrimination is to avoid unjust discrimination in the first place. The second-best method is to avoid making the same mistake twice.

Should Reparations Be to Individuals or to Groups?

James W. Nickel

The discussion occasioned by my note "Discrimination and Morally Relevant Characteristics" has helped to clarify some of the available positions on the justification of special benefits for victims of discrimination. J. L. Cowan ("Inverse Discrimination") agrees that the justification for special help lies in the fact that one has been wronged, not in the fact, say, that one is black. But he thinks that it is important to emphasize that the special benefits which are due to many blacks are due only because they are individuals who have been wronged, not because of any fact relating to their race. In his view, "reparations for blacks" must be understood as "reparations for wronged individuals who happen to be black." P. W. Taylor and M. D. Bayles criticize my approach from the opposite direction. They think that my approach pays insufficient attention to the moral status of wronged groups. In what follows I shall attempt to point out some weaknesses in my critics' positions and to elaborate further my own.

The "reverse discrimination argument" alleges that special benefits for blacks are unjust because they continue to base special treatment on an irrelevant characteristic (viz., being black) and hence continue to discriminate. The counterargument that I offered has two premises:

P_1: For differential treatment to be discriminatory (and unjust for that reason) it must be based on a morally irrelevant characteristic.

Reprinted from *Analysis* 34 (1974) by permission of the author.

P_2: Differential treatment of blacks for purposes of reparations is not based on an irrelevant characteristic (as it would be if it were based on race instead of the fact of having been wronged).

From these premises I drew the conclusion that differential treatment of blacks for purposes of reparations is not unjust on account of being discriminatory.

Cowan's criticism is that the formulation of the argument is ambiguous because it fails to make clear whether it is defending special help to individuals or special help to groups:

> Nickel's reasoning thus does not really, as it might be taken to do, provide any support at all for the kind of self-contradictory thinking the original argument was surely intended to rebut. This is the reasoning that since blacks ... have suffered unjust discrimination, we should now give them special treatment to make it up to them. Once again there is no problem insofar as this simply means that where individual blacks have suffered injustice it should, as with anyone else, insofar as possible be made up to those individuals who have so suffered. The fallacy arises when rather than individuals it is the group which is intended, and individuals are regarded merely as members of that group rather than in their individuality. (chap. 2, p. 6)

But it was indeed my intention to provide support for the kind of thinking that Cowan finds contradictory. I intended to suggest that since almost all American blacks have been victimized by discrimination it would be justifiable to design and institute programs of special benefits for blacks. Such programs, which are probably the only effective and administratively feasible way to provide reparations to blacks, would be justified in terms of the injuries that almost all of the recipients have suffered—not in terms of the race of the recipients. To make this clearer one needs to distinguish between the justifying and the administrative basis for a program.[1] The justifying basis for such a program would be the injuries that many blacks suffer and the special needs that many blacks have because of discrimination. The administrative basis for distributing the program's benefits might be the presence in an individual of these needs and injuries, but it is more likely that it would be some other characteristics (such as race and present income) which were easier to detect and which were highly correlated with the justifying basis. My assumption here is that it is sometimes justifiable for reasons of administrative efficiency to use as part of the administrative basis for a program of benefits a characteristic, such as race, which would be implausible as a justifying basis. Cowan argues that special advantages to blacks as a group are "out of the question, since in the moral context there is no such group" (chap. 2, p. 7). I agree with the premise that there

21

is no such group insofar as this means that race or ancestry can never be a justifying basis for differential treatment. But I do not agree that race or ancestry can never serve as a morally acceptable administrative basis for a program of differential treatment which provides compensation for past wrongs, and hence I reject the unqualified conclusion that special advantages to blacks as a group are out of the question.

Bayles and Taylor want to go further than this. They want to give direct moral status to the defining characteristics of wronged groups, and argue that special help to blacks as a group can be justified in terms of a principle requiring reparations to wronged groups. They hold the view, paradoxical but not contradictory, that although race is irrelevant in a context where persons of a given race are being unjustly harmed, it is not irrelevant in a context where the obligation to give reparations to wronged groups is being met. Bayles, unlike Taylor, does not offer positive grounds for his own view; he simply offers it as an alternative to my approach—which he thinks can be discredited by refutation by analogy. In response to my claim that having been wronged rather than being black is the justifying basis for special help, he says,

> By parallel reasoning it can be argued that the original discrimination was not on the basis of a morally irrelevant characteristic. Racists do not discriminate against blacks simply because they are black. Rather they claim that blacks as a class are inferior in certain relevant respects, e.g., they lack certain abilities and virtues such as industriousness, reliability, and cleanliness. Thus, reasoning similarly to Nickel and Cowan, racists could contend that they do not discriminate on the basis of a morally irrelevant characteristic, but the morally relevant ones which are thought to be associated with being black. (chap. 3, p. 9)

Bayles's complaint is that if those who favor reparations can use this argument, then so can racists. He thinks that if it works for the one then it will work for the other. And since it is obvious that it won't work for the racist as a way of showing that he doesn't discriminate, he concludes that it won't work for those who favor reparations.

One response to this complaint is to argue that the second premise of my counterargument to the "reverse discrimination argument" would not be true when used by the racist. The racist's version of the second premise would be:

RP$_2$: My differential treatment of blacks is not based on an irrelevant characteristic (as it would be if it were based on race instead of the fact of being lazy, unreliable, and unclean).

In most cases this would not be, I submit, a true claim. It would rather be a self-serving rationalization. In B. A. O. Williams's words, the racist is "paying, in very poor coin, the homage of irrationality to reason."[2] Most racists could not use this defense of their differential treatment of blacks because its premise about their real reasons would not be true.

But to avoid being doctrinaire about this we must allow that some racists might be able to make this claim about their real reasons without falsehood and rationalization. And Bayles is right in suggesting that this possibility requires me to modify or give up my counterargument. Bayles's approach is to give up this defense and use a much stronger principle about reparations to wronged groups to defend programs of reparations to blacks from the charge of unjust discrimination. But before adopting Bayles's approach we will do well, I think, to consider modifying the first premise of my counterargument. This premise holds that for differential treatment to be discriminatory (and unjust for that reason) it must be based on an irrelevant characteristic. But it should be changed to one which holds that for differential treatment to be discriminatory (and unjust for that reason) it is necessary that it be based on an irrelevant characteristic *or* on a false claim about the correlation between characteristics. This is, in effect, to modify one's definition of "discrimination." When this modification is made, the defender of reparations is not able to move directly from the fact that preferential treatment was not based on an irrelevant characteristic to the conclusion that it was not unjustly discriminatory. To get to this conclusion he would also have to show that there was in fact a very high correlation between being an American black and being a victim of discriminatory and harmful treatment. I think that the defender of reparations can do this, but the racist cannot make the analogous move. He cannot show that there is in fact a high correlation between being black and lacking industry, reliability, and cleanliness, and hence his actions are based on false beliefs about correlations between characteristics and can—under the modified premise—be condemned as discriminatory. Hence the defender of reparations can use this defense without making an equally good defense available to the racist.

Taylor agrees with Bayles's claim that the justification of special benefits to blacks requires us to appeal to a moral principle about compensation for wronged *groups*. He formulates this principle as follows:

> The principle of compensatory justice is that, in order to restore the balance of justice when an injustice has been committed to a group of persons, some form of compensation or reparation must be made to that group. (chap. 4, p. 13)

When there has been institutionalized discrimination against persons who have a certain morally irrelevant characteristic, the effect of this principle is to *make* this characteristic relevant for purposes of reparations. Taylor insists that in such a case reparations are due to the group, not just to those of its members who were harmed by the discriminatory practice. Since the characteristic which defines the group was essentially involved in the discriminatory practice, reparations must be made available to all those who have this characteristic.

An interesting aspect of Taylor's article is his suggestion that the principles of compensatory justice can be chosen from the perspective which John Rawls advocates for choosing principles of distributive justice. If it can be argued plausibly that persons in the Rawlsian original position would choose compensatory principles that include a principle providing benefits directly to wronged groups, then any lingering suspicion that Taylor's principle is ad hoc and has been invented specifically to deal with the issue of special benefits for blacks could be laid to rest.

Rawls has very little to say about compensatory and retributive justice in *A Theory of Justice*, but the principles of distributive justice that he thinks would be chosen in the original position would themselves require a good deal of compensatory activity on the part of government. These principles embody a general conception of justice which holds that "all social values . . . are to be distributed equally unless an unequal distribution of any, or all, of these values is to everyone's advantage."[3] A consequence of this is that heavier-than-average burdens are unjust unless they can be justified by showing that even the person who suffers the most from bearing the burden would be worse off if that kind of burden were shifted or compensated. But it will be impossible to show this with regard to many types of burdens, and hence these will have to be shifted to others with lighter loads or compensated. Since it is often impossible to shift such burdens (e.g., a heavy workload resulting from skills that are much in demand, or disabilities resulting from an accident), compensation in the form of balancing benefits will be required in many cases by Rawls's principles of distributive justice. This applies to all unjustifiable burdens, no matter what their origin, and would include unequal burdens resulting from discrimination. The latter, being unjustifiable, would have to be shifted or compensated. It appears, therefore, that Rawls's principles of distributive justice by themselves would take us some distance toward remedying the effects of discrimination.

Since the compensation of unjustifiable burdens would be required by Rawls's principles of distributive justice, it is not entirely clear that *any* distinct principles of compensatory justice would be chosen by persons in the original position. From the Rawlsian perspective, such principles would not be chosen merely because it was thought to be "fitting" that wrongdoers should repay their victims. They would be chosen only if their use would maximize the life prospects of those who would live in the projected society.

But assume, for purposes of argument, that persons in the original position would choose to have compensatory principles among their principles of justice. These principles would require persons and institutions to compensate the victims of their wrongdoing and negligence, and would require government to provide compensation when the wrongdoer was financially unable. The question, then, is whether persons in the original position would also choose a principle which would compensate *groups* as such for injuries suffered by their members as members. Since the members of these groups could obtain compensation as individuals under the other reparations principles, would there be any reason to provide compensation to groups as such?

I am unable to think of any such reason, and I think that the reason that Taylor presents is unsound. He contends that a program of reparations which is justified by reference to the wrongs suffered by individuals "completely disregards what, morally speaking, is the most hideous aspect of the injustices of human history: those carried out systematically and directed toward whole groups of men and women *as groups*" (chap. 4, pp. 15–16). If Taylor is right in claiming that providing reparations to groups as groups is the only alternative to ignoring these hideous injustices, then persons in the original position would have a reason for choosing principles requiring such reparations. One function of requiring the performance of acts of reparations is to provide a symbolic denunciation of the evil that was done and to provide the wrongdoer with an opportunity to declare in a concrete and meaningful way his turning away from that evil. Perhaps it is this element that those, like Taylor, who demand reparations to blacks as a group feel would be missing in any approach to reparations which proceeded on an individual basis. A person of strong moral feeling may hold that such an approach allows America to bury its racist past rather than to confront it and repent of it. A symbolic denunciation of racism is desired, and it is held that only a program of reparations to blacks as a group can do this.

But surely Taylor presents us with a false dilemma when he suggests that compensation to groups as such is the only alternative to disregarding the injustices of institutionalized discrimination against groups. We can give great emphasis to the injustices involved in such discrimination through means other than those of imitating the structure of such injustices in our compensatory mechanisms. We can denounce such practices, teach our children to notice their silent but sinister operations and avoid them, make them illegal and provide effective enforcement mechanisms, and provide reparations to their victims which is justified—but not necessarily administered—on an individual basis. If we succeed in doing these things, then it can scarcely be said that we have disregarded the most hideous aspects of institutionalized discrimination against groups. Direct compensation to groups of the sort advocated by Taylor is not the only effective way of demonstrating our aversion to this kind of injustice.

The upshot of this is that there do not seem to be any reasons why the life prospects of persons in the original position would be bettered by their choosing a principle requiring reparations to wronged groups. Furthermore, there is at least one reason for thinking that these prospects would be worsened. . This is that there might well be cases in which the result of following Taylor's principle would be to waste resources on substantial numbers of persons who were completely unaffected by discrimination directed against a group to which they belonged. Suppose that there was a group which was evenly distributed throughout the country but which was subject to discriminatory treatment in only some sections, and as a result of this, half of the members of this group were completely unaffected by this discrimination—even though it was based on a characteristic which all of them shared.[4] Would we be willing to agree with the conclusion of Taylor's principle that all of them should receive compensation whether they had been harmed or not? This problem does not arise in the case of American blacks since all, or almost all, of them have suffered significantly from discrimination, and hence there is no great unfairness or waste of resources if benefits are provided for all. But in dealing with a group in which only a portion of the members had been affected by the discrimination it is far from clear that a principle requiring compensation to all would be desirable.

Notes

1. This distinction is elaborated in my essay "Classification by Race in Compensatory Programs," *Ethics* 84, no. 2 (January 1974): 146–50.
2. "The Idea of Equality," in Peter Laslett and W. G. Runciman, eds., *Philosophy, Politics and Society*, Second Series (Oxford: Oxford University Press, 1962), p. 113.
3. John Rawls, *A Theory of Justice* (Cambridge, MA: Harvard University Press, 1971), p. 62.
4. This example was suggested by Kent Greenawalt [Professor of Law at Columbia University —Ed.].

Reparations to Individuals or Groups?

Alan H. Goldman

James Nickel bases his latest argument for reparations to groups upon a distinction between the justifying and administrative basis for a program of reparations. I have argued against compensatory hiring for groups elsewhere,[1] but had not considered there this most recent argument. Its novelty lies in the shift from abstract or ideal principles of compensatory justice to the necessity in practice of balancing claims so as to maximize (imperfect) justice. The justification for favored treatment for groups, according to Nickel, derives from the administrative feasibility of such a program by comparison with the high cost and impracticality of administering compensatory justice in this area on an individual basis. Thus while there is only a high correlation between being black, for example, and having been discriminated against and so deserving compensation (justifying basis), so that preferential treatment for the group will occasionally result in undeserved benefits for individuals, the balance of justice in practice favors such treatment. The viable alternatives seem to be either award of deserved compensation in the great majority of cases and occasional undeserved benefit and hence injustice to white job applicants, or compensation on an individual basis, which would require demonstration of past injustice in court or before a special administrative body, so that the cost and difficulty of the operation would result in far fewer awards of deserved reparation. It is better, the argument holds, to have compensation which is only almost always deserved than a program which in practice would amount to almost no compensation at all, so that a policy which would not be accepted in

Reprinted from *Analysis* 35 (1975) by permission of the author.

an ideally just world (a world which became ideally just after compensation was paid) becomes best in the present situation.

In reply, one would first of all like to ask how high the correlation between group membership and past discrimination, and hence the proportion of deserved to undeserved compensation, must be. Presumably a ratio of 51 to 49 will not do, since in the case of compensation by preferential hiring policies, there are two injustices involved in every case of undeserved compensation: first, the payment for the undeserved benefit made by society in accepting less efficient service (since the candidate will not be as competent if hired only because of preferred treatment), but, more important, the injustice to the white male applicant who is best qualified. The correlation is presumably not as high in the case of women as a group as in the case of blacks, and not as high for middle-class as for lower-class blacks. The latter comparison suggests narrowing the specification of the group so as to maximize the correlation, but of course at the limit of such narrowing is a program administered on an individual basis.

Thus far it still seems we must balance ideal theory against practice, but the far more serious point completely forgotten in Nickel's argument is the effect of the operation of market criteria upon hiring even within a compensatory program of preferential treatment. Since hiring within the preferred group still depends upon relative qualifications and hence upon past opportunities for acquiring qualifications, there is in fact an inverse ratio established between past discrimination and present benefits, so that those who benefit most from the program, those who actually obtain jobs, are those who deserve to least. Given that those individuals will always be hired first who have suffered least from prior discrimination, this effect of competence requirements completely destroys the rationale of arguing by correlation unless the correlation is extremely close to perfect, for as long as there are some members in the market who have not unfairly lost opportunities, they will be the ones getting the jobs. But the establishment of such high correlation for a specific group, or the narrowing of specifications for group membership until virtually all members have been treated unjustly, amounts to administering a program on an individual basis. It will have to be determined for each individual whether he belongs to the narrowly specified group and have to be determined for individuals within that group whether virtually all have been discriminated against and thereby suffered harm.[2] These two steps, when the group is sufficiently narrowly specified, will, I suspect, be as difficult as handling cases on an individual basis from the beginning.

Since Nickel's argument wrongly assumes that the majority of compensation cases will tend to be fair if the correlation of past injustice to group membership is above 50 percent, it is unsound. Nor can the practice of hiring by competence itself be blamed or held therefore unjust. If efficiency is Nickel's basis for arguing for group compensation, he cannot condemn a general practice which in the long run results in more goods for all in favor of some less efficient alternative. It would at least be strange to recommend hiring the least competent as a general practice within some preferred group, and in this case efficiency would be gained, not lost, by moving away from a group program. In order, then, not to create a policy which in practice singles out for benefits within a generally unjustly treated minority just that minority which has not been unjustly treated, and thus does treat unfairly members of the "majority group" applying for jobs, a compensatory program of preferential hiring must be administered on an individual basis. Where there are significant departures from this toward preferential treatment for loosely defined large groups, we must suspect further injustice not only to "majority group" members, but to members of the minority who have suffered previous injustice and are now passed over in favor of other members who have at least suffered less. There are surely degrees of injustice, and the market here will invert the ratio of past injustice to present compensation if the program is directed toward a group.

Notes

1. "The Justification of Reverse Discrimination," presented at the Eastern Division meeting of the American Philosophical Association, December 27, 1974.
2. I suggest that for the past generation of blacks this might be found to be the case, but not for the generation currently in school, and certainly not for women, who are benefiting most from the current practice in universities.

What's Wrong with Discrimination?

Paul Woodruff

The trouble with compensatory discrimination in favor of a group, say its crit-ics, is that it is discrimination. It is morally wrong because it accords differen-tial treatment on morally irrelevant grounds—it distributes reparations on the basis of group membership, whereas if reparations are to be made, they should be made to the individuals who have been wronged (see William A. Nunn III, chapter 5, and Alan H. Goldman, chapter 7, this volume). The defenders of compensatory discrimination for groups tend to deny that its criteria are morally irrelevant. A person's membership in a group, they say, may become morally relevant when there has been systematic discrimination against that group (see Paul W. Taylor, chapter 4).

No one, it seems, stops to consider the relevance of moral relevance to the issue. The important question is why discrimination is wrong when it is wrong. When we know the answer to that we shall know who it is that is wronged by it.

For brevity's sake, and because it is the hardest case to make out, I shall con-sider only discrimination in hiring by private employers. The problem is that it does not always seem to be wrong. Suppose a private banker hires his cousin in preference to a better-qualified applicant from another family. Hiring bankers this way is discriminatory, for it uses a criterion (kinship) that is irrelevant to banking. Is it morally wrong?

We need to know more about the case. Suppose that our banker's bank is the only bank in the country, that it is entirely a family affair, and that it dominates the modern economy of the country. Then, whenever our banker hires a cousin,

Reprinted from *Analysis* 36 (1976) by permission of the author.

he helps to exclude those outside his family from power and to raise over them a class with birthright privileges. He participates in a pattern of discrimination that wrongs *everyone* who is not a member of his family by making their parentage a reason for failure. This is insulting to every member of the excluded class, and damages their self-respect and the respect in which they are held by others.

On the other hand, if our banker's bank were a small business in a land of many and various banks, which were not in general ruled by a privileged class, then what moral wrong would he commit in hiring his cousin? If the cousin is idle, it would be foolish to hire him. If an applicant is disappointed, it is sad not to hire him. But I am not aware that it is generally wrong to disappoint people.

The disappointed applicant may have valid complaints against the banker that have nothing to do with discrimination. For example, in advertising the job, our banker may have promised to give it to the best applicant. Or using customary hiring practices like interviews may oblige him to hire the best applicant. But he can discriminate without violating obligations of that sort. Also, it may turn out that no one hires the applicant. Whatever the cause of this, and whether or not discrimination was involved, his unemployment may be a social injustice. If so, the banker does wrong by contributing to that injustice. But discrimination and the fate to which it may bring its victims are wrong in different ways. For example, it does not matter how people are made slaves; their slavery is an injustice whether they came to it by stupidity, conquest, discrimination, or an impartial lottery. Slavery is an injustice to the slaves. But enslaving people *for their race* would add a wrong to slavery, and not to slaves only, but to every member of the insulted race.

Notice that the moral relevance of the criteria used is not decisive. Kinship would be morally relevant to our banker's decision if he himself had benefited from the hiring of cousins. But what really matters is whether or not it is right to hire cousins.

I suggest that an act of discrimination is wrong when it is wrong not simply because it is discriminatory, but because it is part of a pattern of discrimination that is wrong. A pattern of discrimination is wrong when it makes membership in a group burdensome by unfairly reducing the respect in which the group is held. It may accomplish this, for example, by making group membership a prima facie reason for failure. One act of discrimination cannot do that. If an applicant fails at one bank because of his race, and at other banks for other reasons, his race is not the reason for his unemployment, and his failure is not an insult to his race. Discriminating, like walking on the grass, is to be judged with reference to how much of it is being done. Walking on the grass is harmful only if enough people are in the habit of doing it to ruin the grass. So it is with walking over the feelings of a group.

My account of discrimination yields two conclusions for the debate on compensatory discrimination.

(1) The objection that compensatory discrimination is wrong because it is discriminatory may be dismissed. Compensatory discrimination is not part of a pattern that is wrong. Since it is compensatory it is limited to a scale which will not reduce *unfairly* the respect in which the compensating group is held. Though it may cause certain people to be unemployed, it does not increase unemployment, which is an evil however it is distributed.

I do not consider the objection that compensatory discrimination violates the principle that the best people deserve the best jobs (the meritocratic principle). The merits of that principle are much in question, and raise too large an issue for this brief note. In any case, the chief complaints against discrimination are based not on that principle but on egalitarian beliefs. I have tried to make the burden of those complaints precise.

(2) It is now clear that compensation for discrimination is owed to all members of the relevant group in virtue of their membership in that group. An individual disappointed by discrimination has no special claim to redress on that score. He has been wronged, not because he has been disappointed, but because he is a member of a group that has been wronged. Every member of the group finds membership in the group unfairly burdensome as a result of the pattern of discrimination; every member has an equal claim to compensation. Conversely, every member is benefited equally by an act that tends to break the pattern. Our banker would do well by the noncousins if he hires even a privileged noncousin, one who has not yet been disappointed, if in doing so he increases the accessibility of bank jobs to noncousins.

Of course in the history of any pattern of discrimination there are usually at least two wrongs to be righted. Thus if people have been enslaved on the basis of race, then (i) every member of the race deserves redress for discrimination, and (ii) every slave deserves redress for enslavement. Slavery, poverty, and the like are borne by individuals; discrimination is borne by groups.

But what precisely is a group for our purposes? Consider the group of those who are either black women or hold degrees in law from Harvard. Few of its members in proportion to its number enjoy jobs of importance. Yet no white Harvard lawyer is wronged by the snubbing of a black woman, and it would be no consolation to black women to see a Harvard lawyer advanced to a good job, if he is white. We need to restrict what counts as a group for our purposes. As consistent egalitarians, we must avoid certain moral and natural criteria for grouphood, on pain of undermining our objection to discrimination. The relevant group in each case is the group that has been insulted. What that is is a question for social scientists.

Justice and Compensation

Preferential Hiring

Judith Jarvis Thomson

Many people are inclined to think preferential hiring an obvious injustice.[1] I should have said "feel" rather than "think": it seems to me the matter has not been carefully thought out, and that what is in question, really, is a gut reaction.

I am going to deal with only a very limited range of preferential hirings: that is, I am concerned with cases in which several candidates present themselves for a job, in which the hiring officer finds, on examination, that all are equally qualified to hold that job, and he then straightway declares for the black, or for the woman, because he or she *is* a black or a woman. And I shall talk only of hiring decisions in the universities, partly because I am most familiar with them, partly because it is in the universities that the most vocal and articulate opposition to preferential hiring is now heard—not surprisingly, perhaps, since no one is more vocal and articulate than a university professor who feels deprived of his rights.

I suspect that some people may say, Oh well, in *that* kind of case it's all right, what we object to is preferring the less qualified to the better qualified. Or again, What we object to is refusing even to consider the qualifications of white males. I shall say nothing at all about these things. I think that the argument I shall give for saying that preferential hiring is not unjust in the cases I do concentrate on can also be appealed to to justify it outside that range of cases. But I won't draw any conclusions about cases outside it. Many people do have that

Reprinted from *Philosophy and Public Affairs* 2 (1973). Copyright © 1973 by Princeton University Press. Reprinted by permission of Princeton University Press.

gut reaction I mentioned against preferential hiring in any degree or form; and it seems to me worthwhile bringing out that there is good reason to think they are wrong to have it. Nothing I say will be in the slightest degree novel or original. It will, I hope, be enough to set the relevant issues out clearly.

I

But first, something should be said about qualifications.

I said I would consider only cases in which the several candidates who present themselves for the job are equally qualified to hold it; and there plainly are difficulties in the way of saying precisely how this is to be established, and even what is to be established. Strictly academic qualifications seem at a first glance to be relatively straightforward: the hiring officer must see if the candidates have done equally well in courses (both courses they took, and any they taught), and if they are recommended equally strongly by their teachers, and if the work they submit for consideration is equally good. There is no denying that even these things are less easy to establish than first appears: for example, you may have a suspicion that Professor Smith is given to exaggeration, and that his "great student" is in fact less strong than Professor Jones's "good student"—but do you *know* that this is so? But there is a more serious difficulty still: as blacks and women have been saying, strictly academic indicators may themselves be skewed by prejudice. My impression is that women, white and black, may possibly suffer more from this than black males. A black male who is discouraged or downgraded for being black is discouraged or downgraded out of dislike, repulsion, a desire to avoid contact; and I suspect that there are very few teachers nowadays who allow themselves to feel such things, or, if they do feel them, to act on them. A woman who is discouraged or downgraded for being a woman is not discouraged or downgraded out of dislike, but out of a conviction that she is not serious, and I suspect that while there are very few teachers nowadays who allow themselves to feel that women generally are not serious, there are many who allow themselves to feel of the particular individual women students they confront that Ah, this one isn't serious, and in fact that one isn't either, nor is that other one—women generally are, of course, one thing, but these particular women, really they're just girls in search of husbands, are quite another. And I suspect that this will be far harder to root out. A teacher could not face himself in the mirror of a morning if he had downgraded anyone out of dislike; but a teacher can well face himself in the mirror if he downgrades someone out of a conviction that that person is not serious: after all, life is serious, and jobs and work, and who can take the unserious seriously? Who pays attention to the dilettante? So the hiring officer must read very very carefully between the lines in the candidates' dossiers even to assess their strictly academic qualifications.

And then of course there are other qualifications besides the strictly academic ones. Is one of the candidates exceedingly disagreeable? A department is not merely a collection of individuals, but a working unit; and if anyone is going to disrupt that unit, and to make its work more difficult, then this counts against him—he may be as well qualified in strictly academic terms, but he is not as well qualified. Again, is one of the candidates incurably sloppy? Is he going to mess up his records, is he going to have to be nagged to get his grades in, and worse, is he going to lose students' papers? This too would count against him: keeping track of students' work, records, and grades, after all, is part of the job.

What seems to me to be questionable, however, is that a candidate's race or sex is itself a qualification. Many people who favor preferential hiring in the universities seem to think it is; in their view, if a group of candidates is equally well qualified in respect of those measures I have already indicated, then if one is of the right race (black) or of the right sex (female), then that being itself a qualification, it tips the balance, and that one is the best qualified. If so, then of course no issue of injustice, or indeed of any other impropriety, is raised if the hiring officer declares for that one of the candidates straightway.

Why does race or sex seem to many to be, itself, a qualification? There seem to be two claims in back of the view that it is. First, there is the claim that blacks learn better from a black, women from a woman. One hears this less often in respect of women; blacks, however, are often said to mistrust the whites who teach them, with the result that they simply do not learn as well, or progress as far, as they would if taught by blacks. Second, and this one hears in respect of women as well as blacks, what is wanted is *role models*. The proportion of black and women faculty members in the larger universities (particularly as one moves up the ladder of rank) is very much smaller than the proportion of blacks and women in the society at large—even, in the case of women, than the proportion of them amongst recipients of Ph.D. degrees from those very same universities. Black and women students suffer a constricting of ambition because of this. They need to see members of their race or sex who are accepted, successful professionals. They need concrete evidence that those of their race or sex *can* become accepted, successful professionals.

And perhaps it is thought that it is precisely by virtue of having a role model right in the classroom that blacks do learn better from a black, women from a woman.

Now it is obviously essential for a university to staff its classrooms with people who can teach, and so from whom its students can learn, and indeed learn as much and as well as possible—teaching, after all, is, if not the whole of the game, then anyway a very large part of it. So if the first claim is true, then race and sex *do* seem to be qualifications. It obviously would not follow that a university should continue to regard them as qualifications indefinitely; I suppose, however, that it would follow that it should regard them as qualifications at

37

least until the proportion of blacks and women on the faculty matches the proportion of blacks and women among the students.

But in the first place, allowing this kind of consideration to have a bearing on a hiring decision might make for trouble of a kind that blacks and women would not be at all happy with. For suppose it could be made out that white males learn better from white males? (I once, years ago, had a student who said he really felt uncomfortable in a class taught by a woman, it was interfering with his work, and did I mind if he switched to another section?) I suppose we would feel that this was due to prejudice, and that it was precisely to be discouraged, certainly not encouraged by establishing hiring ratios. I don't suppose it is true of white males generally that they learn better from white males; I am concerned only with the way in which we should take the fact, if it were a fact, that they did—and if it would be improper to take it to be reason to think being a white male is a qualification in a teacher, then how shall we take its analogue to be reason to think being black, or being a woman, is a qualification in a teacher?

And in the second place, I must confess that, speaking personally, I do not find the claim we are looking at borne out in experience; I do not think that as a student I learned any better, or any more, from the women who taught me than from the men, and I do not think that my own women students now learn any better or any more from me than they do from my male colleagues. Blacks, of course, may have, and may have had, very different experiences, and I don't presume to speak for them—or even for women generally. But my own experience being what it is, it seems to *me* that any defense of preferential hiring in the universities which takes this first claim as premise is so far not an entirely convincing one.

The second claim, however, does seem to me to be plainly true: black and women students do need role models, they do need concrete evidence that those of their race or sex can become accepted, successful, professionals—plainly, you won't try to become what you don't believe you can become.

But do they need these role models right there in the classroom? Of course it might be argued that they do: that a black learns better from a black teacher, a woman from a woman teacher. But we have already looked at this. And if they are, though needed, not needed in the classroom, then is it the university's job to provide them?

For it must surely be granted that a college, or university, has not the responsibility—or perhaps, if it is supported out of public funds, even the right—to provide just *any* service to its students which might be good for them, or even which they may need, to be provided with. Sports seem to me plainly a case in point. No doubt it is very good for students to be offered, and perhaps even required to become involved in, a certain amount of physical exercise; but I can see no reason whatever to think that universities should be expected to provide facilities for it, or taxpayers to pay for those facilities. I suspect others may disagree, but my own feeling is that it is the same with medical and psychiatric services: I am sure that at least some students need medical and psychiatric help, but I cannot see why it should be provided for them in the universities, at public expense.

So the further question which would have to be answered is this: granting that black and female students need black and female role models, why should the universities be expected to provide them within their faculties? In the case of publicly supported universities, why should taxpayers be expected to provide them?

I don't say these questions can't be answered. But I do think we need to come at them from a quite different direction. So I shall simply sidestep this ground for preferential hiring in the universities. The defense I give will not turn on anyone's supposing that of two otherwise equally well-qualified candidates, one may be better qualified for the job by virtue, simply, of being of the right race or sex.

II

I mentioned several times in the preceding section the obvious fact that it is the taxpayers who support public universities. Not that private universities are wholly private: the public contributes to the support of most of them, for example by allowing them tax-free use of land, and of the dividends and capital gains on investments. But it will be the public universities in which the problem appears most starkly: as I shall suggest, it is the fact of public support that makes preferential hiring in the universities problematic.

For it seems to me that—other things being equal—there is no problem about preferential hiring in the case of a wholly private college or university, that is, one which receives no measure of public support at all, and which lives simply on tuition and (non-tax-deductible) contributions.

The principle here seems to me to be this: no perfect stranger has a right to be given a benefit which is yours to dispose of; no perfect stranger even has a right to be given an equal chance at getting a benefit which is yours to dispose of. You not only needn't give the benefit to the first perfect stranger who walks in and asks for it, you needn't even give him a chance at it, as, e.g., by tossing a coin.

I should stress that I am here talking about *benefits*, that is, things which people would like to have, which would perhaps not merely please them, but improve their lives, but which they don't actually *need*. (I suspect the same holds true of things people do actually need, but many would disagree, and as it is unnecessary to speak here of needs, I shall not discuss them.) If I have extra apples (they're mine: I grew them, on my own land, from my own trees), or extra money, or extra tickets to a series of lectures I am giving on How to Improve Your Life through Philosophy, and am prepared to give them away, word of this may get around, and people may present themselves as candidate recipients. I do not have to give to the first, or to proceed by letting them all draw straws; if I really do own the things, I can give to whom I like, on any ground I please, and in so doing, I violate no one's *rights*, I treat no one *unjustly*. None of the candidate recipients has a right to the benefit, or even to a chance at it.

There are four caveats. (1) Some grounds for giving or refraining from giving are less respectable than others. Thus, I might give the apples to the first who asks for them simply because he is the first who asks for them. Or again, I might give the apples to the first who asks for them because he is black, and because I am black and feel an interest in and concern for blacks which I do not feel in and for whites. In either case, not merely do I do what it is within my rights to do, but more, my ground for giving them to that person is a not immoral ground for giving them to him. But I might instead give the apples to the sixth who asks, and this because the first five were black and I hate blacks—or because the first five were white and I hate whites. Here I do what I have a right to do (for the apples are *mine*), and I violate no one's rights in doing it, but my ground for disposing of the apples as I did was a bad one; and it might even, more strongly, be said that I ought not to have disposed of the apples in the way I did. But it is important to note that it is perfectly consistent, on the one hand, that a man's ground for acting as he did was a bad one, and even that he ought not have done what he did, and, on the other hand, that he had a right to do what he did, that he violated no one's rights in doing it, and that no one can complain he was unjustly treated.

The second caveat (2) is that although I have a right to dispose of my apples as I wish, I have no right to harm, or gratuitously hurt or offend. Thus I am within my rights to refuse to give the apples to the first five because they are black (or because they are white); but I am not within my rights to say to them, "I refuse to give you apples because you are black (or white) and because those who are black (or white) are inferior."

And (3) if word of my extra apples, and of my willingness to give them away, got around because I advertised, saying or implying First Come First Served Till Supply Runs Out, then I cannot refuse the first five because they are black, or white. By so advertising I have *given* them a right to a chance at the apples. If they come in one at a time, I must give out apples in order, till the supply runs out; if they come in together, and I have only four apples, then I must either cut up the apples, or give them each an equal chance, as, e.g., by having them draw straws.

And last (4), there may be people who would say that I don't really, or don't fully own those apples, even though I grew them on my own land, from my own trees, and therefore that I don't have a right to give them away as I see fit. For after all, I don't own the police who protected my land while those apples were growing, or the sunlight because of which they grew. Or again, wasn't it just a matter of luck for me that I was born with a green thumb?—and why should I profit from a competence that I didn't deserve to have, that I didn't earn? Or perhaps some other reason might be put forward for saying that I don't own those apples. I don't want to take this up here. It seems to me wrong, but I want to let it pass. If anyone thinks that I don't own the apples, or, more generally, that no one really or fully owns anything, he will regard what I shall say in the remainder of this section, in which I talk about what may be done with what is privately owned, as an idle academic exercise. I'll simply ask that anyone who does think this be patient: we will come to what is publicly owned later.

Now what was in question was a job, not apples: and it may be insisted that to give a man a job is not to give him a benefit, but rather something he needs. Well, I am sure that people do need jobs, that it does not fully satisfy people's needs to supply them only with food, shelter, and medical care. Indeed, I am sure that people need, not merely jobs, but jobs that interest them, and that they can therefore get satisfaction from the doing of. But on the other hand, I am not at all sure that any candidate for a job in a university needs a job in a university. One would very much like it if all graduate students who wish it could find jobs teaching in universities; it is in some measure a tragedy that a person should spend three or four years preparing for a career, and then find there is no job available, and that he has in consequence to take work which is less interesting than he had hoped and prepared for. But one thing seems plain: no one *needs* that work which would interest him most in all the whole world of work. Plenty of people have to make do with work they like less than other work—no economy is rich enough to provide everyone with the work he likes best of all—and I should think that this does not mean they lack something they *need*. We are all of us prepared to tax ourselves so that no one shall be in need; but I should imagine that we are not prepared to tax ourselves (to tax barbers, truck drivers, salesclerks, waitresses, and factory workers) in order that everyone who wants a university job, and is competent to fill it, shall have one made available to him.

All the same, if a university job is a benefit rather than something needed, it is anyway not a "pure" benefit (like an apple), but an "impure" one. To give a man a university job is to give him an opportunity to do work which is interesting and satisfying; but he will only be interested and satisfied if he actually does the work he is given an opportunity to do, and does it well.

What this should remind us of is that certain cases of preferential hiring might well be utterly irrational. Suppose we have an eating club, and need a new chef; we have two applicants, a qualified French chef and a Greek who happens to like to cook, though he doesn't do it very well. We are fools if we say to ourselves, "We like the Greeks and dislike the French, so let's hire the Greek." We simply won't eat as well as we could have, and eating, after all, was the point of the club. On the other hand, it's *our* club, and so *our* job. And who shall say it is not within a man's rights to dispose of what really is his in as foolish a way as he likes?

And there is no irrationality, of course, if one imagines that the two applicants are equally qualified French chefs, and one is a cousin of one of our members, the other a perfect stranger. Here if we declare directly for the cousin, we do not act irrationally, we violate no one's rights, and indeed do not have a morally bad ground for making the choice we make. It's not a morally splendid ground, but it isn't a morally bad one either.

Universities differ from eating clubs in one way which is important for present purposes: in an eating club, those who consume what the club serves are the members, and thus the owners of the club themselves—by contrast, if the university is wholly private, those who consume what it serves are not among the owners. This makes a difference: the owners of the university have a responsibility not merely to themselves (as the owners of an eating club do), but also to those who come to buy what it offers. It could, I suppose, make plain in its advertising that it is prepared to allow the owner's racial or religious or other preferences to outweigh academic qualifications in its teachers. But in the absence of that, it must, in light of what a university is normally expected to be and to aim at, provide the best teachers it can afford. It does not merely act irrationally, but indeed violates the rights of its student-customers if it does not.

On the other hand, this leaves it open to the university that in case of a choice between equally qualified candidates, it violates no one's rights if it declares for the black because he is black, or for the white because he is white. To the wholly *private* university, that is, for that is all I have so far been talking of. Other things being equal—that is, given it has not advertised the job in a manner which would entitle applicants to believe that all who are equally qualified will be given an equal chance at it, and given it does not gratuitously give offense to those whom it rejects—the university may choose as it pleases, and violates no one's rights in doing so. Though no doubt its grounds for choosing may be morally bad ones, and we may even wish to say, more strongly, that it ought not choose as it does.

What will have come out in the preceding is that the issue I am concerned with is a moral, and not a legal one. My understanding is that the law does prevent an employer wholly in the private sector from choosing a white rather than a black on ground of that difference alone—though not from choosing a black rather than a white on ground of that difference alone. Now if, as many people say, legal rights (or perhaps, legal rights in a relatively just society) create moral rights, then even a moral investigation should take the law into account; and indeed, if I am not mistaken as to the law, it would have to be concluded that blacks (but not whites) do have rights of the kind I have been denying. I want to sidestep all this. My question can be re-put: would a private employer's choosing a white (or black) rather than a black (or white) on ground of that difference alone be a violation of anyone's rights if there were no law making it illegal? And the answer seems to me to be: it would not.

III

But hardly any college or university in America is purely private. As I said, most enjoy some public support, and the moral issues may be affected by the extent of the burden carried by the public. I shall concentrate on universities which are entirely publicly funded, such as state or city universities, and ignore the complications which might arise in case of partial private funding.

The special problem which arises here, as I see it, is this: where a community pays the bills, the community owns the university.

I said earlier that the members, who are therefore the owners, of a private eating club may declare for whichever chef they wish, even if the man they declare for is not as well qualified for the job as some other; in choosing amongst applicants, they are *not* choosing amongst fellow members of the club who is to get some benefit from the club. But now suppose, by contrast, that two of us who are members arrive at the same time, and there is only one available table. And suppose also that this has never happened before, and that the club has not voted on any policy for handling it when it does happen. What seems to me to be plain is this: the headwaiter cannot indulge in preferential seating, he cannot simply declare for one or the other of us on just any ground he pleases. He must randomize: as it might be, by tossing a coin.

Or again, suppose someone arrives at the dining room with a gift for the club: a large and very splendid apple tart. And suppose that this, too, has never happened before, and that the club has not voted on any policy for handling it when it does happen. What seems to me plain is this: the headwaiter cannot distribute that tart in just any manner, and on any ground he pleases. If the tart won't keep till the next meeting, and it's impossible to convene one now, he must divide the tart amongst us equally.

Consideration of these cases might suggest the following principle: every owner of a jointly owned property has a right to either an equal chance at, or an equal share in, any benefit which that property generates, and which is available for distribution amongst the owners—equal chance rather than equal share if the benefit is indivisible, or for some reason is better left undivided.

Now I have all along been taking it that the members of a club jointly own the club, and therefore jointly own whatever the club owns. It seems to me possible to view a community in the same way: to suppose that its members jointly own it, and therefore jointly own whatever it owns. If a community is properly viewed in this way, and if the principle I set out above is true, then every member of the community is a joint owner of whatever the community owns, and so in particular, a joint owner of its university; and therefore every member of the community has a right to an equal chance at, or equal share in, any benefit which the university generates, which is available for distribution amongst the owners. And that includes university jobs, if, as I argued, a university job is a benefit.

Alternatively, one might view a community as an imaginary Person: one might say that the members of that community are in some sense participants in that Person, but that they do not jointly own what the Person owns. One might in fact say the same of a club: that its members do not jointly own the club or anything which the club owns, but only in some sense participate in the Person which owns the things. And then the cases I mentioned might suggest an analogous principle: every "participant" in a Person (Community-Person, Club-Person) has a right to either an equal chance at, or an equal share in, any benefit which is generated by a property which that Person owns, which is available for distribution amongst the "participants."

On the other hand, if we accept any of this, we have to remember that there are cases in which a member may, without the slightest impropriety, be deprived of this equal chance or equal share. For it is plainly not required that the university's hiring officer decide who gets the available job by randomizing amongst *all* the community members, however well- or ill-qualified, who want it. The university's student-customers, after all, have rights too; and their rights to good teaching are surely more stringent than each member's right (if each has such a right) to an equal chance at the job. I think we do best to reserve the term "violation of a right" for cases in which a man is unjustly deprived of something he has a right to, and speak rather of "overriding a right" in cases in which, though a man is deprived of something he has a right to, it is not unjust to deprive him of it. So here the members' rights to an equal chance (if they have them) would be not violated, but merely overridden.

It could of course be said that these principles hold only of benefits of a kind I pointed to earlier, and called "pure" benefits (such as apples and apple tarts), and that we should find some other, weaker, principle to cover "impure" benefits (such as jobs).

Or it could be said that a university job is not a benefit which is available for distribution amongst the community members—that although a university job is a benefit, it is, in light of the rights of the students, available for distribution only amongst those members of the community who are best qualified to hold it. And therefore that they alone have a right to an equal chance at it.

It is important to notice, however, that unless *some* such principle as I have set out is true of the publicly owned university, there is no real problem about preferential hiring in it. Unless the white male applicant who is turned away had a right that this should not be done, doing so is quite certainly not violating any of his rights. Perhaps being joint owner of the university (on the first model) or being joint participant in the Person which owns the university (on the second model), does not give him a right to an equal chance at the job; perhaps he is neither joint owner nor joint participant (some third model is preferable), and it is something else which gives him his right to an equal chance at the job. Or perhaps he hasn't a right to an equal chance at the job, but has instead some other right which is violated by declaring for the equally qualified black or woman straightway. It is here that it seems to me it emerges most clearly that opponents of preferential hiring are merely expressing a gut reaction against it: for they have not asked themselves precisely what right is in question, and what it issues from.

Perhaps there is lurking in the background some sense that everyone has a right to "equal treatment," and that it is this which is violated by preferential hiring. But what on earth right is this? Mary surely does not have to decide between Tom and Dick by toss of a coin, if what is in question is marrying. Nor even, as I said earlier, if what is in question is giving out apples which she grew on her own land, on her own trees.

It could, of course, be argued that declaring for the black or woman straightway isn't violation of the white male applicant's rights, but is all the same wrong, bad, something which ought not be done. As I said, it is perfectly consistent that one ought not do something which is, nevertheless, no violation of anyone's rights to do. So perhaps opponents of preferential hiring might say that rights are not in question, and still argue against it on other grounds. I say they *might*, but I think they plainly do better not to. If the white male applicant has no rights which would be violated, and appointing the black or woman indirectly benefits other blacks or women (remember that need for role models), and thereby still more indirectly benefits us all (by widening the available pool of talent), then it is very hard to see how it could come out to be morally objectionable to declare for the black or woman straightway.

I think we should do the best we can for those who oppose preferential hiring: I think we should grant that the white male applicant has a right to an equal chance at the job, and see what happens for preferential hiring if we do. I shall simply leave open whether this right issues from considerations of the kind I drew attention to, and so also whether or not every member of the community, however well- or ill-qualified for the job, has the same right to an equal chance at it.

Now it is, I think, widely believed that we may, without injustice, refuse to grant a man what he has a right to only if *either* someone else has a conflicting and more stringent right, *or* there is some very great benefit to be obtained by doing so—perhaps that a disaster of some kind is thereby averted. If so, then there really is trouble for preferential hiring. For what more stringent right could be thought to override the right of the white male applicant for an equal chance? What great benefit obtained, what disaster averted, by declaring for the black or the woman straightway? I suggested that benefits are obtained, and they are not small ones. But are they large enough to override a right? If these questions cannot be satisfactorily answered, then it looks as if the hiring officer does act unjustly, and does violate the rights of the white males, if he declares for the black or woman straightway.

But in fact there are other ways in which a right may be overriden. Let's go back to that eating club again. Suppose that now it has happened that two of us arrive at the same time when there is only one available table; we think we had better decide on some policy for handling it when it happens. And suppose that we have of late had reason to be especially grateful to one of the members, whom I'll call Smith: Smith has done a series of very great favors for the club. It seems to me we might, out of gratitude to Smith, adopt the following policy: for the next six months, if two members arrive at the same time, and there is only one available table, then Smith gets in first, if he's one of the two; whereas if he's not, then the headwaiter shall toss a coin.

We might even vote that for the next year, if he wants apple tart, he gets more of it than the rest of us.

It seems to me that there would be no impropriety in our taking these actions—by which I mean to include that there would be no injustice in our taking them. Suppose another member, Jones, votes No. Suppose he says, "Look. I admit we all benefited from what Smith did for us. But still, I'm a member, and a member in as good standing as Smith is. So I have a right to an equal chance (and equal share), and I demand what I have a right to." I think we may rightly feel that Jones merely shows insensitivity: he does not adequately appreciate what Smith did for us. Jones, like all of us, has a right to an equal chance at such benefits as the club has available for distribution to the members; but there is no injustice in a majority's refusing to grant the members this equal chance, in the name of a debt of gratitude to Smith.

It is worth noticing an important difference between a debt of gratitude and debts owed to a creditor. Suppose the club had borrowed $1,000 from Dickenson, and then was left as a legacy a painting appraised at $1,000. If the club has no other saleable assets, and if no member is willing to buy the painting, then I take it that justice would precisely require *not* randomizing amongst the members who is to get that painting, but would instead require our offering it to Dickenson. Jones could not complain that to offer it to Dickenson is to treat him, Jones, unjustly: Dickenson has a right to be paid back, and that right is more stringent than any member's right to an equal chance at the painting. Now Smith, by contrast, did not have a right to be given anything, he did not have a right to our adopting a policy of preferential seating in his favor. If we fail to do anything for Dickenson, we do him an injustice; if we fail to do anything for Smith, we do *him* no injustice—our failing is not injustice, but ingratitude. There is no harm in speaking of debts of gratitude and in saying that they are owed to a benefactor, by analogy with debts owed to a creditor; but it is important to remember that a creditor has, and a benefactor does not have, a right to repayment.

To move now from clubs to more serious matters, suppose two candidates for a civil service job have equally good test scores, but that there is only one job available. We could decide between them by coin tossing. But in fact we do allow for declaring for A straightway, where A is a veteran, and B is not.[2] It may be that B is a nonveteran through no fault of his own: perhaps he was refused induction for flat feet or a heart murmur. That is, those things in virtue of which B is a nonveteran may be things which it was no more in his power to control or change than it is in anyone's power to control or change the color of his skin. Yet the fact is that B is not a veteran and A is. On the assumption that the veteran has served his country,[3] the country owes him something. And it seems plain that giving him preference is a not unjust way in which part of that debt of gratitude can be paid.

And now, finally, we should turn to those debts which are incurred by one who wrongs another. It is here we find what seems to me the most powerful argument for the conclusion that the preferential hiring of blacks and women is not unjust.

I obviously cannot claim any novelty for this argument: it's a very familiar one. Indeed, not merely is it familiar, but so are a battery of objections to it. It may be granted that if we have wronged A, we owe him something: we should make amends, we should compensate him for the wrong done him. It may even be granted that if we have wronged A, we must make amends, that justice requires it, and that a failure to make amends is not merely callousness, but injustice. But (a) are the young blacks and women who are amongst the current applicants for university jobs amongst the blacks and women who were wronged? To turn to particular cases, it might happen that the black applicant is middle class, son of professionals, and has had the very best in private schooling; or that the woman applicant is plainly the product of feminist upbringing and encouragement. Is it proper, much less required, that the black or woman be given preference over a white male who grew up in poverty, and has to make his own way and earn his encouragements? Again, (b) did we, the current members of the community, wrong any blacks or women? Lots of people once did; but then isn't it for them to do the compensating? That is, if they're still alive. For presumably nobody now alive owned any slaves, and perhaps nobody now alive voted against women's suffrage. And (c) what if the white male applicant for the job has never in any degree wronged any blacks or women? If so, *he* doesn't owe any debts to them, so why should *he* make amends to them?

These objections seem to me quite wrongheaded.

Obviously the situation for blacks and women is better than it was a hundred and fifty, fifty, twenty-five years ago. But it is absurd to suppose that the young blacks and women now of an age to apply for jobs have not been wronged. Large-scale, blatant, overt wrongs have presumably disappeared; but it is only within the last twenty-five years (perhaps the last ten years, in the case of women) that it has become at all widely agreed in this country that blacks and women must be recognized as having not merely this or that particular right normally recognized as belonging to white males, but all of the rights and respect which go with full membership in the community. Even young blacks and women have lived through downgrading for being black or female: they have not merely not been given that very equal chance at the benefits generated by what the community owns which is so firmly insisted on for white males, they have not until lately even been felt to have a right to it.

And even those who were not themselves downgraded for being black or female have suffered the consequences of the downgrading of other blacks and women: lack of self-confidence, and lack of self-respect. For where a community accepts that a person's being black, or being a woman, are right and proper grounds for denying that person full membership in the community, it can hardly be supposed that any but the most extraordinarily independent black or woman will escape self-doubt. All but the most extraordinarily independent of them have had to work harder—if only against self-doubt—than all but the most deprived white males, in the competition for a place amongst the best qualified.

If any black or woman has been unjustly deprived of what he or she has a right to, then of course justice does call for making amends. But what of the blacks and women who haven't actually been deprived of what they have a right to, but only made to suffer the consequences of injustice to other blacks and women? *Perhaps* justice doesn't require making amends to them as well; but common decency certainly does. To fail, at the very least, to make what counts as public apology to all, and to take positive steps to show that it is sincerely meant, is, if not injustice, then anyway a fault at least as serious as ingratitude.

Opting for a policy of preferential hiring may of course mean that some black or woman is preferred to some white male who as a matter of fact has had a harder life than the black or woman. But so may opting for a policy of veterans' preference mean that a healthy, unscarred, middle-class veteran is preferred to a poor, struggling, scarred nonveteran. Indeed, opting for a policy of settling who gets the job by having all equally qualified candidates draw straws may also mean that in a given case the candidate with the hardest life loses out. Opting for any policy other than hard-life preference may have this result.

I have no objection to anyone's arguing that it is precisely hard-life preference that we ought to opt for. If all, or anyway all of the equally qualified, have a right to an equal chance, then the argument would have to draw attention to something sufficiently powerful to override that right. But perhaps this could be done along the lines I followed in the case of blacks and women: perhaps it could be successfully argued that we have wronged those who have had hard lives, and therefore owe it to them to make amends. And then we should have in more extreme form a difficulty already present: how are these preferences to be ranked? Shall we place the hard-lifers ahead of blacks? Both ahead of women? And what about veterans? I leave these questions aside. My concern has been only to show that the white male applicant's right to an equal chance does not make it unjust to opt for a policy under which blacks and women are given preference. That a white male with a specially hard history may lose out under this policy cannot possibly be any objection to it, in the absence of a showing that hard-life preference is not unjust and, more important, takes priority over preference for blacks and women.

Last, it should be stressed that to opt for such a policy is not to make the young white male applicants themselves make amends for any wrongs done to blacks and women. Under such a policy, no one is asked to give up a job which is already his; the job for which the white male competes isn't his, but is the community's, and it is the hiring officer who gives it to the black or woman in the community's name. Of course the white male is asked to give up his equal chance at the job. But that is not something he pays to the black or woman by way of making amends; it is something the community takes away from him in order that *it* may make amends.

Still, the community does impose a burden on him: it is able to make amends for its wrongs only by taking something away from him, something which, after all, we are supposing he has a right to. And why should *he* pay the cost of the community's amends-making?

If there were some appropriate way in which the community could make amends to its blacks and women, some way which did not require depriving anyone of anything he has a right to, then that would be the best course of action for it to take. Or if there were anyway some way in which the costs could be shared by everyone, and not imposed entirely on the young white male job applicants, then that would be, if not the best, then anyway better than opting for a policy of preferential hiring. But in fact the nature of the wrongs done is such as to make jobs the best and most suitable form of compensation. What blacks and women were denied was full membership in the community; and nothing can more appropriately make amends for that wrong than precisely what will make them feel they now finally have it. And that means jobs. Financial compensation (the cost of which could be shared equally) slips through the fingers; having a job, and discovering you do it well, yield—perhaps better than anything else—that very self-respect which blacks and women have had to do without.

But of course choosing this way of making amends means that the costs are imposed on the young white male applicants who are turned away. And so it should be noticed that it is not entirely inappropriate that those applicants should pay the costs. No doubt few, if any, have themselves, individually, done any wrongs to blacks and women. But they have profited from the wrongs the community did. Many may actually have been direct beneficiaries of policies which excluded or downgraded blacks and women—perhaps in school admissions, perhaps in access to financial aid, perhaps elsewhere; and even those who did not directly benefit in this way had, at any rate, the advantage in the competition which comes of confidence in one's full membership, and of one's rights being recognized as a matter of course.

49

Of course it isn't only the young white male applicant for a university job who has benefited from the exclusion of blacks and women; the older white male, now comfortably tenured, also benefited, and many defenders of preferential hiring feel that he should be asked to share the costs. Well, presumably we can't demand that he give up his job, or share it. But it seems to me in place to expect the occupants of comfortable professorial chairs to contribute in some way, to make some form of return to the young white male who bears the cost and is turned away. It will have been plain that I find the outcry now heard against preferential hiring in the universities objectionable; it would also be objectionable that those of us who are now securely situated should placidly defend it, with no more than a sigh of regret for the young white male who pays for it.

IV

One final word: "discrimination." I am inclined to think we so use it that if anyone is convicted of discriminating against blacks, women, white males, or what have you, then he is thereby convicted of acting unjustly. If so, and if I am right in thinking that preferential hiring in the restricted range of cases we have been looking at is *not* unjust, then we have two options: (a) we can simply reply that to opt for a policy of preferential hiring in those cases is not to opt for a policy of discriminating against white males, or (b) we can hope to get usage changed— e.g., by trying to get people to allow that there is discriminating against and discriminating against, and that some is unjust, but some is not.

Best of all, however, would be for that phrase to be avoided altogether. It's at best a blunt tool: there are all sorts of nice moral discriminations [*sic*] which one is unable to make while occupied with it. And that bluntness itself fits it to do harm: blacks and women are hardly likely to see through to what precisely is owed them while they are being accused of welcoming what is unjust.

Notes

1. This essay is an expanded version of a talk given at the Conference on the Liberation of Female Persons, held at North Carolina State University at Raleigh, on March 26–28, 1973, under a grant from the S & H Foundation. I am indebted to James Thomson and the members of the Society for Ethical and Legal Philosophy for criticism of an earlier draft.
2. To the best of my knowledge, the analogy between veterans' preference and the preferential hiring of blacks has been mentioned in print only by Edward T. Chase, in a letter to the editor, *Commentary*, February 1973.
3. Many people would reject this assumption, or perhaps accept it only selectively, for veterans of this or that particular war. I ignore this. What interests me is what follows if we make the assumption—as, of course, many other people do; more, it seems, than do not.

Preferential Hiring: A Reply to Judith Jarvis Thomson

Robert Simon

Judith Jarvis Thomson has defended preferential hiring of women and black persons in universities.[1] She restricts her defense of the assignment of preference to only those cases where candidates from preferred groups and their white male competitors are equally qualified, although she suggests that her argument can be extended to cover cases where the qualifications are unequal as well. The argument in question is compensatory; it is because of pervasive patterns of unjust discrimination against black persons and women that justice, or at least common decency, requires that amends be made.

While Thomson's analysis surely clarifies many of the issues at stake, I find it seriously incomplete. I will argue that even if her claim that compensation is due victims of social injustice is correct (as I think it is), it is questionable nevertheless whether preferential hiring is an acceptable method of distributing such compensation. This is so, even if, as Thomson argues, compensatory claims override the right of the white male applicant to equal consideration from the appointing officer. For implementation of preferential hiring policies may involve claims, perhaps even claims of right, other than the above right of the white male applicant. In the case of the claims I have in mind, the best that can be said is that where preferential hiring is concerned, they are arbitrarily ignored. If so, and if such claims are themselves warranted, then preferential hiring, while *perhaps* not unjust, is open to far more serious question than Thomson acknowledges.

I

A familiar objection to special treatment for blacks and women is that, if such a practice is justified, other victims of injustice or misfortune ought to receive special treatment too. While arguing that virtually all women and black persons have been harmed, either directly or indirectly, by discrimination, Thomson acknowledges that in any particular case, a white male may have been victimized to a greater extent than have the blacks or women with whom he is competing. However, she denies that other victims of injustice or misfortune ought automatically to have priority over blacks and women where distribution of compensation is concerned. Just as veterans receive preference with respect to employment in the civil service, as payment for the service they have performed for society, so can blacks and women legitimately be given preference in university hiring, in payment of the debt owed them. And just as the former policy can justify hiring a veteran who in fact had an easy time of it over a nonveteran who made great sacrifices for the public good, so too can the latter policy justify hiring a relatively undeprived member of a preferred group over a more disadvantaged member of a nonpreferred group.

But surely if the reason for giving a particular veteran preference is that he performed a service for his country, that same preference must be given to anyone who performed a similar service. Likewise, if the reason for giving preference to a black person or to a woman is that the recipient has been injured due to an unjust practice, then preference must be given to anyone who has been similarly injured. So, it appears, there can be no relevant *group* to which compensation ought to be made, other than that made up of and only of those who have been injured or victimized.[2] Although, as Thomson claims, all blacks and women may be members of that latter group, they deserve compensation *qua* victim and not *qua* black person or woman.

There are at least two possible replies that can be made to this sort of objection. First, it might be agreed that anyone injured in the same way as blacks or women ought to receive compensation. But then, "same way" is characterized so narrowly that it applies to no one except blacks and women. While there is nothing logically objectionable about such a reply, it may nevertheless be morally objectionable. For it implies that a nonblack male who has been terribly injured by a social injustice has less of a claim to compensation than a black or woman who has only been minimally injured. And this implication may be morally unacceptable.

A more plausible line of response may involve shifting our attention from compensation of individuals to collective compensation of groups.[3] Once this shift is made, it can be acknowledged that as individuals, some white males may have stronger compensatory claims than blacks or women. But as compensation is owed the group, it is group claims that must be weighed, not individual ones. And surely, at the group level, the claims of black persons and women to compensation are among the strongest there are.

Suppose we grant that certain groups, including those specified by Thomson, are owed collective compensation. What should be noted is that the conclusion of concern here—that preferential hiring policies are acceptable instruments for compensating groups—does not directly follow. To derive such a conclusion validly, one would have to provide additional premises specifying the relation between collective compensation to groups and distribution of that compensation to individual members. For it does not follow from the fact that some group members are compensated that the group is compensated. Thus, if through a computer error, every member of the American Philosophical Association was asked to pay additional taxes, then if the government provided compensation for this error, it would not follow that it had compensated the association. Rather, it would have compensated each member *qua* individual. So what is required, where preferential hiring is concerned, are plausible premises showing how the preferential award of jobs to group members counts as collective compensation for the group.

Thomson provides no such additional premises. Moreover, there is good reason to think that if any such premises were provided, they would count against preferential hiring as an instrument of collective compensation. This is because although compensation is owed to the group, preferential hiring policies award compensation to an arbitrarily selected segment of the group; namely, those who have the ability and qualifications to be seriously considered for the jobs available. Surely, it is far more plausible to think that collective compensation ought to be equally available to all group members, or at least to all kinds of group members.[4] The claim that although compensation is owed collectively to a group, only a special sort of group member is eligible to receive it, while perhaps not incoherent, certainly ought to be rejected as arbitrary, at least in the absence of an argument to the contrary.

Accordingly, the proponent of preferential hiring faces the following dilemma. Either compensation is to be made on an individual basis, in which case the fact that one is black or a woman is irrelevant to whether one ought to receive special treatment, or it is made on a group basis, in which case it is far from clear that preferential hiring policies are acceptable compensatory instruments. Until this dilemma is resolved, assuming it can be resolved at all, the compensatory argument for preferential hiring is seriously incomplete at a crucial point.

II

Even if the above difficulty could be resolved, however, other problems remain. For example, once those entitled to compensatory benefits have been identified, questions arise concerning how satisfactorily preferential hiring policies honor such entitlements.

Consider, for example, a plausible principle of compensatory justice which might be called the Proportionality Principle (PP). According to the PP, the strength of one's compensatory claim and the quantity of compensation one is entitled to is, *ceteris paribus*, proportional to the degree of injury suffered. A corollary of the PP is that equal injury gives rise to compensatory claims of equal strength. Thus, if X and Y were both injured to the same extent, and both deserve compensation for their injury, then *ceteris paribus*, each has a compensatory claim of equal strength and each is entitled to equal compensation.

Now, it is extremely unlikely that a hiring program which gives preference to blacks and women will satisfy the PP because of the arbitrariness implicit in the search for candidates on the open market. Thus, three candidates, each members of previously victimized groups, may well wind up with highly disparate positions. One may secure employment in a prestigious department of a leading university while another may be hired by a university which hardly merits the name. The third might not be hired at all.

The point is that where the marketplace is used to distribute compensation, distribution will be by market principles, and hence only accidentally will be fitting in view of the injury suffered and compensation provided for others. While any compensation may be better than none, this would hardly appear to be a satisfactory way of making amends to the victimized.

"Compensation according to ability" or "compensation according to marketability" surely are dubious principles of compensatory justice. On the contrary, those with the strongest compensatory claims should be compensated first (and most). Where compensatory claims are equal, but not everybody can actually be compensated, some fair method of distribution should be employed, e.g., a lottery. Preferential hiring policies, then, to the extent that they violate the PP, *arbitrarily* discriminate in favor of some victims of past injustice and against others. The basis on which compensation is awarded is independent of the basis on which it is owed, and so distribution is determined by application of principles which are irrelevant from the point of view of compensatory justice.

Now, perhaps this is not enough to show that the use of preferential hiring as a compensatory instrument is unjust, or even unjustified. But perhaps it is enough to show that the case for the justice or justification of such a policy has not yet been made. Surely, we can say, at the very least, that a policy which discriminates in the arbitrary fashion discussed above is not a particularly satisfactory compensatory mechanism. If so, the direction in which considerations of compensatory justice and common decency point are far less apparent than Thomson suggests.

III

So far, I have considered arbitrariness in the distribution of compensatory benefits by preferential hiring policies. However, arbitrariness involved in the assessment of costs is also of concern.

Thus, it is sometimes argued that preferential hiring policies place the burden of providing compensation on young white males who are just entering the job market. This is held to be unfair, because, first, there is no special reason for placing the burden on that particular group and, second, because many members of that group are not responsible for the injury done to blacks and women. In response to the first point, Thomson acknowledges that it seems to her "in place to expect the occupants of comfortable professorial chairs to contribute in some way, to make some form of return to the young white male who bears the cost" (chap. 9, p. 50). In response to the second point, Thomson concedes that few, if any, white male applicants to university positions individually have done any wrong to women or black persons. However, she continues, many have profited by the wrongs inflicted by others. So it is not unfitting that they be asked to make sacrifices now.

However, it is far from clear, at least to me, that this reply is satisfactory. For even if the group which bears the cost is expanded to include full professors, why should that new group be singled out? The very same consideration that required the original expansion would seem to require a still wider one. Indeed, it would seem this point can be pressed until costs are assessed against society as a whole. This is exactly the position taken by Paul Taylor, who writes, "The obligation to offer such benefits to [the previously victimized] group . . . is an obligation that falls on society in general, not on any particular person. For it is the society in general, that through its established [discriminatory] social practice, brought upon itself the obligation" (chap. 4, pp. 14–15).

Perhaps, however, the claim that preferential hiring policies arbitrarily distribute burdens can be rebutted. For presumably the advocate of preferential hiring does not want to restrict such a practice to universities but rather would wish it to apply throughout society. If so, and *if* persons at the upper echelons are expected to share costs with young white male job applicants, then perhaps a case can be made that burdens are equitably distributed throughout society.

Even here, however, there are two points an opponent of preferential hiring can make. First, he can point out that burdens are not equitably distributed now. Consequently, to the extent that preferential policies are employed at present, then to that extent are burdens arbitrarily imposed now. Second, he can question the assumption that if someone gains from an unjust practice for which he is not responsible and even opposes, the gain is not really his and can be taken from him without injustice. This assumption is central to the compensatory argument for preferential hiring since if it is unacceptable, no justification remains for requiring "innocent bystanders" to provide compensation.

If X benefits at the expense of Y because of the operation of an unjust social institution, then is the benefit which accrues to X really deserved by Y? It seems to me that normally the answer will be affirmative. But it also seems to me that there is a significant class of cases where an affirmative response *may* not be justified. Suppose X himself is the victim of a similarly unjust social practice so that Z benefits at his expense. In such circumstances, it is questionable whether X ought to compensate Y, especially if X played no personal role in the formation of the unjust institutions at issue. Perhaps *both* X and Y ought to receive (different degrees of) compensation from Z.

If this point is sound, it becomes questionable whether *all* members of non-preferred groups are equally liable (or even liable at all) for provision of compensation. It is especially questionable in the case where the individual from the nonpreferred group has been unjustly victimized to a far greater extent than the individual from the preferred group. Hence, even if it were true that all members of nonpreferred groups have profited from discrimination against members of preferred groups, it does not automatically follow that all are equally liable for providing compensation. Insofar as preferential hiring policies do not take this into account, they are open to the charge of arbitrariness in assessing the costs of compensation.

One more point seems to require mention here. If preferential hiring policies are expanded, as Thomson suggests, to cases where the candidates are not equally qualified, a further difficulty arises. To the extent that lowering quality lowers efficiency, members of victimized groups are likely to lose more than others. This may be particularly important in educational contexts. Students from such groups may have been exposed to poorer instruction than was made available to others. But they might have greater need for better instruction than, say, middle-class students from affluent backgrounds.

Suppose that members of previously discriminated against groups deserve special support in developing their capacities and talents. Then, it would seem that educational institutions charged with promoting such development have a corresponding obligation to develop those capacities and talents to the best of their ability. Presumably, this requires hiring the best available faculty and administration.

What we seem to have here is a conflict within the framework of compensatory justice itself. Even if preferential hiring is an acceptable method for distributing compensation, the compensation so distributed may decrease the beneficial effects of education. And this may adversely affect more members of the preferred groups than are helped by the preferential policy.[5]

IV

The argument of this paper is not directed against the view that victims of grave social injustice in America deserve compensation. On the contrary, a strong case can be made for providing such compensation.[6] Rather, I have tried to show that the case for using preferential hiring as a *means* of providing such compensation is incomplete at three crucial points:

(1) It is not clear to whom compensation should be made, groups or individuals. If the former, it has not been shown that preferential hiring compensates the group. If the latter, it has not been shown why membership in a group (other than that composed of, and only of, the victimized) is relevant to determining who should be compensated.

(2) It has not been shown that compensation should be awarded on grounds of marketability, grounds that certainly seem to be irrelevant from the compensatory point of view.

(3) It has not been shown that arbitrariness and inequity are or can be avoided in distributing the costs of preferential hiring policies of the sort in question.

If these charges have force, then whether or not preferential hiring can be justified on other grounds, the compensatory argument for such a practice is far more doubtful than Thomson's article suggests.

Notes

I am grateful to the American Council of Learned Societies and to Hamilton College for their support during the period the arguments set forth here were first formulated.

1. See chapter 9 of this volume.
2. This point also has been argued for recently by J. L. Cowan, "Inverse Discrimination." See chapter 2 of this volume.
3. Such a position has been defended by Paul Taylor, in his "Reverse Discrimination and Compensatory Justice." See chapter 4 of this volume.
4. Taylor would apparently agree. See chapter 4, p. 14.
5. This will not apply as frequently as might be thought, however, if it is true that membership in a preferred group is itself an *educational* qualification. That this is so is sometimes argued on the grounds, for example, that women and black professors are necessary as "role models" for women and black students. Thomson, however, expresses doubts about arguments of this sort (pp. 38–39). More important, if such arguments were strong, it would seem that a case could be made for hiring black and women professors on grounds of merit. That is, they should be hired because they can do the job better than others, not (only) because they are owed compensation. In any case, however, my argument in the text would still apply to those instances in which the candidate from the preferred group was not as qualified (in the broad sense of "qualified," in which membership in the preferred group is one qualification) as the candidates from nonpreferred groups.
6. For a defense of the provision of monetary compensation or reparations, see Hugo Bedau, "Compensatory Justice and the Black Manifesto," *The Monist* 56, no. 1 (1972): 20–42.

Justifying Reverse Discrimination
in Employment

George Sher

A currently favored way of compensating for past discrimination is to afford preferential treatment to the members of those groups which have been discriminated against in the past. I propose to examine the rationale behind this practice when it is applied in the area of employment. I want to ask whether, and if so under what conditions, past acts of discrimination against members of a particular group justify the current hiring of a member of that group who is less than the best qualified applicant for a given job. Since I am mainly concerned about exploring the relations between past discrimination and present claims to employment, I shall make the assumption that each applicant is at least minimally competent to perform the job he seeks; this will eliminate the need to consider the claims of those who are to receive the services in question. Whether it is ever justifiable to discriminate in favor of an incompetent applicant, or a less than best qualified applicant for a job such as teaching, in which almost any increase in employee competence brings a real increase in services rendered, will be left to be decided elsewhere. Such questions, which turn on balancing the claim of the less than best qualified applicant against the competing claims of those who are to receive his services, are not as basic as the question of whether the less than best qualified applicant ever *has* a claim to employment.[1]

I

It is sometimes argued, when members of a particular group have been barred from employment of a certain kind, that since this group has in the past received *less* than its fair share of the employment in question, it now deserves to receive *more* by way of compensation.[2] This argument, if sound, has the virtue of showing clearly why preferential treatment should be extended even to those current group members who have not themselves been denied employment: if the point of reverse discrimination is to compensate a wronged *group*, it will presumably hardly matter if those who are preferentially hired were not among the original victims of discrimination. However, the argument's basic presupposition, that groups as opposed to their individual members are the sorts of entities that can be wronged and deserve redress, is itself problematic.[3] Thus the defense of reverse discrimination would be convincing only if it were backed by a further argument showing that groups can indeed be wronged and have deserts of the relevant sort. No one, as far as I know, has yet produced a powerful argument to this effect, and I am not hopeful about the possibilities. Therefore I shall not try to develop a defense of reverse discrimination along these lines.

Another possible way of connecting past acts of discrimination in hiring with the claims of current group members is to argue that even if these current group members have not (yet) been denied *employment*, their membership in the group makes it very likely that they have been discriminatorily deprived of *other* sorts of goods. It is a commonplace, after all, that people who are forced to do menial and low-paying jobs must often endure corresponding privations in housing, diet, and other areas. These privations are apt to be distributed among young and old alike, and so to afflict even those group members who are still too young to have had their qualifications for employment bypassed. It is, moreover, generally acknowledged by both common sense and law that a person who has been deprived of a certain amount of one sort of good may sometimes reasonably be compensated by an equivalent amount of a good of another sort. (It is this principle, surely, that underlies the legal practice of awarding sums of money to compensate for pain incurred in accidents, damaged reputations, etc.) Given these facts and this principle, it appears that the preferential hiring of current members of discriminated-against groups may be justified as compensation for the *other* sorts of discrimination these individuals are apt to have suffered.[4]

But, although this argument seems more promising than one presupposing group deserts, it surely cannot be accepted as it stands. For one thing, insofar as the point is simply to compensate individuals for the various sorts of privations they have suffered, there is no special reason to use reverse discrimination rather than some other mechanism to effect compensation. There are, moreover, certain other mechanisms of redress which seem prima facie preferable. It seems, for instance, that it would be most appropriate to compensate for past privations simply by making preferentially available to the discriminated-against individuals equivalent amounts of the very same sorts of goods of which they have been deprived; simple cash settlements would allow a far greater precision in the adjustment of compensation to privation than reverse discriminatory hiring ever could. Insofar as it does not provide any reason to adopt reverse discrimination rather than these prima facie preferable mechanisms of redress, the suggested defense of reverse discrimination is at least incomplete.

Moreover, and even more important, if reverse discrimination is viewed simply as a form of compensation for past privations, there are serious questions about its fairness. Certainly the privations to be compensated for are not the sole responsibility of those individuals whose superior qualifications will have to be bypassed in the reverse discriminatory process. These individuals, if responsible for those privations at all, will at least be no more responsible than others with relevantly similar histories. Yet reverse discrimination will compensate for the privations in question at the expense of these individuals alone. It will have no effect at all upon those other, equally responsible persons whose qualifications are inferior to begin with, who are already entrenched in their jobs, or whose vocations are noncompetitive in nature. Surely it is unfair to distribute the burden of compensation so unequally.[5]

These considerations show, I think, that reverse discriminatory hiring of members of groups that have been denied jobs in the past cannot be justified simply by the fact that each group member has been discriminated against in other areas. If this fact is to enter into the justification of reverse discrimination at all, it must be in some more complicated way.

II

Consider again the sorts of privations that are apt to be distributed among the members of those groups restricted in large part to menial and low-paying jobs. These individuals, we said, are apt to live in substandard homes, to subsist on improper and imbalanced diets, and to receive inadequate educations. Now, it is certainly true that adequate housing, food, and education are goods in and of themselves; a life without them is certainly less pleasant and less full than one with them. But, and crucially, they are also goods in a different sense entirely. It is an obvious and well-documented fact that (at least) the sorts of nourishment and education a person receives as a child will causally affect the sorts of skills and capacities he will have as an adult—including, of course, the very skills which are needed if he is to compete on equal terms for jobs and other goods. Since this is so, a child who is deprived of adequate food and education may lose not only the immediate enjoyments which a comfortable and stimulating environment bring but also the subsequent ability to compete equally for other things of intrinsic value. But to lose this ability to compete is, in essence, to lose one's access to the goods that are being competed for; and this, surely, is itself a privation to be compensated for if possible. It is, I think, the key to an adequate justification of reverse discrimination to see that practice, not as the redressing of *past* privations, but rather as a way of neutralizing the *present* competitive disadvantage *caused* by those past privations and thus as a way of restoring equal access to those goods which society distributes competitively.[6] When reverse discrimination is justified in this way, many of the difficulties besetting the simpler justification of it disappear.

For whenever someone has been irrevocably deprived of a certain good and there are several alternative ways of providing him with an equivalent amount of another good, it will *ceteris paribus* be preferable to choose whichever substitute comes closest to actually replacing the lost good. It is this principle that makes preferential access to decent housing, food, and education especially desirable as a way of compensating for the experiential impoverishment of a deprived childhood. If, however, we are concerned to compensate not for the experiential poverty, but for the effects of childhood deprivations, then this principle tells just as heavily for reverse discrimination as the proper form of compensation. If the lost good is just the *ability* to compete on equal terms for first-level goods like desirable jobs, then surely the most appropriate (and so preferable) way of substituting for what has been lost is just to remove the *necessity* of competing on equal terms for these goods—which, of course, is precisely what reverse discrimination does.

When reverse discrimination is viewed as compensation for lost ability to compete on equal terms, a reasonable case can also be made for its fairness. Our doubts about its fairness arose because it seemed to place the entire burden of redress upon those individuals whose superior qualifications are bypassed in the reverse discriminatory process. This seemed wrong because these individuals are, of course, not apt to be any more responsible for past discrimination than others with relevantly similar histories. But, as we are now in a position to see, this objection misses the point. The crucial fact about these individuals is not that they are more *responsible* for past discrimination than others with relevantly similar histories (in fact, the dirty work may well have been done before any of their generation attained the age of responsibility), but rather than unless reverse discrimination is practiced, they will *benefit* more than the others from its effects on their competitors. They will benefit more because unless they are restrained, they, but not the others, will use their competitive edge to claim jobs which their competitors would otherwise have gotten. Thus, it is only because they stand to *gain* the most from the relevant effects of the *original* discrimination, that the bypassed individuals stand to *lose* the most from *reverse* discrimination.[7] This is surely a valid reply to the charge that reverse discrimination does not distribute the burden of compensation equally.

III

So far, the argument has been that reverse discrimination is justified insofar as it neutralizes competitive disadvantages caused by past privations. This may be correct, but it is also oversimplified. In actuality, there are many ways in which a person's environment may affect his ability to compete; and there may well be logical differences among these ways which affect the degree to which reverse discrimination is called for. Consider, for example, the following cases:

(1) An inadequate education prevents someone from acquiring the degree of a certain skill that he would have been able to acquire with a better education.

(2) An inadequate diet, lack of early intellectual stimulation, etc., lower an individual's ability, and thus prevent him from acquiring the degree of competence in a skill that he would otherwise have been able to acquire.

(3) The likelihood that he will not be able to use a certain skill because he belongs to a group which has been discriminated against in the past leads a person to decide, rationally, not even to try developing that skill.

(4) Some aspect of this childhood environment renders an individual incapable of putting forth the sustained effort needed to improve his skills.

These are four different ways in which past privations might adversely affect a person's skills. Ignoring for analytical purposes the fact that privation often works in more than one of these ways at a time, shall we say that reverse discrimination is equally called for in each case?

It might seem that we should say it is, since in each case a difference in the individual's environment would have been accompanied by an increase in his mastery of a certain skill (and, hence, by an improvement in his competitive position with respect to jobs requiring that skill). But this blanket counterfactual formulation conceals several important distinctions. For one thing, it suggests (and our justification of reverse discrimination seems to require) the possibility of giving *just enough* preferential treatment of the disadvantaged individual in each case to restore to him the competitive position that he would have had, had he not suffered his initial disadvantage. But in fact, this does not seem to be equally possible in all cases. We can roughly calculate the difference that a certain improvement in education or intellectual stimulation would have made in the development of a person's skills if his efforts had been held constant (cases 1 and 2), for achievement is known to be a relatively straightforward compositional function of ability, environmental factors, and effort. We cannot, however, calculate in the same way the difference that improved prospects or environment would have made in degree of *effort* expended; for although effort is affected by environmental factors, it is not a known compositional function of them (or of anything else). Because of this, there would be no way for us to decide how much preferential treatment is just enough to make up for the efforts that a particular disadvantaged individual would have made under happier circumstances.

There is also another problem with (3) and (4). Even if there were a way to afford a disadvantaged person just enough preferential treatment to make up for the efforts he was prevented from making by his environment, it is not clear that he *ought* to be afforded that much preferential treatment. To allow this, after all, would be to concede that the effort he *would* have made under other conditions is worth just as much as the effort that his rival actually *did* make; and this, I think, is implausible. Surely a person who *actually has* labored long and hard to achieve a given degree of a certain skill is more deserving of a job requiring that skill than another who is equal in all other relevant respects, but who merely *would* have worked and achieved the same amount under different conditions. Because actual effort creates desert in a way that merely possible effort does not, reverse discrimination to restore precisely the competitive position that a person would have had if he had not been prevented from working harder would not be desirable even if it were possible.

There is perhaps also a further distinction to be made here. A person who is rationally persuaded by an absence of opportunities not to develop a certain skill (case 3) will typically not undergo any sort of character transformation in the process of making this decision. He will be the same person after his decision as before it, and, most often, the same person without his skill as with it. In cases such as (4), this is less clear. A person who is rendered incapable of effort by his environment does in a sense undergo a character transformation; to become truly incapable of sustained effort is to become a different (and less meritorious) person from the person one would otherwise have been. Because of this (and somewhat paradoxically, since his character change is itself apt to stem from factors beyond his control), such an individual may have less of a claim to reverse discrimination than one whose lack of effort does not flow from even an environmentally induced character fault, but rather from a justified rational decision.[8]

IV

When reverse discrimination is discussed in a nontheoretical context, it is usually assumed that the people most deserving of such treatment are blacks, members of other ethnic minorities, and women. In this last section, I shall bring the results of the foregoing discussion to bear on this assumption. Doubts will be raised both about the analogy between the claims of blacks and women to reverse discrimination and about the propriety, in absolute terms, of singling out either group as the proper recipient of such treatment.

For many people, the analogy between the claims of blacks and the claims of women to reverse discrimination rests simply upon the undoubted fact that both groups have been discriminatorily denied jobs in the past. But on the account just proposed, past discrimination justifies reverse discrimination only insofar as it has adversely affected the competitive position of present group members. When this standard is invoked, the analogy between the claims of blacks and those of women seems immediately to break down. The exclusion of blacks from good jobs in the past has been only one element in an interlocking pattern of exclusions and often has resulted in a poverty issuing in (and in turn reinforced by) such other privations as inadequate nourishment, housing, and health care, lack of time to provide adequate guidance and intellectual stimulation for the young, dependence on (often inadequate) public education, etc. It is this whole complex of privations that undermines the ability of the young to compete; and it is largely because of its central causal role in this complex that the past unavailability of good jobs for blacks justifies reverse discrimination in their favor now. In the case of women, past discrimination in employment simply has not played the same role. Because children commonly come equipped with both male *and* female parents, the inability of the female parent to get a good job need not, and usually does not, result in a poverty detracting from the quality of the nourishment, education, housing, health, or intellectual stimulation of the female child (and, of course, when such poverty does result, it affects male and female children indifferently). For this reason, the past inaccessibility of good jobs for women does not seem to create for them the same sort of claim on reverse discrimination that its counterpart does for blacks.

Many defenders of reverse discrimination in favor of women would reply at this point that although past discrimination in employment has of course not played the *same* causal role in the case of women which it has in the case of blacks, it has nevertheless played *a* causal role in both cases. In the case of women, the argument runs, that role has been mainly psychological: past discrimination in hiring has led to a scarcity of female "role models" of suitably high achievement. This lack, together with a culture which in many other ways subtly inculcates the idea that women should not or cannot do the jobs that men do, has in turn made women psychologically less able to do these jobs. This argument is hard to assess fully, since it obviously rests on a complex and problematic psychological claim.[9] The following objections, however, are surely relevant. First, even if it is granted without question that cultural bias and absence of suitable role models do have some direct and pervasive effect upon women, it is not clear that this effect must take the form of a reduction of women's *abilities* to do the jobs men do. A more likely outcome would seem to be a reduction of women's *inclinations* to do these jobs—a result whose proper compensation is not preferential treatment of those women who have sought the jobs in question, but rather the encouragement of others to seek those jobs as well. Of course, this disinclination to do these jobs may in turn lead some women not to develop the relevant skills; to the extent that this occurs, the competitive position of these women will indeed be affected, albeit indirectly, by the scarcity of female role models. Even here, however, the resulting disadvantage will not be comparable to those commonly produced by the poverty syndrome. It will flow solely from lack of effort, and so will be of the sort (cases 3 and 4) that neither calls for nor admits of full equalization by reverse discrimination. Moreover, and conclusively, since there is surely the same dearth of role models, etc., for blacks as for women, whatever psychological disadvantages accrue to women because of this will beset blacks as well. Since blacks, but not women, must also suffer the privations associated with poverty, it follows that they are the group more deserving of reverse discrimination.

Strictly speaking, however, the account offered here does not allow us to speak this way of *either* group. If the point of reverse discrimination is to compensate for competitive disadvantages caused by past discrimination, it will be justified in favor of only those group members whose abilities have actually been reduced; and it would be most implausible to suppose that *every* black (or *every* woman) has been affected in this way. Blacks from middle-class or affluent backgrounds will surely have escaped many, if not all, of the competitive handicaps besetting those raised under less fortunate circumstances; and if they have, our account provides no reason to practice reverse discrimination in their favor. Again, whites from impoverished backgrounds may suffer many, if not all, of the competitive handicaps besetting their black counterparts; and if they do, the account provides no reason *not* to practice reverse discrimination in their favor. Generally, the proposed account allows us to view racial (and sexual) boundaries only as roughly suggesting which individuals are likely to have been disadvantaged by past discrimination. Anyone who construes these boundaries as playing a different and more decisive role must show us that a different defense of reverse discrimination is plausible.

Notes

I am grateful to Michael Levin, Edward Erwin, and my wife, Emily Gordon Sher, for helpful discussion of this topic.

1. In what follows I will have nothing to say about utilitarian justifications of reverse discrimination. There are two reasons for this. First, the winds of utilitarian argumentation blow in too many directions. It is certainly socially beneficial to avoid the desperate actions to which festering resentments may lead—but so too is it socially

useful to confirm the validity of qualifications of the traditional sort, to assure those who have amassed such qualifications that "the rules of the game have not been changed in the middle," that accomplishment has not been downgraded in society's eyes. How could these conflicting utilities possibly be measured against one another?

Second and even more important, to rest a defense of reverse discrimination upon utilitarian considerations would be to ignore what is surely the guiding intuition of its proponents, that this treatment is *deserved* where discrimination has been practiced in the past. It is the intention that reverse discrimination is a matter not (only) of social good but of right which I want to try to elucidate.

2. This argument, as well as the others I shall consider, presupposes that jobs are (among other things) *goods*, and so ought to be distributed as fairly as possible. This presupposition seems to be amply supported by the sheer economic necessity of earning a living, as well as by the fact that some jobs carry more prestige and are more interesting and pay better than others.

3. As Robert Simon has pointed out in "Preferential Hiring: A Reply to Judith Jarvis Thomson" (chap. 10) it is far from clear that the preferential hiring of its individual members could be a proper form of compensation for any wronged group that did exist.

4. A version of this argument is advanced by Judith Jarvis Thomson in "Preferential Hiring," chapter 9.

5. Cf. Simon, "Preferential Hiring," chap. 10, pp. 53–54.

6. A similar justification of reverse discrimination is suggested, but not ultimately endorsed, by Thomas Nagel in "Equal Treatment and Compensatory Discrimination," *Philosophy and Public Affairs* 2, no. 4 (summer 1973): 348–63. Nagel rejects this justification on the grounds that a system distributing goods solely on the basis of performance determined by native ability would itself be unjust, even if not as unjust as one distributing goods on a racial or sexual basis. I shall not comment on this, except to remark that our moral intuitions surely run the other way: the average person would certainly find the latter system of distribution *far* more unjust than the former, if, indeed, he found the former unjust at all. Because of this, the burden is on Nagel to show exactly why a purely meritocratic system of distribution would be unjust.

7. It is tempting, but I think largely irrelevant, to object here that many who are now entrenched in their jobs (tenured professors, for example) have already benefited from the effects of past discrimination at least as much as the currently best qualified applicant will if reverse discrimination is not practiced. While many such individuals have undoubtedly benefited from the effects of discrimination upon their *original* competitors, few if any are likely to have benefited from a reduction in the abilities of the *currently best qualified applicant's* competitor. As long as none of them have so benefited, the best qualified applicant in question will still stand to gain the most from that *particular* effect of past discrimination, and so reverse discrimination against him will remain fair. Of course, there will also be cases in which an entrenched person *has* previously benefited from the reduced abilities of the currently best qualified applicant's competitor. In these cases, the best qualified applicant will *not* be the single main beneficiary of his rival's handicap, and so reverse discrimination against him will *not* be entirely fair. I am inclined to think there may be a case for reverse discrimination even here, however, for if it is truly impossible to dislodge the entrenched previous beneficiary of his rival's handicap, reverse discrimination against the best qualified applicant may at least be the fairest (or least unfair) of the practical alternatives.

8. A somewhat similar difference might seem to obtain between cases (1) and (2). One's ability to learn is more intimately a part of him than his actual degree of education; hence, someone whose ability to learn is lowered by his environment (case 2) is a

changed person in a way in which a person who is merely denied education (case 1) is not. However, one's ability to learn is not a feature of *moral* character in the way ability to exert effort is, and so this difference between (1) and (2) will have little bearing on the degree to which reverse discrimination is called for in these cases.

9. The feminist movement has convincingly documented the ways in which sexual bias is built into the information received by the young; but it is one thing to show that such information is received, and quite another to show how, and to what extent, its reception is causally efficacious.

Preferential Hiring and Compensation

Robert K. Fullinwider

> If a man shall steal an ox, or a sheep, and kill it, or sell it; he shall restore
> five oxen for an ox, and four sheep for a sheep.
>
> —Exodus 22

Persons have rights; but sometimes a right may justifiably be overridden. Can
we concede to all job applicants a right to equal consideration, and yet support
a policy of preferentially hiring female over white male applicants?

Judith Thomson, in her article "Preferential Hiring" (chap. 9) appeals to the
principle of compensation as a ground which justifies us in sometimes overriding a person's rights. She applies this principle to a case of preferential hiring of
a woman in order to defend the claim that such preferential hiring is not
unjust. Her defense rests upon the contention that a debt of compensation is
owed to women, and that the existence of this debt provides us with a justification of preferential hiring of women in certain cases even though this involves
setting aside or overriding certain rights of white male applicants.

Although she is correct in believing that the right to compensation sometimes allows us or requires us to override or limit other rights, I shall argue that
Thomson has failed to show that the principle of compensation justifies preferential hiring in the case she constructs. Thus, by implication, I argue that she

Reprinted from *Social Theory and Practice* 3 (1975) by permission of the journal and
the author.

has failed to show that preferential hiring of women in such cases is not unjust. I proceed by setting out Thomson's argument, by identifying the crucial premise. I then show that Thomson fails to defend the premise, and that, given her statement of the principle of compensation, the premise is implausible.

Thomson's Case

Thomson asks us to imagine the following case. Suppose for some academic job a white male applicant (WMA) and a female applicant (FA) are under final consideration.[1] Suppose further that we grant that WMA and FA each has a *right to equal consideration* by the university's hiring officer. This means that each has a right to be evaluated for the job solely in terms of his or her possession of job-related qualifications. Suppose, finally, that the hiring officer hires FA because she is a woman. How can the hiring officer's choice avoid being unjust?

Since being a woman is, by hypothesis, not a job-related qualification in this instance, the hiring officer's act of choosing FA because she is a woman seems to violate WMA's right to equal consideration. The hiring officer's act would not be unjust only if in this situation there were some sufficient moral ground for setting aside or overriding WMA's right.

Consider, Thomson asks us, "those debts which are incurred by one who wrongs another. *It is here we find what seems to me the most powerful argument for the conclusion that preferential hiring of . . . women is not unjust*" (chap. 9, p. 47, emphasis added). We are promised that the basis for justly overriding WMA's acknowledged right is to be found in the principle of compensation. But, at this crucial point in her paper, Thomson stops short of setting out the actual derivation of her conclusion from the application of the principle of compensation to her imagined case. The reader is left to construct the various steps in the argument. From remarks Thomson makes in dealing with some objections to preferential hiring, I offer the following as a fair construction of the argument she intends.

Women, as a group, are owed a debt of compensation. Historically women, because they were women, have been subject to extensive and damaging discrimination, socially approved and legally supported. The discriminatory practices have served to limit the opportunities for fulfillment open to women and have disadvantaged them in the competition for many social benefits. Since women have been the victims of injustice, they have a moral right to be compensated for the wrongs done to them.

The compensation is owed by the community. The community as a whole is responsible, since the discriminatory practices against women have not been limited to isolated, private actions. These practices have been widespread, and public as well as private. Nowhere does Thomson argue that the case for preferring FA over WMA lies in a debt to FA directly incurred by WMA. In fact,

Thomson never makes an effort to show any direct connection between FA and WMA. The moral relationship upon which Thomson's argument must rely exists between women and the community. The sacrifice on WMA's part is exacted from him by the community so it may pay its debt to women. This is a crucial feature of Thomson's case, and creates the need for the next premise: The right to compensation on the part of women justifies the community in overriding WMA's right to equal consideration. This premise is necessary to the argument. If the setting aside of WMA's right is to be justified by appeal to the principle of compensation, and the debt of compensation exists between the community and women, then something like the fourth premise is required to gain the application of the principle of compensation to WMA. This premise grounds the justness of WMA's sacrifice in the community's debt.

In short, Thomson's argument contains the following premises:

1. Women, as a group, are owed a debt of compensation.

2. The compensation is owed to women by the community.

3. The community exacts a sacrifice from WMA (i.e., sets aside his right to equal consideration) in order to pay its debt.[2]

4. The right to compensation on the part of women against the community justifies the community in setting aside WMA's right.

If we assume that the community may legitimately discharge its debt to women by making payments to *individual women*, then from premises 1–4 the conclusion may be drawn that WMA's right to equal consideration may be overridden in order to prefer FA, and, hence, that it is not unjust for the hiring officer to choose FA because she is a woman.

I shall not quarrel with premises 1–3, nor with the assumption that *groups* can be wronged and have rights.[3] My quarrel here is with premise 4. I shall show that Thomson offers no support for 4, and that it does not involve a correct application of the principle of compensation as used by Thomson. I will examine the case for premise 4 later. In the next section I pause to look at Thomson's statement of the principle of compensation.

The Principle of Compensation

In the passage quoted earlier, Thomson speaks of those debts incurred by one who wrongs another. These are the debts of compensation. Using Thomson's own language, we may formulate the principle of compensation as the declaration that *he who wrongs another owes the other*.[4] The principle of compensation tells us that, for some person B, B's act of wronging some person A creates a special moral relationship between A and B. The relationship is a species of the relationship of *being indebted to*. In the case of compensation, the indebtedness arises as a result of a wrongdoing, and involves the wrongdoer owing the wronged. To say that B owes something to A is to say that B's liberty of action with respect to what is owed is limited. B is under an obligation to yield to A what he owes him, and A has a right to it.[5] *What* B must yield will be a matter of the kind of wrong he has done A, and the optional means of compensation open to him. Thus, it is clearly the case that debts of compensation are grounds for limiting or overriding rights. But our being owed compensation by someone, though giving us some purchase on his liberty, does not give us carte blanche in limiting his rights. The debt is limited to what makes good our loss (restores our right), and is limited to us, his victims.

It might be that, for some reason, WMA directly owes FA compensation. If so, it would immediately follow that FA has a moral claim against WMA which limits WMA's liberty with respect to what he owes her. Furthermore, the nature of WMA's wrong may be such as to require a form of compensation interfering with the particular right we are focusing on—his right to equal consideration. Suppose the wrong done by WMA involved his depriving FA of fair opportunities for employment. Such a wrong might be the basis for requiring WMA, in compensation, to forgo his right to equal consideration if he and FA were in direct competition for some job. This case would conform precisely to the model of Thomson's stated principle of compensation.

Thomson makes no effort to show that WMA has interfered with FA's chances at employment, or done her any other harm. She claims that it is "wrongheaded" to dwell upon the question of whether WMA has wronged FA or any other woman (chap. 9, p. 47). As we have already seen, Thomson maintains that the relevant moral relationship exists between *women* and the *community*. Consequently, the full weight of her argument rests on premise 4, and I now turn to it.

Applying the Principle of Compensation to Groups

Thomson asserts that there is a relationship of indebtedness between the community and women. Yet it is the overriding of WMA's right which is purportedly justified by this fact. The sacrifice imposed upon WMA is not due to his directly owing FA. The community owes FA (as a woman), and exacts the sacrifice from WMA in order that *it* may pay its debt. This is supposed to be justified by premise 4.

May the community take *any* act it sees fit in order to pay its debts?[6] This question goes to the heart of Thomson's case: what support is there for her premise 4? What is the connection between the community's liability to women (or FA), and WMA's membership in the community? Can we find in the fact that the community owes something to women a moral justification for overriding WMA's right? In this section I explore two attempts to provide a positive answer to this last question. These are not Thomson's attempts; I consider her own words in the next section.

First, one might attempt to justify the imposition of a sacrifice on WMA by appeal to distributive liability. It might be urged that since the community owes FA, then every member of the community owes FA and thus WMA owes FA. This defense of premise 4 is unconvincing. While it is true that if the community owes FA then its members collectively owe FA, it does not follow that they distributively owe FA. It is not the case that, as a general rule, distributive liability holds between organized groups and their members.[7] What reason is there to suppose it does in this case?

Though this attempt to defend premise 4 is unsatisfactory, it is easy to see why it would be very appealing. Even though the indebtedness is established, in the first instance, between the community and FA, if distributive liability obtained we could derive a debt WMA owed to FA, a debt that arose as a result of the application of the principle of compensation to the community. In imposing a sacrifice on WMA, the community would be enforcing *his* (derived) obligation to FA.

Second, imagine a 36-hole, two-round golf tournament among FA, WMA, and a third party, sanctioned and governed by a tournament organizing committee. In previous years FA switched to a new-model club, which improved her game. Before the match the third player surreptitiously substitutes for FA's clubs a set of the old type. This is discovered after 18 holes have been played. If we suppose that the match cannot be restarted or canceled, then the committee is faced with the problem of compensating FA for the unfair disadvantage caused her by the substitution. By calculating her score averages over the years, the committee determines that the new clubs have yielded FA an average two-stroke improvement per 18 holes over the old clubs. The committee decides to compensate FA by penalizing the third player by two strokes in the final 18 holes.

But the committee must also penalize WMA two strokes. If FA has been put at a disadvantage by the wrongful substitution, she has been put at a disadvantage with respect to every player in the game. She is in competition with all the players; what the third player's substitution has done is to deprive her of a fair opportunity to defeat all the other players. That opportunity is not restored by penalizing the third player alone. If the committee is to rectify in mid-match the wrong done to FA, it must penalize WMA as well, though WMA had no part in the wrong done to FA.

Now, if it is right for the committee to choose this course of action, then this example seems promising for Thomson's argument. Perhaps in it can be found a basis for defending premise 4. This example seems appropriately similar to Thomson's case: in it an organization penalizes WMA to compensate FA, though WMA is innocent of any wrong against FA. If the two situations are sufficiently alike and in the golfing example it is not unjust for the committee to penalize WMA, then by parity of reasoning it would seem that the community is not unjust in setting aside WMA's right.

Are the committee's action and the community's action to be seen in the same light? Does the committee's action involve setting aside any player's rights? The committee constantly monitors the game, and intervenes to balance off losses or gains due to infractions or violations. Unfair gains are nullified by penalties; unfair losses are offset by awards. In the end no player has a complaint because the interventions ensure that the outcome has not been influenced by illegitimate moves or illegal actions. Whatever a player's position at the end of the game, it is solely the result of his own unhindered efforts. In penalizing WMA two strokes (along with the third player), the committee does him no injustice nor overrides any of his rights.

The community, or its government, is responsible for preserving fair employment practices for its members. It can penalize those who engage in unfair discrimination; it can vigorously enforce fair employment rules; and, if FA has suffered under unfair practices, it may consider some form of compensation for FA. However, compensating FA by imposing a burden on WMA, when he is not culpable, is *not* like penalizing WMA in the golf match. The loss imposed by the community upon WMA is not part of a gamelike scheme, carefully regulated and continuously monitored by the community, wherein it intervenes continually to offset unfair losses and gains by distributing penalties and advantages, ensuring that over their lifetimes WMA's and FA's chances at employment have been truly equal. WMA's loss may endure; and there is no reason to believe that his employment position at the end of his career reflects only his unhindered effort. If the community exacts a sacrifice from WMA to pay FA, *it merely redistributes losses and gains without balancing them.*

Even though the golfing example looked promising as a source of clues for a defense of premise 4, on examination it seems not to offer any support for that premise. Indeed, in seeing how the golfing case is different from the hiring case, we may become even more dubious that Thomson's principle of compensation can justify the community in overriding WMA's right to equal consideration in the absence of his culpability.[8]

Thomson's Words

Since Thomson never explicitly expresses premise 4 in her paper, she never directly addresses the problem of its defense. In the one place where she seems to take up the problem raised by premise 4, she says:

Still, the community does impose a burden upon him (WMA): it is able to make amends for its wrongs only by taking something away from him, something which, after all, we are supposing he has a right to. And why should *he* pay the cost of the community's amends-making?

> If there were some appropriate way in which the community could make amends to its . . . women, some way which did not require depriving anyone of anything he has a right to, then that would be the best course of action for it to take. Or if there were anyway some way in which the costs could be shared by everyone, and not imposed entirely on the young white male job applicants, then that would be, if not the best, then anyway better than opting for a policy of preferential hiring. But in fact *the nature of the wrongs done is such as to make jobs the best and most suitable form of compensation* (chap. 9, p. 49, emphasis added).

How does this provide an answer to our question? Is this passage to be read as suggesting, in support of premise 4, the principle that a group may override the rights of its (nonculpable) members in order to pay the "best" form of compensation?[9] If WMA's right to equal consideration stood in the way of the community's paying best compensation to FA, then this principle would entail premise 4. This principle, however, will not withstand scrutiny.

Consider an example: Suppose that you have stolen a rare and elaborately engraved hunting rifle from me. Before you can be made to return it, the gun is destroyed in a fire. By coincidence, however, your brother possesses one of the few other such rifles in existence; perhaps it is the only other model in existence apart from the one you stole from me and which was destroyed. From my point of view, having my gun back, or having one exactly like it, is the best form of compensation I can have from you. No other gun will be a suitable replacement, nor will money serve satisfactorily to compensate me for my loss. I prized the rifle for its rare and unique qualities, not for its monetary value. You can pay me the best form of compensation by giving me your brother's gun. However, this is clearly not a morally justifiable option. I have no moral title to your brother's gun, nor are you (solely in virtue of your debt to me) required or permitted to take your brother's gun to give to me. The gun is not yours to give; and nothing about the fact that you owe me justifies you in taking it.

In this example it is clear that establishing what is the best compensation (best makes up the wrongful loss) does not determine what is the morally appropriate form of compensation. Thus, as a defense of premise 4, telling us that preferential hiring is the best compensation begs the question.

The question of the best form of compensation may properly arise only after we have determined who owes whom, and what are the morally permissible means of payment open to the debtor. The question of the best form of compensation arises, in other words, only after we have settled the moral justifiability of exacting something from someone, and settled the issue of what it is that the debtor has that he can pay.

The case of preferential hiring seems to me more like the case of the stolen rifle than like the case of the golfing match. If WMA has a right to equal consideration, then he, not the community, owns the right. In abridging his right in order to pay FA, the community is paying in stolen coin, just as you would be were you to expropriate your brother's rifle to compensate me. The community is paying with something that does not belong to it. WMA has not been shown by Thomson to owe anybody anything. Nor has Thomson defended or made plausible premise 4, which on its face ill fits her own expression of the principle of compensation. If we reject the premise, then Thomson has not shown what she claimed—that it is not unjust to engage in preferential hiring of women. I fully agree with her that it would be appropriate, if not obligatory, for the community to adopt measures of compensation to women.[10] I cannot agree, on the basis of her argument, that it may do so by adopting a policy of preferential hiring.

Benefit and Innocence

Thomson seems vaguely to recognize that her case is unconvincing without a demonstration of culpability on the part of WMA. At the end of her essay, after having made her argument without assuming WMA's guilt, she assures us that after all WMA is not so innocent, and it is not unfitting that he should bear the sacrifice required in preferring FA.

> It is not entirely inappropriate that those applicants [like WMA] should pay the costs. No doubt few, if any, have themselves, individually, done any wrongs to . . . women. But they have profited from the wrongs the community did. Many may actually have been direct beneficiaries of policies which excluded or downgraded . . . women—perhaps in school admissions, perhaps in access to financial aid, perhaps elsewhere; and even those who did not directly benefit in this way had, at any rate, the advantage in the competition which comes of confidence in one's full membership, and of one's rights being recognized as a matter of course. (chap. 9, p. 49)

Does this passage make a plausible case for WMA's diminished "innocence," and the appropriateness of imposing the costs of compensation on him? The principle implied in the passage is, "He who benefits from a wrong shall pay for the wrong." Perhaps Thomson confuses this principle with the principle of compensation itself ("He who wrongs another shall pay for the wrong"). At any rate, the principle, "He who benefits from a wrong shall pay for the wrong," is surely suspect as an acceptable moral principle.

Consider the following example. While I am away on vacation, my neighbor contracts with a construction company to repave his driveway. He instructs the workers to come to his address, where they will find a note describing the driveway to be repaired. An enemy of my neighbor, aware somehow of this arrangement, substitutes for my neighbor's instructions a note describing *my* driveway. The construction crew, having been paid in advance, shows up on the appointed day while my neighbor is at work, finds the letter, and faithfully following its instructions paves my driveway. In this example my neighbor has been wronged and damaged. He is out a sum of money, and his driveway is unimproved. I benefited from the wrong, for my driveway is considerably improved. Yet, am I morally required to compensate my neighbor for the wrong done him? Is it appropriate that the costs of compensating my neighbor fall on me? I cannot see why. My paying the neighbor the cost he incurred in hiring the construction company would be an act of supererogation on my part, not a discharge of an obligation to him. If I could afford it, it would be a decent thing to do; but it is not something I *owe* my neighbor. I am not less than innocent in this affair because I benefited from my neighbor's misfortune; and no one is justified in exacting compensation from me.

The very obvious feature of the situation just described which bears on the fittingness of compensation is the fact of *involuntariness*. Indeed I benefited from the wrong done my neighbor, but the benefit was involuntary and undesired. If I knowingly and voluntarily benefit from wrongs done to others, though I do not commit the wrongs myself, then perhaps it is true to say that I am less than innocent of these wrongs, and perhaps it is morally fitting that I bear some of the costs of compensation. But it is not like this with involuntary benefits.

Though young white males like WMA have undeniably benefited in many ways from the sexist social arrangements under which they were reared, to a large extent, if not entirely, these benefits are involuntary. From an early age the male's training and education inculcate in him the attitudes and disposition, the knowledge and skills, which give him an advantage over women in later life. Such benefits are unavoidable (by him) and ineradicable. Most especially is this true of "that advantage . . . which comes of confidence in one's full membership [in the community] and of one's rights being recognized as a matter of course."

The principle, "He who *willingly* benefits from wrong must pay for the wrong," may have merit as a moral principle. To show a person's uncoerced and knowledgeable complicity in wrongdoing is to show him less than innocent, even if his role amounts to no more than ready acceptance of the fruits of wrong. Thomson makes no effort to show such complicity on WMA's part. The principle that she relies upon, "He who benefits from a wrong must pay for the wrong," is without merit. So, too, is her belief that "it is not entirely inappropriate" that WMA (and those like him) should bear the burden of a program of compensation to women. What Thomson ignores is the moral implication of the fact that the benefits of sexism received by WMA may be involuntary and unavoidable. This implication cannot be blinked, and it ruins Thomson's final pitch to gain our approval of a program which violates the rights of some persons.[11]

Notes

1. Thomson asks us to imagine two such applicants *tied* in their qualifications. Presumably, preferring a less qualified teacher would violate students' rights to the best available instruction. If the applicants are equally qualified, then the students' rights are satisfied whichever one is picked. In cases where third-party rights are not involved, there would seem to be no need to include the tie stipulation, for if the principle of compensation is strong enough to justify preferring a woman over a man, it is strong enough whether the woman is equally qualified or not, so long as she is minimally qualified. (Imagine hiring a librarian instead of a teacher.) Thus, I leave out the requirement that the applicants be tied in their qualifications. Nothing in my argument turns on whether the applicants are equally qualified. The reader may, if he wishes, mentally reinstate this feature of Thomson's example.

2. The comments from which propositions 1–3 are distilled occur on pages 48–49.

3. For a discussion of these issues, see chapter 10, "Preferential Hiring: A Reply to Judith Jarvis Thomson," by Robert Simon.

4. There are broader notions of compensation, where it means making up for any deficiency or distortion, and where it means recompense for work. Neither of these notions plays a role in Thomson's argument.

5. On page 45, Thomson says: "Now it is, I think, widely believed that we may, without injustice, refuse to grant a man what he has a right to only if *either* someone else has a conflicting and more stringent right, *or* there is some very great benefit to be obtained by doing so—perhaps that a disaster of some kind is thereby averted . . . . But in fact there are other ways in which a right may be overridden." The "other way" which Thomson mentions derives from the force of debts. A debt consists of rights and obligations, and the force of debts can perhaps be accounted for in terms of superior rights. Then, debts would not be a third ground, independent of the first listed by Thomson, for overriding a right.

6. The U.S. government owes Japanese companies compensation for losses they incurred when the president imposed an illegal import surtax. May the government justly discharge its debt by taxing only Japanese Americans in order to pay the Japanese companies?

7. See Joel Feinberg, "Collective Responsibility," *Journal of Philosophy* 65 (1968); and Virginia Held, "Can a Random Collection of Individuals Be Morally Responsible?" *Journal of Philosophy* 67 (1970).

8. George Sher, in "Justifying Reverse Discrimination in Employment," defends reverse discriminations to "neutralize competitive disadvantages caused by past privations" (chapter 11, page 61). He seems to view the matter along the lines of my golfing example. Thus, my comments here against the sufficiency of that model apply to Sher's argument. Also, see the last section of this chapter for arguments that bear on Sher's contention that the justification for discriminating against white male applicants is not that they are most responsible for injustice, but benefit the most from it.

9. In the passage quoted, Thomson is attempting to morally justify the community's imposing a sacrifice on WMA. Thus, her reference to "best" compensation cannot be construed to mean "morally best," since morally best means morally justified. By best compensation Thomson means that compensation which will best make up the loss suffered by the victim. This is how I understand the idea of best compensation in the succeeding example and argument.

10. And there are many possible modes of compensation open to the community which are free of any moral taint. At the worst, monetary compensation is always an alternative. This may be second- or third-best compensation for the wrongs done, but when the best is not available, second-best has to do. For the loss of my gun, I am

going to have to accept cash from you (assuming you have it), and use it to buy a less satisfactory substitute.

11. But, if FA is *not* given preferential treatment in hiring (the best compensation), are *her* rights violated? In having a right to compensation, FA does not have a right to anything at all that will compensate her. She has a right to the best of the morally available options open to her debtor. Only if the community refuses to pay her this is her right violated. We have seen no reason to believe that setting aside the right of white male applicants to equal consideration is an option morally available to the community.

Compensatory Justice: The Question of Costs

Robert Amdur

An adequate theory of compensatory justice should include answers to two sets of questions. First, who is to receive compensation, and how much should they receive? Second, who should pay the costs of compensation, and how much should each pay?

In the literature on preferential hiring, reverse discrimination, and affirmative action, the first set of questions has received far more attention than the second. Several writers have argued in favor of preferential treatment without considering the costs of compensation at all—suggesting either that the distribution of costs is not a major issue or that the solution to the problem is too obvious to require discussion. Others have dealt with the question of who should pay, but only briefly, after detailed and rigorous examinations of who should be compensated. By the time these writers reach the question of distribution of costs, everything else, including the proper mode of compensation, has been decided on. At this point, there are very few options left: the mode of compensation determines how the burden will be distributed.

I want to suggest that the question of who should pay is a fundamental one. It is too important to be postponed until after the rest of the problems concerning compensatory justice have been settled. In Part I of this essay, I put forward three principles intended to regulate distribution of the costs of compensation. In Parts II and III, I ask whether these principles can be satisfied by programs involving preferential treatment for blacks and women.

Reprinted from *Political Theory* 7 (1979). Copyright © 1979 by *Political Theory*. Reprinted by permission of Sage Publications Inc.

I

Assume that it will sometimes be necessary to compensate certain individuals or groups, either for past injustices committed against them or for present competitive disadvantages resulting from past injustices. Who should pay the costs of compensation? There are two obvious answers:

First principle: Compensation should be paid by the perpetrators of injustice, those whose unjust actions gave rise to the need for compensation.

Second principle: Compensation should be paid by those who benefited from injustice, whether directly or indirectly (for example, inheriting wealth originally acquired by unjust means).

These principles do not comprise a complete theory of just compensation; at best, they provide the beginnings of such a theory. I want to comment briefly on four issues that require further attention: identification of the perpetrators of injustice; the question of intentions; the distribution of costs among perpetrators (or among beneficiaries); and the relationship between the two principles.

(1) The first principle is intended to impose costs on those persons responsible for injustice. But how do we determine who was responsible for instituting and perpetuating a particular unjust practice? Discussing the theft of Indian lands, Robert E. Litan observes: "Certainly more individuals were responsible ... than just those in the U.S. Army. What about the political leaders who founded such activities, individuals who voted for these leaders, and the like? Where does the buck of responsibility come to rest?"[1]

To answer this question, information about who did what to whom is necessary, but not sufficient. Whether we are responsible for starvation in Bangladesh depends in part on the history of our relations with that country. But it also depends on whether we have a duty to supply starving people with food. To answer Litan's question, we would need both historical information *and* a theory of responsibility, a theory that tells us when individuals are obliged to act to alleviate suffering and when they are to be held accountable for their actions or failures to act. Although philosophers have begun to address these questions,[2] a satisfactory theory of responsibility does not yet exist.

In the absence of such a theory, it is not surprising that there is little agreement (even among supporters of compensatory programs) about who is responsible for injustice against blacks and women in America. According to one view, the perpetrators of injustice are those individuals who have engaged in overt racial or sexual discrimination, particularly hiring discrimination. At the opposite extreme is the view that every person has a duty to struggle against injustice wherever it exists, and hence that anyone not currently fighting for equality is a perpetrator of injustice. As Alison Jaggar puts it, "Everyone who acquiesces in a racist and sexist system helps to 'cause' discrimination."[3] Most supporters of compensation fall somewhere between these extremes; they see the perpetrators of injustice as including all those who have engaged in a variety of social and economic practices which tend to perpetuate the inferior position of blacks and women.[4]

(2) Several writers have endorsed the second principle but suggested that it should apply only to those who have benefited intentionally or voluntarily. According to Robert K. Fullinwider,

> If I knowingly and voluntarily benefit from wrongs done to others, though I do not commit the wrongs myself, then perhaps it is true to say that I am less than innocent of these wrongs, and perhaps it is morally fitting that I bear some of the costs of compensation. But it is not like this with involuntary benefits. (chap. 12, p. 76)

Is such a restriction necessary? If we were concerned with guilt and innocence, blame and responsibility, then Fullinwider would undoubtedly be correct: intention would be a relevant consideration. But most of the writers who endorse the second principle are not concerned with guilt and innocence. For them, the idea behind the second principle is not that those who are to blame for an injustice should be made to pay. Rather, they are interested in restoring the competitive balance that would have existed had the injustice in question never taken place. They believe that the natural way to accomplish this goal is simply to ask those who have gained from injustice to give up what they have gained. Whether the beneficiaries are "innocent of these wrongs" is, according to this view, irrelevant.

(3) Another issue involves the distribution of costs *among* beneficiaries or perpetrators. While many people may benefit from an unjust practice or policy, some are likely to benefit more than others. Responsibility raises more complicated problems, but most theorists seem to agree that it too can be divided unevenly. Here it seems reasonable to amend the first and second principles in the following manner: in applying these principles, the costs of compensation should be distributed in proportion to the degree of responsibility or to the benefits received. In some instances a demand for strict proportionality will make little sense, but even in these cases it is appropriate that those who are more responsible (those who have contributed more to initiating or perpetuating unjust policies) or those who have benefited more should pay a larger share. If for some reason it becomes necessary to assign the costs of compensation to some group within the general population of beneficiaries and/or perpetrators, costs ought to be assigned to those who have benefited most, or those most responsible. When an individual is asked to pay part of the costs of compensation, while others who benefited more than he did from the injustice in question are *not* being asked to pay a share of the costs, he may rightly complain that

he is being singled out unfairly. He is justified in asking "Why me?" In this case, it is not sufficient to answer, "Because you did, after all, benefit from injustice."

(4) Finally, what is the relationship between the two principles? We might want to apply both principles at the same time (with a proviso to deal with perpetrators of injustice who are also beneficiaries). Alternatively, we could specify a priority rule—for example: apply the first principle whenever possible; in other cases, apply the second. I am not sure how the two principles should fit together, though clearly this is a question that a comprehensive theory of compensation would have to answer.

Although many details have yet to be worked out, I believe that the principles discussed above should ideally regulate allocation of the costs of compensating individuals or groups for the effects of past injustice. Not surprisingly, these principles have been put forward, in one form or another, in many discussions of compensatory justice. The problem is that it is extremely difficult—perhaps impossible—to apply these principles, in any rigorous way, to actual cases.

This is probably clearer with regard to the second principle. It is never easy to determine exactly who has benefited from a particular social practice or policy; witness the ongoing debates on the left over whether members of the white working class gain or lose from racial discrimination and economic imperialism. When a practice and its effects extend over several generations, the difficulties become more serious and the possibilities of error increase. Where we must not only identify gainers and losers but also determine how much different individuals have gained, the problems become still more complex.[5] To apply the second principle to an historical case, one would have to answer an enormous number of questions not only about what in fact happened but also about what *would have* happened under a different set of social practices. Efforts to determine who benefited (and how much) from discriminatory practices are likely to yield results too crude to serve as a just basis for decisions about the allocation of costs.[6]

When we turn to the first principle, the problems are no less serious. Given a generally accepted theory of responsibility and a detailed knowledge of the relevant historical facts, it will often be possible to identify the perpetrators of injustice. However, many of the most interesting cases are likely to involve unjust practices carried out over a long period of time, or past injustices, the effects of which are still being felt. All or nearly all of the perpetrators (particularly those who appear most responsible for initiating and maintaining the unjust practices in question) are likely to be dead. Since responsibility (unlike benefits) cannot be inherited, it will often be impossible to apply the first principle, even in those cases where the perpetrators can be identified. In general, it will be difficult to apply this principle when the most important injustices requiring compensation, and the compensation itself, do not take place within the same generation.

These considerations give rise to the question: who should pay the costs of compensation in those cases where it is not possible to assign costs either to the perpetrators or to the beneficiaries of injustice? One possible answer is that in situations of this sort no one should pay. From this point on, it might be argued, we should prohibit all racial and sexual discrimination. We should guarantee those individuals previously victimized by injustice an equal opportunity to advance as far as their talents will carry them. But that is all we should do. If we are unable to assign the costs to the "right" people, then there should be no compensation at all. The results of past injustice must be allowed to fall wherever they happen to fall.

This position might be described as the libertarian solution to the problem of costs. In some ways it is an appealing solution. It is the only alternative which guarantees that no one will be treated unfairly by the compensation process itself. That is to say, it is the only alternative which guarantees that the process of compensation will not make anyone worse off than he would have been if there had never been any injustice in the first place. As such, it must recommend itself to anyone opposed to using some people as means to promote the good of others.

Nevertheless, there are good reasons for rejecting the libertarian position. I want to emphasize two of these. First, the effects of past injustice generally do not "wash away" with time; frequently, the disadvantages resulting from unjust practices are transmitted from one generation to the next. Contrary to the expectations of many nineteenth- and early-twentieth-century egalitarians, formal equality of opportunity is not sufficient to eliminate the effect of past privations on the present generation. At least in many cases, victims of injustice who do not receive some sort of compensation are likely to remain seriously disadvantaged, despite the existence of equality of opportunity.

The second point concerns the arbitrariness involved in compensating some victims of injustice, but not others. Imagine two victimized groups, both equally (and seriously) disadvantaged as a result of past wrongs. In one case it is possible to identify the perpetrators (and/or beneficiaries) of injustice; in the other case it is not—we have no knowledge about them, or our knowledge is not sufficiently certain, or we know the class to which they belong but cannot identify particular individuals. Most of us will agree that if the first group of victims is entitled to compensation, then so is the second. Their claim to receive compensation should depend on the nature of the injustice they have suffered and the effects of that injustice, not on whether it is possible to locate the perpetrators of injustice and hold them accountable. If the victims ought to receive compensation when the perpetrators of injustice can be found, then it will seem unfair to deny them compensation in those cases where the perpetrators cannot be found.

I believe these considerations are sufficient to outweigh the arguments in favor of the libertarian position. The most plausible alternative is close to the mirror image of the libertarian view.

Third principle: When it is not possible to assign the costs of compensation either to the perpetrators or to the beneficiaries of injustice, those costs should be distributed evenly among the entire community.

In short, everyone should pay. The costs of compensation should be divided so as to equalize sacrifice as nearly as possible; they should be distributed, in other words, just the way we distribute the costs of any public good.[7]

This suggestion is not original; a number of writers have argued in favor of having the entire community pay the costs of compensation. Generally, however, those who take this position couch their arguments in terms of collective responsibility. Thus, according to Paul W. Taylor (chap. 4), when injustice has resulted from a discriminatory social practice, "the obligation to compensate for the past injustice does not fall upon any particular individual but upon the society as a whole" (p. 12) excepting, of course, the victims of past discrimination. Taylor believes that "the perpetrator of the original injustice was the whole society" (p. 15); therefore, "society is morally at fault if it ignores the group which it has discriminated against" (p. 16). The duty to provide compensation follows from "the society's past use of a certain characteristic or set of characteristics as the criterion for identification of the group, membership in which was taken as a ground for unjust treatment" (p. 16).

When the case for payment by the entire community is made in this fashion, there is an obvious reply. "The society in general" is made up of a large number of individuals, many of whom will not have engaged in discriminatory or otherwise unjust behavior. What about recent immigrants? What about those who were children when the discriminatory acts took place? What about those people who disapproved of unjust practices and fought to eliminate them? What about persons who simply had no opportunity to engage in discrimination? Even if one takes a very broad view concerning the locus of responsibility for social practices, it will be impossible to maintain that *everyone* is responsible for *every* unjust practice. When we talk about "society as a whole" perpetrating injustices or using certain characteristics as a basis for unjust treatment, we are using a kind of shorthand. That shorthand may be appropriate for some purposes, but not for assigning responsibility. When we are concerned with assigning responsibility, we are necessarily concerned with individuals.

These objections are, in my view, persuasive. Even if there are cases in which (nearly) everyone bears responsibility for an unjust social practice, there will be many cases in which responsibility is far less widely diffused. For that reason, it is not possible to base the demand for equal sacrifice on a notion of collective responsibility. If something like the third principle can be defended, it must be defended on the ground that an even distribution of costs among the entire community is simply more equitable (or perhaps less inequitable) than any other distribution that might be suggested, given the impossibility of assigning the costs to the "right" people. It is difficult to make a positive argument for this position. On the other hand, once we are agreed that *someone* will have to pay the costs of compensation, it seems equally difficult to think of another principle of distribution that is, on its face, superior.

It is important to emphasize that distributing costs *evenly* is very different from distributing costs *randomly*. At first glance, the two may seem to be based on the same philosophical principle; and some of those who have written about compensatory justice appear to believe that payment by the community and payment by a random sample of the community are equivalent.[8] But payment by randomly selected individuals is different from payment by the entire community, and, from a moral point of view, distinctly inferior.

We can support this conclusion, and thereby strengthen the case for the third principle, on either utilitarian or Rawlsian grounds. There are two utilitarian reasons for preferring to have costs spread out as evenly as possible. First, if we accept the standard utilitarian assumptions about diminishing marginal utility, "equality of sacrifice" is likely to be superior to any principle that assigns costs to a randomly selected few; small sacrifices by large numbers of people will have a less serious impact on overall utility than larger sacrifices by smaller numbers.[9] Second, a scheme that distributes costs evenly among the entire community is most likely to allow people to plan their lives in a rational manner. On the other hand, a program that assigns larger burdens to a few randomly selected individuals will make planning more difficult, and life more insecure, for everyone.

From a Rawlsian perspective, the case for equal sacrifice is also compelling. Rawls ignores compensation in *A Theory of Justice*, along with most other branches of what he calls non-ideal theory. But he acknowledges that a comprehensive theory of justice would include principles to regulate compensation, and he clearly believes that such principles would have to be chosen in the original position. It is, of course, one of his major contentions that the features of the original position force the hypothetical contractees to choose conservatively; when we place ourselves behind the veil of ignorance, we will feel constrained "to adopt the alternative, the worst outcome of which is superior to the worst outcomes of the others."[10] When the parties in the original position meet to choose non-ideal principles, each will seek to avoid the risk of having to pay a disproportionate share of the costs of compensation. This should lead to a unanimous preference for equal sacrifice over any principle that assigns larger costs to fewer people.

The point of the third principle is to divide costs as evenly as possible among the entire community, not to assign costs by lot. It is grossly unfair to impose the costs of compensation on individuals chosen at random from the population. Nor is the injustice mitigated by the fact that every person has an equal chance to be among those selected.

What if we cannot avoid assigning costs to a smaller group? In such situations it may be necessary to select people at random. But the third principle suggests that we should try to avoid situations of this sort whenever possible. In choosing among alternative modes of compensation, the possibility of dividing costs evenly should be an important consideration. Other things being equal, one mode of compensation is superior to another if its costs can be spread evenly among the entire community rather than assigned to any smaller group (except, of course, those groups identified by the first two principles). Even when other things are not equal, the need to distribute costs evenly may be an overriding consideration. It may be enough to tip the scales in favor of a mode of compensation which is, in all other respects, second best.

II

Can programs requiring preferential treatment for blacks or women satisfy the first two principles? If one takes a narrow view of the injustice requiring rectification, then it might be possible to imagine a preferential hiring program that assigned costs to the perpetrators and beneficiaries of injustice. In universities, in particular, it may be possible to identify those persons who have engaged in or benefited from discriminatory hiring practices. They will be some, though obviously not all, of the white males currently holding faculty and administrative positions. If we were concerned solely with compensating for (fairly recent) university hiring discrimination, we might be able to devise a scheme that would force the beneficiaries and perpetrators of injustice to give up their jobs, to be replaced by the most qualified black and female candidates currently available. Even in this case our task would not be easy: how can we be certain which professors would have achieved their present positions under a perfectly just selection procedure; how can we know whether professor x voted against candidate y for unjust reasons? Still, such a program might be feasible. It would, of course, be different from anything yet instituted in an American university— or anything seriously recommended in the literature on preferential treatment.

What about the sorts of preferential hiring and preferential admissions programs that have been proposed and implemented during the past decade? Is it possible to justify *these* programs in terms of the first two principles discussed above? In his article "Justifying Reverse Discrimination in Employment" (chap. 11) George Sher tries to defend preferential hiring by an appeal to something close to the second principle. Sher begins by suggesting that

> If reverse discrimination is viewed simply as a form of compensation for past privations, there are serious questions about its fairness. Certainly the privations to be compensated for are not the sole responsibility of those individuals whose superior qualifications will have to be bypassed

in the reverse discriminatory process. These individuals, if responsible for those privations at all, will at least be no more responsible than others with relevantly similar histories. Yet reverse discrimination will compensate for the privations in question at the expense of these individuals alone. It will have no effect at all upon those other, equally responsible persons. . . . Surely it is unfair to distribute the burden of compensation so unequally. (p. 60)

But this does not mean that we should abandon reverse discrimination. Rather, we should view "that practice, not as the redressing of *past* privations, but rather as a way of neutralizing the *present* competitive disadvantage *caused* by those past privations and thus as a way of restoring equal access to those goods which society distributes competitively" (p. 61). Sher continues:

When reverse discrimination is viewed as compensation for lost ability to compete on equal terms, a reasonable case can also be made for its fairness. Our doubts about its fairness arose because it seemed to place the entire burden of redress upon those individuals whose superior qualifications are bypassed in the reverse discriminatory process. This seemed wrong because these individuals are, of course, not apt to be any more responsible for past discrimination than others with relevantly similar histories. But, as we are now in a position to see, this objection misses the point. The crucial fact about these individuals is not that they are more *responsible* for past discrimination than others with relevantly similar histories (in fact, the dirty work may well have been done before any of their generation attained the age of responsibility), but rather that unless reverse discrimination is practiced, they will *benefit* more than the others from its effects on their competitors. They will benefit more because unless they are restrained, they, but not the others, will use their competitive edge to claim jobs which their competitors would otherwise have gotten. Thus, it is only because they stand to *gain* the most from the relevant effects of the *original* discrimination, that the bypassed individuals stand to *lose* the most from *reverse* discrimination. This is surely a valid reply to the charge that reverse discrimination does not distribute the burden of compensation equally. (pp. 61–62)

Is it? The answer depends at least in part on whether the people who are bypassed in the reverse discrimination process are the same ones who would not have gotten jobs had there been no past discrimination. If they are, then we can say to those people: "Look, if not for past discrimination, there would be a larger number of highly qualified applicants today, and you would not be in line for jobs at all." The crucial word in this sentence is "you." It is *not* sufficient to say:

"Look, if not for past discrimination, there would be a larger number of highly qualified applicants today, and *some* white males would not be in line for jobs at all." Though he is not explicit, Sher does seem to believe that today's marginal applicants are exactly the same people who would have lost out in the competition for jobs had there been no history of discrimination. I find this assumption implausible. It is extremely difficult to determine what society would look like today if radically different social practices had been instituted a century ago. Surely, it is reasonable to think that racial injustice has affected whites differentially, that some who are now advantaged would have been less well off under a different set of rules and that some who are now "marginal" would have been better off. At the very least, Sher's assumption seems open to question.

Even if we accept Sher's assumption, one feature of his argument remains puzzling. Why allow the present generation of white male job applicants to bear *all* the costs of compensation? In a footnote Sher concedes that "many who are now entrenched in their jobs (tenured professors, for example) have already benefited from the effects of past discrimination at least as much as the currently best qualified applicant will if reverse discrimination is not practiced." But he sees that as "largely irrelevant" (p. 66). He appears to believe that we ought to assist disadvantaged members of this generation by depriving contemporaries who would otherwise benefit at their expense. But why is such symmetry desirable? Why should all compensation be intragenerational? Intuitively it seems that those who "have already benefited from the effects of past discrimination" should be asked to sacrifice as much as those who were about to benefit, before the advent of reverse discrimination. Perhaps they should be asked to bear *more* of the costs since they, at least, have had an opportunity to enjoy the benefits.

III

If it is not possible to assign the costs of compensation either to the perpetrators or to the beneficiaries of injustice, then, according to the third principle, those costs should be divided as evenly as possible among all the members of the community. Obviously, no program of preferential hiring or preferential admissions will satisfy the requirement of equality of sacrifice. It is arguable that, by singling out young white males of lower-middle or working-class background, such programs assign the costs of compensation to those members of society *least* likely to have engaged in or benefited from past discrimination.[11] Whether or not that is true, it is clear that preferential programs do not distribute costs evenly and cannot be made to do so.

The programs that satisfy the third principle most easily are programs involving monetary compensation, paid for through taxation. The most interesting historical example is the program of reparations to Jews victimized by the

Nazis, instituted in West Germany after World War II. Under this program large numbers of individual Jews received direct cash payments to compensate for the losses they had suffered under the Nazi regime. Individuals were eligible to receive payments if they could demonstrate damage to health, reduction of income, loss of freedom, property losses, or impairment of professional or economic advancement. Under certain circumstances, dependents of those killed by the Nazis also received compensation. In addition to the payments to individuals, beginning in 1953 the German Federal Republic paid hundreds of millions of dollars in reparations to the state of Israel and to an international claims conference which was responsible for the relief, rehabilitation, and resettlement of non-Israeli Jews.[12]

It should be noted that the German political leaders who supported reparations did not attempt to justify those payments in terms of collective guilt. Nearly every participant in the parliamentary debates over reparations explicitly rejected the argument that all Germans were responsible for the crimes of the Nazis. Several speakers echoed Konrad Adenauer's assertion that "the overwhelming majority of the German people abominated the crimes committed against the Jews, and did not participate in them." Nevertheless, the leaders of nearly all of Germany's postwar political parties agreed on two points: first, compensation for the Jews was morally necessary, and second, the community as a whole would have to bear the cost.[13]

Boris Bittker provides a second (hypothetical) example in *The Case for Black Reparations*. Bittker advances a number of plans designed to compensate black Americans for damages inflicted by slavery and subsequent racial discrimination. One alternative would involve money payments to blacks, "graduated by reference to a few readily ascertainable characteristics (such as the claimant's age and marital status)."[14] Another alternative would entail payments not to individuals but to representative groups, to be used for projects beneficial to the black community as a whole. It is also possible to imagine various combinations. Whatever alternative might be selected, Bittker believes that the payments would have to be at least large enough to "close the economic gap between blacks and whites"; that is to say, they would have to be sufficient to erase the current disparities both in income and in net worth. He is also sympathetic to additional allowances to compensate for "the humiliation inflicted by segregation."[15] As with the West German reparations program, the necessary money would be raised by taxation.

If my argument is correct, there is a presumption in favor of programs such as these and against preferential hiring and preferential admissions. Are there any reasons to override this presumption? Judith Jarvis Thomson has argued that there are. Her argument deserves close examination, for she is one of the few supporters of preferential hiring programs to acknowledge that there is a strong case for equality of sacrifice.

Thomson believes that "if there were . . . some way in which the costs could be shared by everyone, and not imposed on the young white male applicants, then that would be, if not the best, then anyway better than opting for a policy of preferential hiring." But she insists that

> the nature of the wrongs done is such as to make jobs the best and most suitable form of compensation. What blacks and women were denied was full membership in the community; and nothing can more appropriately make amends for that wrong than precisely what will make them feel they now finally have it. And that means jobs. Financial compensation (the cost of which could be shared equally) slips through the fingers; having a job, and discovering you do it well, yield—perhaps better than anything else—that very self-respect which blacks and women have had to do without. (chap. 9, p. 49)

This argument seems wrong on a number of crucial issues. It is not at all clear that the jobs provided by preferential hiring programs will make women and blacks feel they now have full membership in the community. These jobs *may* buttress the self-respect of the individual blacks and women who receive them, but these people are fairly certain to be a small group (and, arguably, not the ones whose self-respect is in greatest need of reinforcement).[16] There is little reason to believe that jobs for a few blacks and women will do anything for the self-respect of the majority; and this is especially true if, as Thomson asserts, "having a job, and discovering you do it well" is the key to self-respect.

Concerning the alternative to preferential hiring, it is also not clear what Thomson means by the assertion that "financial compensation . . . slips through the fingers." Clearly, very small amounts of money—such as, for example, the "fifteen dollars per nigger" demanded in the Black Manifesto of 1969—would do very little to improve the living conditions of blacks as a group. Such payments would undoubtedly be spent quickly, leaving their recipients no better off than before. If this what Thomson means, she is right. But there is no reason to assume that compensatory payments would have to be so small. Bittker, in proposing to "close the economic gap between blacks and whites," clearly envisions payments much larger than those proposed in the Manifesto.

If Thomson is not simply pointing out that insignificant amounts of money are not very useful, what could she mean? Perhaps she has in mind something like E. C. Banfield's view that members of the "lower class" have an almost unlimited capacity to waste money.[17] If we accept this view as correct, then even a very ambitious program of money payments will indeed be pointless; it will make no positive long-term difference in the lives of recipients. If this is Thomson's argument, it is necessary to make two points in response. First, Banfield's assertion, and the larger theory of which it forms a part, have been widely criticized.[18] It is, to say the least, a matter of dispute whether large numbers of people actually display the attitudes and personality traits attributed by Banfield to the lower class. (Banfield himself appears to believe that the "radically improvident" constitute only 10 to 20 percent of those with incomes below the poverty line.) But second, if the claim under consideration is correct, it hardly does very much to advance the argument for preferential treatment. For if there are large numbers of people who should not receive transfer payments because of their lower-class attitudes, it is difficult to argue that those people ought to be given jobs teaching in universities, or places in law and medical schools.

In short, I do not believe Thomson has shown that jobs are a particularly appropriate, or transfer payments a particularly inappropriate, form of compensation. Perhaps others will offer more persuasive arguments to support these contentions. To make such an argument successfully, however, it would *not* be sufficient to demonstrate that provision of jobs (or places in professional schools) for blacks and women would achieve some desirable goal. It would also be necessary to show that the same goal could not be achieved by means of transfer payments. In discussion of the *Bakke* case, the most common argument for preferential admissions has focused on the need to improve medical care in the black community. This is obviously a worthwhile goal. But money payments on the scale envisioned by Bittker would almost certainly do more to improve medical care for blacks than any preferential admissions program that might be devised.

In any case, it should be emphasized that even if someone were to demonstrate convincingly that jobs are "the best and most suitable form of compensation" from the point of view of those to be compensated, that still would not clinch the argument in favor of preferential treatment. For the people being asked to pay *also* have claims that must be taken into account. In particular, they have a claim not to be singled out to pay the costs of compensation, unless they can be identified as either the perpetrators or the beneficiaries of injustice. Clearly, it would be unfair to the victims of discrimination not to provide compensation at all. But sometimes it may be necessary to choose a form of compensation other than the "best and most suitable" form, so as to avoid doing injustice to those who must pay the costs.

Notes

1. Robert E. Litan, "On Rectification in Nozick's Minimal State," *Political Theory* 5 (1977): 243.
2. See especially Joel Feinberg, *Doing and Deserving: Essays in the Theory of Responsibility* (Princeton, NJ: Princeton University Press, 1970); and the essays in *Individual and Collective Responsibility*, ed. Peter A. French (Cambridge, MA: Schenkman, 1972).
3. Alison Jaggar, "Relaxing the Limits on Preferential Treatment," *Social Theory and Practice* 4 (1977): 231.

4. These may include practices and policies which (as in the case of antinepotism rules or the policy of "last hired–first fired") are not inherently discriminatory and which operate to the detriment of blacks and women "only because of certain contingent features of this society." See Mary Anne Warren, "Secondary Sexism and Quota Hiring," *Philosophy and Public Affairs* 6 (1977): 240–61.

5. For an excellent discussion of these complexities, see Litan, "On Rectification in Nozick's Minimal State," pp. 237–40.

6. For a contrary view, see Hardy Jones, "Fairness, Meritocracy, and Preferential Treatment," *Social Theory and Practice* 4 (1977): 211–26.

7. Under the principle of equal sacrifice, every individual need not contribute the same amount. When money payments are at issue, equality of sacrifice is likely to require progressive taxation. For a discussion of the differing interpretations of equal sacrifice, see Walter J. Blum and Harry Kalven, Jr., *The Uneasy Case for Progressive Taxation* (Chicago: University of Chicago Press, 1953), pp. 39–45.

8. I believe this is implied by Taylor.

9. The assumptions underlying this view are summarized in Blum and Kalven, *The Uneasy Case for Progressive Taxation.*

10. John Rawls, *A Theory of Justice* (Cambridge, MA: Harvard University Press, 1971), p. 153. See also Rawls, "Reflections on the Maximin Criterion," *American Economic Review* 64 (1974): 143.

11. This argument has been made most persuasively by Alan H. Goldman. See especially "Affirmative Action," *Philosophy and Public Affairs* 5 (1976): 191–92.

12. The most comprehensive treatment of German reparations is Nicholas Balabkins, *West German Reparations to Israel* (New Brunswick, NJ: Rutgers University Press, 1971). For an excellent summary see Raul Hilberg, *The Destruction of the European Jews* (Chicago: Quadrangle Books, 1961), pp. 746–59. Many important documents are found in *The German Path to Israel,* ed. Rolf Vogel (London: Oswald Wolff, 1969).

13. For excerpts from the parliamentary debates, see Vogel, pp. 32–35, 69–87.

14. Boris Bittker, *The Case for Black Reparations* (New York: Random House, 1973), p. 89.

15. *Ibid.,* pp. 131–32. Bittker estimates the minimum annual cost of a serious reparations program at $34 billion. He also suggests that such a program would have to be carried out "for at least a decade or two."

16. See Goldman, "Affirmative Action," pp. 190–91.

17. Edward C. Banfield, *The Unheavenly City: The Nature and Future of Our Urban Crisis* (Boston: Little, Brown, 1970), pp. 126–27.

18. See, for example, Chandler Davidson, "On the Culture of Shiftlessness," *Dissent* 23 (1976): 349–56.

The BAKKE Case

Who Are Equals?

Carl Cohen

> Equals ought to have equality. But there still remains a question: equality or inequality of what?
>
> —Aristotle, *Politics*

The Fourteenth Amendment to the U.S. Constitution reads in part: "No State shall . . . deny to any person within its jurisdiction the equal protection of the laws." What is the point of this passage? What would a law be like that did not apply equally to those to whom it did apply? Imagine the law: "All citizens eighteen years of age and over shall have the right to vote." Under it, the seventeen-year-old and the nineteen-year-old are treated very differently; all nineteen-year-old citizens are treated in one way (if the law is obeyed) and all seventeen-year-old citizens in another; neither group is denied the equal protection of the law. Suppose, when I went to register to vote, the county clerk responded to my request with an embarrassed smile, saying: "Ah yes, Mr. Cohen, but you see, you're Jewish, so I'm afraid we can't register you." Well! We'd make short work of him.

Now suppose the law were different. Suppose it read: "All citizens eighteen years of age and over *except Jews* shall have the right to vote." The clerk will not smile when he is handed my application in this case. "I'm sorry, Mr. Cohen,"

Reprinted from *National Forum: The Phi Kappa Phi Journal* 58, no. 1 (winter 1978), by permission of the publishers.

one can hear the mechanical voice of that bureaucrat, "but the law prescribes that Jews may not vote." I am stunned as I read the printed statute he puts before me, but there it is: non-Jews (over eighteen) vote, Jews don't. Suppose the clerk is efficient and incorruptible—all Jews are treated alike with utmost scrupulosity. Then it would appear that all were treated justly under that law, receiving its equal protection.

Surely we never supposed that the equal protection of the law entails identical treatment for everyone. We know that would be absurd. Employers have legal obligations that employees have not. Students have legal rights (and duties) that teachers have not. Rich people must pay taxes that poor people need not. Our legal codes are replete with distinctions—hundreds and thousands of distinctions determining the applicability of the laws. I may be angered by a distinction drawn—yet I will reluctantly agree that if that is the law, and if I am in a specific category, it is fair for me to be obliged under that law, as others are who are in the same class.

We argue about these distinctions—but in three very different ways. We may argue (lawyers are constantly arguing) about who are and who are not in the same class. When you defend a contested deduction on your income tax against the IRS, or I insist that as a college professor I am not a "public official" in the sense that would require public disclosure of my finances, we are disputing over the application of the legal categories drawn, not over the categories themselves. We may argue—as students of political science, or as legislators—that it is wise (or unwise) to introduce certain categorial distinctions. For example, should the law distinguish between large and small businesses in the application of industrial safety regulations? Should minimum wage requirements not apply to employees in certain age groups? And so on.

We may also argue about whether categories of a particular kind should be permitted in the law at all. Some legislation duly enacted, or administrative regulations duly authorized, may distinguish categories of persons we think ought not be distinguished. Some discriminations are worse than unwise; they are unjust.

Return now to the Fourteenth Amendment and its equal protection clause. The prohibition in that clause bears chiefly on arguments of the third sort. It does not bar legislatures from categorizing, but is interpreted so as to require categories used in laws to have a rational foundation. Some categorial distinctions will by that clause be prohibited altogether. Under Hitler's Nuremberg Laws all Jews were treated alike, but justice in America does not permit that sort of equal protection. The central thrust of the Fourteenth Amendment was, and is, to forbid the use—in law, or by administrators under color of law—of categories intrinsically unfair.

But which categories are unfair? The amendment itself was clearly designed to ensure that blacks, former slaves, were to be as free as whites. The laws were to protect all races equally. Now, more than a century later, seeking to give redress for long-standing racial injustice, we encounter the problem of fairness from the other side. May we, in the honest effort to achieve real equality among the races, distinguish between black and white (and yellow and brown, etc.) giving preference to some over others? Does our commitment to the equal protection of the laws permit it?

When the courts, and especially the United States Supreme Court, speak to such questions, they decide not simply what the U.S. Constitution requires, but what (in their view) justice requires. High courts must frame principles for the resolution of disputes between real parties, in the case before them and in future cases. Judicial reasoning is often profoundly moral reasoning. Actual cases, faced and decided, are the grist that the mill of American justice grinds. We do well to philosophize with the courts, and as they do, in living contexts. The context now forcing a deeper understanding of "the equal protection of the laws" is that of racially preferential admissions to law schools and medical schools. Some call the problem that of "reverse discrimination," others "benign quotas." Let the name not prejudice the issues. None of the participants in this dispute question the need to give redress for racial injustice and to prevent its reoccurrence. At issue is *what* we may justly do to advance these objectives—what categories we may (or must not) use, how we may (or must not) apply them.

The case of *The Regents of the University of California v. Allan Bakke*,[1] now (in 1977) before the Supreme Court of the United States, puts this problem in sharp focus. Allan Bakke was twice rejected (in 1973 and 1974) by the University of California Davis School of Medicine. His undergraduate performance was fine, his test scores excellent, his character and interview performance admirable; he ranked very high among the more than three thousand applicants for one hundred seats. But sixteen of those seats were reserved for minority-group applicants who faced admission standards deliberately and markedly lower than did majority group students like Bakke. The University of California (like many of its sister universities) was determined to enroll a representative proportion of blacks and members of other minority groups in its medical school—however distasteful the double standard believed necessary to accomplish that end.

The Davis medical school established a special committee to fill the reserved slots; this committee evaluated only the minority-group candidates, who competed only against one another. Officially, any disadvantaged person could seek admission under the special program; in fact, all persons admitted under that program, from its inception in 1969, were minority-group members. Officially, that committee reported to the admissions committee; in fact, the applicants chosen by the special committee were invariably admitted. In each of the years Bakke was rejected some minority-group admittees had grade-point averages so low (2.11 in 1973, 2.21 in 1974) that, if they had been white, they would have been summarily rejected. The University of California does not deny that the overall ranking of many of the minority-group applicants who were accepted—

after interviews, and with character, interests, test scores, and averages all considered—was substantially below that of many majority applicants who were rejected. Bakke contends that had his skin been of a darker color he would certainly have been admitted. He argues that, refused admission solely because of his race, he was denied "the equal protection of the laws" guaranteed him by the Fourteenth Amendment to the U.S. Constitution.

All sides in this litigation agree that professional schools may properly use, in screening for admission, a host of factors other than test scores and grade-point averages: dedication or dexterity, compassion or professional aims. All sides agree that persons unfairly injured are entitled to full, appropriate, and timely redress. What remains at issue in this case is one thing only: *preference by race*.

The advocates of racially preferential systems reason as follows: Equal protection of the laws requires different treatment for people in different circumstances. Minority-group members are in very special circumstances. Preference by race is here a reasonable instrument to achieve, for members of minority groups, objectives both just and compelling.

Such preference (not denied by the medical school) is thus defended by two central arguments. The first is grounded in alleged demands of justice: Only by deliberately preferring minority applicants can we give adequate compensation for generations of oppressive maltreatment. The second is grounded in the alleged needs of society: If we do not continue to give deliberate racial preference, our medical and law schools will again become what they long were—white enclaves. *Compensation* is the heart of the first argument, *integration* of the second. Both arguments are profoundly mistaken.

Redress is rightly given for injury—not for being black or brown. Members of minority groups have been cruelly damaged, but whatever damage is rightly compensated for (cultural or economic deprivation, inferior schooling, or other), *any* applicant so unfairly damaged is fully entitled to the same special consideration, regardless of his or her race or ethnic group. The prohibition of special favor by race—any race—is the central thrust of a constitutional guarantee that all will receive the protection of the laws equally. Classification by race for the distribution of goods or opportunities is intrinsically odious, always invidious, and morally impermissible, no matter how laudable the goals in view.

What of the school-desegregation cases in which the U.S. Supreme Court has approved the use of racial categories to ensure racial integration? Don't these show that racial preference is permissible if the aim is good? Certainly not. In these cases attention to race was allowed in order to ascertain whether school boards that had been discriminating wrongfully by race had really ceased to do so. Racial identification was there permitted—but only to ensure that all students, of whatever race, received absolutely equal treatment. The distinction between that use of racial counting, and the use of racial categories to reintroduce special preference, is sharp and profound.

Can the University of California be defended on the ground that its system of racial preference is not injurious but benign? No. Results, not intentions, determine benignity. All racial quotas have injurious results and therefore cannot be benign. When the goods being distributed are in short supply, and some get more of those goods because of their race, then others get less because of their race. There is no escaping that cold logic. Bakke and others like him are seriously penalized for no other reason than their race. Such a system, as even the Washington State Supreme Court in the *DeFunis* case agreed, "is certainly not benign with respect to non-minority students who are displaced by it."[2]

All this says not an iota against compensation. If redress is due, let us give it, and give it fully. If compensation is to be offered through special favor in professional-school admissions—a questionable mode of payment but a possible one—then let us be certain we look in every case to the injury for which we give redress, and not to the race of the applicant.

If the requirements of justice cannot support racial preference, perhaps the society's interest in integration can. The Supreme Court of California, while upholding Bakke's claim, allowed, *arguendo*, that integration is a compelling interest. "Integration" has different meanings, of course. That ambiguity invites the university's most appealing complaint. "You have told us to integrate," the university has said, in effect, "and when we devise admissions systems designed to do just that, you tell us we may not use racial preference. But the problem is a racial one. We cannot achieve racial balance unless we give special preference to racial minorities. Do not ask the impossible of us. And do not ask us to do in indirect ways what you will not permit us to do directly."

That argument by the University of California is not sound. The reply is fourfold.

First, some of the ends in view are important, some are questionable. That the entire package is "compelling" is very doubtful.

1. Better medical and legal services for minorities is a pressing need, but it is far from obvious that minority professionals reared in city slums will return to practice there. And it is patently unfair to burden them with this restrictive expectation. If the intention to give service to particular segments of the community is to be a consideration in admission to professional school, let that be known, and let all persons, of whatever race, make their case for establishing such intentions, if they claim them.

2. Some defend preferential admission on the ground that many persons seeking professional help will be "more comfortable" with a lawyer or a doctor of their own race or religion. Possibly true. But the argument based upon

this interest, now to serve as a justification of institutionalized racial preference, has long been used to exclude blacks from white hospitals and Jews from Christian law firms. It is an argument in which bigots of every color will take satisfaction.

3. Diversity of cultural background in the professional schools, and in the professions themselves, will increase the richness of education and of service, and will provide role models for youngsters from cultural groups long oppressed. These are genuine and worthy interests, but are they compelling? What *is* compelling is integration in the classical sense: the removal of every obstruction to genuinely equal opportunity, the elimination of every racial qualification. Integration in the now fashionable sense—entailing some *de facto* mix of races approaching proportionality—may be desirable in many contexts, but is in any case certainly not compelling.

Second, the Supreme Court of California emphasized that no party has shown that preference by race in admissions (which all agree is objectionable) is necessary to achieve appropriate social goals. Even if arbitrary numerical ratios are established as the only acceptable standard of success, that cannot be shown. But from whence comes that numerical standard? The entire history of our nation has been one of ethnic layering, in which different interests and activities tend to be pursued by different cultural and ethnic groups. That is not unwholesome. The effort to homogenize society in spite of this natural tendency is already proving to be divisive, frustrating, and unworkable. Substantial increases of diversity in some professions are reasonably sought. With nonpreferential forms of affirmative action pursued vigorously, and admissions criteria enlarged and enriched and applied evenhandedly to all applicants, diversity and de facto integration may be much advanced. Still more might be accomplished if various compensatory schemes were introduced, but they must be applied in a racially neutral way. Some majority applicants who deserve compensatory preference will also benefit under such programs, but this is entirely fitting.

There is nothing crafty about this reply. The claim that these are but devious ways to reach the same ends is simply false, and betrays an inclination to introduce racial preference somehow, "through the back door" if necessary. That would be ugly. There is no reason to fear or to be ashamed of an honest admissions program, or of an honest compensatory program, honestly applied. The racial count that results may not be the same as that when racial preference is used, but perhaps it ought not be. Even if the count were the same, the individuals (admitted using morally relevant principles, not race) would be different, and that makes all the difference. It is certain that substantial progress in diversifying and integrating professional school classes can be achieved without racial preference.

Third, we must see that granting favor on the basis of race alone is a nasty business, however honorable the goal. The moral issue comes in classic form: Terribly pressing objectives (integrated professions, adequate legal and medical service for members of minority groups) appear to require impermissible means. Might we not wink at the Constitution, this once, in view of the importance and decency of our objectives?

Such winking is precisely the hope of every party having aims that are, to that party's profound conviction, of absolutely overriding importance. Constitutional shortcuts have been and will be urged for the sake of national security (e.g., the internment of Japanese Americans during World War II), for the enforcement of criminal laws (e.g., admission of illegally seized evidence), and in other spheres. But wink we must not. Each party in its turn must abide the restrictions of constitutional process. The single most important feature of a constitution, if it is more than paper, is its preclusion of unjust means. Hence the preciousness and power of the guarantee of equality before the law. When good process and laudable objectives conflict, long experience teaches the priority of process. Means that are corrupt will infect the result and (with societies as with individuals) will corrupt the user in the end. So it is with wiretapping, with censorship, and with every shortcut taken knowingly at the expense of the rights of individuals. So it is also with racial preference, even when well-intended.

The *fourth* response to the integration argument adds bitter irony. Hating the taste of racial preference in admissions, the advocates of these programs swallow them only because of a conviction that they are so good for us. Bitter but (they think) medicinal. In this, too, they are mistaken. Racial preference is good for nobody, black or white, majority or minority. However much the advocates of such systems may hope for ultimate integration (though some do not share that ideal) the consequence of preferential systems is ever greater attention to race, agitation and tension about race. All comment about race, even scholarship with constructive intent, comes to be viewed as invidious. Rewards and penalties based on race are widely thought to be unfair, undeserved. Unfairness breeds resentment; resentment grows to anger. Racial preference does not integrate the races but *dis*integrates them, exciting envy, fostering ill will and even hatred.

Racial preference is dynamite. Many who play with such preference are now blinded by honest zeal and hide from themselves the explosions likely in the sequel. Justice John Marshall Harlan, dissenting in 1896 from the Supreme Court ruling that established the "separate but equal" doctrine, insisted that the U.S. Constitution was and must be color-blind. Some would have the law be color-conscious now so that it may become color-blind in the future. That cannot be. One is reminded of political leaders who "suspend" constitutions to "build a firmer base for democracy." Once established as constitutionally acceptable grounds for discriminatory distribution, racial categories will wax, not wane, in importance. No prescription for racial disharmony could be surer of success.

Official favoritism by race or national origin is poison in society. In American society, built of manifold racial and ethnic layers, it is deadly poison. How gravely mistaken it will be to take new doses of the same stuff, while still suffering the pains of recovery from the old.

Notes

1. *Regents of The University of California v. Bakke*, 438 U.S. 265, 403 (1978).
2. *DeFunis v. Odegaard*, 416 U.S. 312 (1974).

Bakke's Case: Are Quotas Unfair?

Ronald Dworkin

On October 12, 1977, the Supreme Court heard oral argument in the case of *The Regents of the University of California v. Allan Bakke*. No lawsuit has ever been more widely watched or more thoroughly debated in the national and international press before the Court's decision. Still, some of the most pertinent facts set before the Court have not been clearly summarized.

The University of California Davis School of Medicine has an affirmative action program (called the "task force program") designed to admit more black and other minority students. It sets sixteen places aside for which only members of "educationally and economically disadvantaged minorities" compete. Allan Bakke, white, applied for one of the remaining eighty-four places; he was rejected but, since his test scores were relatively high, the medical school has conceded that it could not prove that he would have been rejected if the sixteen places reserved had been open to him. Bakke sued, arguing that the task force program deprived him of his constitutional rights. The California Supreme Court agreed, and ordered the medical school to admit him. The university appealed to the Supreme Court.

The Davis program for minorities is in certain respects more forthright (some would say cruder) than similar plans now in force in many other American universities and professional schools. Such programs aim to increase the enrollment of black and other minority students by allowing the fact of their race to count affirmatively as part of the case for admitting them. Some schools set a

Reprinted from the *New York Review of Books*, November 10, 1977, © Ronald Dworkin, by permission of the *New York Review of Books*.

"target" of a particular number of minority places instead of setting aside a flat number of places. But Davis would not fill the number of places set aside unless there were sixteen minority candidates it considered clearly qualified for medical education. The difference is therefore one of administrative strategy and not of principle.

So the constitutional question raised by *Bakke* is of capital importance for higher education in the United States, and a large number of universities and schools have entered briefs *amicus curiae* urging the Court to reverse the California decision. They believe that if they are not free to use explicit racial criteria in their admissions programs, they will be unable to fulfill what they take to be their responsibilities to the nation.

It is often said that affirmative action programs aim to achieve a racially conscious society divided into racial and ethnic groups, each entitled as a group to some proportionable share of resources, careers, or opportunities. That is a perverse description. American society is currently a racially conscious society; this is the inevitable and evident consequence of a history of slavery, repression, and prejudice. Black men and women, boys and girls, are not free to choose for themselves in what roles—or as members of which social groups—others will characterize them. They are black, and no other feature of personality or allegiance or ambition will so thoroughly influence how they will be perceived and treated by others, and the range and character of the lives that will be open to them.

The tiny number of black doctors and other professionals is both a consequence and a continuing cause of American racial consciousness, one link in a long and self-fueling chain reaction. Affirmative action programs use racially explicit criteria because their immediate goal is to increase the number of members of certain races in these professions. But their long-term goal is to *reduce* the degree to which American society is overall a racially conscious society.

The programs rest on two judgments. The first is a judgment of social theory: that the United States will continue to be pervaded by racial divisions as long as the most lucrative, satisfying, and important careers remain mainly the prerogative of members of the white race, while others feel themselves systematically excluded from a professional and social elite. The second is a calculation of strategy: that increasing the number of blacks who are at work in the professions will, in the long run, reduce the sense of frustration and injustice and racial self-consciousness in the black community to the point at which blacks may begin to think of themselves as individuals who can succeed like others through talent and initiative. At that future point the consequences of nonracial admissions programs, whatever these consequences might be, could be accepted with no sense of racial barriers or injustice.

It is therefore the worst possible misunderstanding to suppose that affirmative action programs are designed to produce a balkanized America, divided into racial and ethnic subnations. They use strong measures because weaker ones will fail; but their ultimate goal is to lessen not to increase the importance of race in American social and professional life.

According to the 1970 census, only 2.1 percent of American doctors were black. Affirmative action programs aim to provide more black doctors to serve black patients. This is not because it is desirable that blacks treat blacks and whites treat whites, but because blacks, through no fault of their own, are now unlikely to be well served by whites, and because a failure to provide the doctors they trust will exacerbate rather than reduce the resentment that now leads them to trust only their own. Affirmative action tries to provide more blacks as classmates for white doctors, not because it is desirable that a medical school class reflect the racial makeup of the community as a whole, but because professional association between blacks and whites will decrease the degree to which whites think of blacks as a race rather than as people, and thus the degree to which blacks think of themselves that way. It tries to provide "role models" for future black doctors, not because it is desirable for a black boy or girl to find adult models only among blacks, but because our history has made them so conscious of their race that the success of whites, for now, is likely to mean little or nothing for them.

The history of the campaign against racial injustice since 1954, when the Supreme Court decided *Brown v. Board of Education*, is a history in large part of failure. We have not succeeded in reforming the racial consciousness of our society by racially neutral means. We are therefore obliged to look upon the arguments for affirmative action with sympathy and an open mind. Of course, if Bakke is right that such programs, no matter how effective they may be, violate his constitutional rights, then they cannot be permitted to continue. But we must not forbid them in the name of some mindless maxim, like the maxim that it cannot be right to fight fire with fire, or that the end cannot justify the means. If the strategic claims for affirmative action are cogent, they cannot be dismissed on the ground that racially explicit tests are distasteful. If such tests are distasteful, it can only be for reasons that make the underlying social realities the programs attack more distasteful still.

It is said that, in a pluralistic society, membership in a particular group cannot be used as a criterion of inclusion or exclusion from benefits. But group membership is, as a matter of social reality rather than formal admission standards, part of what determines inclusion or exclusion for us now. If we must choose between a society that is in fact liberal and an illiberal society that scrupulously avoids formal racial criteria, we can hardly appeal to the ideals of liberal pluralism to prefer the latter.

Archibald Cox of Harvard Law School, speaking for the University of California in oral argument, told the Supreme Court that this is the choice the United States must make. As things stand, he said, affirmative action programs are the only effective means of increasing the absurdly small number of black doctors. The California Supreme Court, in approving Bakke's claim, had urged the university to pursue that goal by methods that do not explicitly take race into account. But that is unrealistic. We must distinguish, Cox said, between two interpretations of what the California court's recommendation means. It might mean that the university should aim at the same immediate goal, of increasing the proportion of black and other minority students in the medical school, by an admissions procedure that on the surface is not racially conscious.

That is a recommendation of hypocrisy. If those who administer the admissions standards, however these are phrased, understand that their immediate goal is to increase the number of blacks in the school, then they will use race as a criterion in making the various subjective judgments the explicit criteria will require, because that will be, given the goal, the only right way to make those judgments. The recommendation might mean, on the other hand, that the school should adopt some nonracially conscious goal, like increasing the number of disadvantaged students of all races, and then hope that that goal will produce an increase in the number of blacks as a by-product. But even if that strategy is less hypocritical (which is far from plain), it will almost certainly fail because no different goal, scrupulously administered in a nonracially conscious way, will significantly increase the number of black medical students.

Cox offered powerful evidence for that conclusion, and it is supported by the recent and comprehensive report of the Carnegie Council on Policy Studies in Higher Education. Suppose, for example, that the medical school sets aside separate places for applicants "disadvantaged" on some racially neutral test, like poverty, allowing only those disadvantaged in that way to compete for these places. If the school selects those from that group who scored best on standard medical school aptitude tests, then it will take almost no blacks, because blacks score relatively low even among the economically disadvantaged. But if the school chooses among the disadvantaged on some basis other than test scores, just so that more blacks will succeed, then it will not be administering the special procedure in a nonracially conscious way.

So Cox was able to put his case in the form of two simple propositions. A racially conscious test for admission, even one that sets aside certain places for qualified minority applicants exclusively, serves goals that are in themselves unobjectionable and even urgent. Such programs are, moreover, the only means that offer any significant promise of achieving these goals. If these programs are halted, then no more than a trickle of black students will enter medical or other professional schools for another generation at least.

If these propositions are sound, then on what ground can it be thought that such programs are either wrong or unconstitutional? We must notice an important distinction between two different sorts of objections that might be made. These programs are intended, as I said, to decrease the importance of race in the United States in the long run. It may be objected, first, that the programs will harm that goal more than they will advance it. There is no way now to prove that that is not so. Cox conceded in his argument that there are costs and risks in these programs.

Affirmative action programs seem to encourage, for example, a popular misunderstanding, which is that they assume that racial or ethnic groups are entitled to proportionate shares of opportunities, so that Italian or Polish ethnic minorities are, in theory, as entitled to their proportionate shares as blacks or Chicanos or American Indians are entitled to the shares the present programs give them. That is a plain mistake: the programs are not based on the idea that those who are aided are entitled to aid, but only on the strategic hypothesis that helping them is now an effective way of attacking a national problem. Some medical schools may well make that judgment, under certain circumstances, about a white ethnic minority. Indeed it seems likely that some medical schools are even now attempting to help white Appalachian applicants, for example, under programs of regional distribution.

So the popular understanding is wrong, but so long as it persists it is a cost of the program because the attitudes it encourages tend to a degree to make people more rather than less conscious of race. There are other possible costs. It is said, for example, that some blacks find affirmative action degrading; they find that it makes them more rather than less conscious of prejudice against their race as such. This attitude is also based on a misperception, I think, but for a small minority of blacks at least it is a genuine cost.

In the view of the many important universities which have such programs, however, the gains will very probably exceed the losses in reducing racial consciousness overall. This view is hardly so implausible that it is wrong for these universities to seek to acquire the experience that will allow us to judge whether they are right. It would be particularly silly to forbid these experiments if we know that the failure to try will mean, as the evidence shows, that the status quo will almost certainly continue. In any case, this first objection could provide no argument that would justify a decision by the Supreme Court holding the programs unconstitutional. The Court has no business substituting its speculative judgment about the probable consequences of educational policies for the judgment of professional educators.

So the acknowledged uncertainties about the long-term results of such programs could not justify a Supreme Court decision making them illegal. But there is a second and very different form of objection. It may be argued that even if the programs *are* effective in making our society less a society dominated by race, they are nevertheless unconstitutional because they violate the individual constitutional rights of those, like Allan Bakke, who lose places in consequence. In the oral argument Reynold H. Colvin of San Francisco, who is Bakke's lawyer, made plain that his objection takes this second form. Mr. Justice White asked him whether he accepted that the goals affirmative action programs seek are important goals. Colvin acknowledged that they were. Suppose, Justice White continued, that affirmative action programs are, as Cox had argued, the only effective means of seeking such goals. Would Colvin nevertheless maintain that the programs are unconstitutional? Yes, he insisted, they would be, because his client has a constitutional right that the programs be abandoned, no matter what the consequences.

Colvin was wise to put his objections on this second ground; he was wise to claim that his client has rights that do not depend on any judgment about the likely consequences of affirmative action for society as a whole, because if he sustains that claim, then the Court must give him the relief he seeks.

But can he be right? If Allan Bakke has a constitutional right so important that the urgent goals of affirmative action must yield, then this must be because affirmative action violates some fundamental principle of political morality. This is not a case in which what might be called formal or technical law requires a decision one way or the other. There is no language in the Constitution whose plain meaning forbids affirmative action. Only the most naive theories of statutory construction could argue that such a result is required by the language of any earlier Supreme Court decision or of the Civil Rights Act of 1964 or of any other congressional enactment. If Colvin is right, it must be because Allan Bakke has not simply some technical legal right but an important moral right as well.

What could that right be? The popular argument frequently made on editorial pages is that Bakke has a right to be judged on his merit. Or that he has a right to be judged as an individual rather than as a member of a social group. Or that he has a right, as much as any black man, not to be sacrificed or excluded from any opportunity because of his race alone. But these catchphrases are deceptive here, because, as reflection demonstrates, the only genuine principle they describe is the principle that no one should suffer from the prejudice or contempt of others. And that principle is not at stake in this case at all. In spite of popular opinion, the idea that the *Bakke* case presents a conflict between a desirable social goal and important individual rights is a piece of intellectual confusion.

Consider, for example, the claim that individuals applying for places in medical school should be judged on merit, and merit alone. If that slogan means that admissions committees should take nothing into account but scores on some particular intelligence test, then it is arbitrary and, in any case, contradicted by the long-standing practice of every medical school. If it means, on the other hand, that a medical school should choose candidates that it supposes will make the most useful doctors, then everything turns on the judgment of what factors make different doctors useful. The Davis medical school assigned to each regular applicant, as well as to each minority applicant, what it called a "benchmark score." This reflected not only the results of aptitude tests and college grade averages, but a subjective evaluation of the applicant's chances of functioning as an effective doctor, in view of society's present needs for medical service. Presumably the qualities deemed important were different from the qualities that a law school or engineering school or business school would seek, just as the intelligence tests a medical school might use would be different from the tests these other schools would find appropriate.

There is no combination of abilities and skills and traits that constitutes "merit" in the abstract; if quick hands count as "merit" in the case of a prospective surgeon, this is because quick hands will enable him to serve the public better and for no other reason. If a black skin will, as a matter of regrettable fact, enable another doctor to do a different medical job better, then that black skin is by the same token "merit" as well. That argument may strike some as dangerous; but only because they confuse its conclusion—that black skin may be a socially useful trait in particular circumstances—with the very different and despicable idea that one race may be inherently more worthy than another.

Consider the second of the catchphrases I have mentioned. It is said that Bakke has a right to be judged as an "individual," in deciding whether he is to be admitted to medical school and thus to the medical profession, and not as a member of some group that is being judged as a whole. What can that mean? Any admissions procedure must rely on generalizations about groups that are justified only statistically. The regular admissions process at Davis, for example, set a cutoff figure for college grade-point averages. Applicants whose averages fell below that figure were not invited to any interview, and therefore rejected out of hand.

An applicant whose average fell one point below the cutoff might well have had personal qualities of dedication or sympathy that would have been revealed at an interview, and that would have made him or her a better doctor than some applicant whose average rose one point above the line. But the former is excluded from the process on the basis of a decision taken for administrative convenience and grounded in the generalization, unlikely to hold true for every individual, that those with grade averages below the cutoff will not have other qualities sufficiently persuasive. Even the use of standard Medical College Aptitude Tests (MCAT) as part of the admissions procedure requires judging people as part of groups, because it assumes that test scores are a guide to medical intelligence, which is in turn a guide to medical ability. Though this judgment is no doubt true statistically, it hardly holds true for every individual.

Allan Bakke was himself refused admission to two other medical schools, not because of his race but because of his age: these schools thought that a student entering medical school at the age of thirty-three was likely to make less of a contribution to medical care over his career than someone entering at the standard age of twenty-one. Suppose these schools relied, not on any detailed investigation of whether Bakke himself had abilities that would contradict the generalization in his specific case, but on a rule of thumb that allowed only the most cursory look at applicants over (say) the age of thirty. Did these two medical schools violate his right to be judged as an individual rather than as a member of a group?

The Davis School of Medicine permitted whites to apply for the sixteen places reserved for members of "educationally or economically disadvantaged minorities," a phrase whose meaning might well include white ethnic minorities. In fact several whites have applied, though none has been accepted, and the California court found that the special committee charged with administering the program had decided, in advance, against admitting any. Suppose that decision had been based on the following administrative theory: it is so unlikely that any white doctor can do as much to counteract racial imbalance in the medical professions as a well-qualified and trained black doctor can do that the committee should for reasons of convenience proceed on the presumption no white doctor could. That presumption is, as a matter of fact, more plausible than the corresponding presumption about medical students over the age of thirty, or even the presumption about applicants whose grade-point averages fall below the cutoff line. If the latter presumptions do not deny the alleged right of individuals to be judged as individuals in an admissions procedure, then neither can the former.

Colvin, in oral argument, argued the third of the catchphrases I mentioned. He said that his client had a right not to be excluded from medical school because of his race alone, and this as a statement of constitutional right sounds more plausible than claims about the right to be judged on merit or as an individual. It sounds plausible, however, because it suggests the following more complex principle. Every citizen has a constitutional right that he not suffer disadvantage, at least in the competition for any public benefit, because the race or religion or sect or region or other natural or artificial group to which he belongs is the object of prejudice or contempt.

That is a fundamentally important constitutional right, and it is that right that was systematically violated for many years by racist exclusions and anti-Semitic quotas. Color bars and Jewish quotas were not unfair just because they made race or religion relevant or because they fixed on qualities beyond individual control. It is true that blacks or Jews do not choose to be blacks or Jews. But it is also true that those who score low in aptitude or admissions tests do not choose their levels of intelligence. Nor do those denied admission because they are too old, or because they do not come from a part of the country underrepresented in the school, or because they cannot play basketball well, choose not to have the qualities that made the difference.

Race seems different because exclusions based on race have historically been motivated not by some instrumental calculation, as in the case of intelligence or age or regional distribution or athletic ability, but because of contempt for the excluded race or religion as such. Exclusion by race was in itself an insult, because it was generated by and signaled contempt.

Bakke's claim, therefore, must be made more specific than it is. He says he was kept out of medical school because of his race. Does he mean that he was kept out because his race is the object of prejudice or contempt? That suggestion is absurd. A very high proportion of those who were accepted (and, presumably, of those who run the admissions program) were members of the same race. He therefore means simply that if he had been black he would have been accepted, with no suggestion that this would have been so because blacks are thought more worthy or honorable than whites.

That is true: no doubt he would have been accepted if he were black. But it is also true, and in exactly the same sense, that he would have been accepted if he had been more intelligent, or made a better impression in his interview, or, in the case of other schools, if he had been younger when he decided to become a doctor. Race is not, in *his* case, a different matter from these other factors equally beyond his control. It is not a different matter because in his case race is not distinguished by the special character of public insult. On the contrary, the program presupposes that his race is still widely if wrongly thought to be superior to others.

In the past it made sense to say that an excluded black or Jewish student was being sacrificed because of his race or religion; that meant that his or her exclusion was treated as desirable in itself, not because it contributed to any goal in which he as well as the rest of society might take pride. Allan Bakke is being "sacrificed" because of his race only in a very artificial sense of the word. He is being "sacrificed" in the same artificial sense because of his level of intelligence, since he would have been accepted if he were more clever than he is. In both cases he is being excluded not by prejudice but because of a rational calculation about the socially most beneficial use of limited resources for medical education.

It may now be said that this distinction is too subtle, and that if racial classifications have been and may still be used for malign purposes, then everyone has a flat right that racial classifications not be used at all. This is the familiar appeal to the lazy virtue of simplicity. It supposes that if a line is difficult to draw, or might be difficult to administer if drawn, then there is wisdom in not making the attempt to draw it. There may be cases in which that is wise, but those would be cases in which nothing of great value would as a consequence be lost. If racially conscious admissions policies now offer the only substantial hope for bringing more qualified black and other minority doctors into the profession, then a great loss is suffered if medical schools are not allowed voluntarily to pursue such programs. We should then be trading away a chance to attack certain and present injustice in order to gain protection we may not need against speculative abuses we have other means to prevent. And such abuses cannot, in any case, be worse than the injustice to which we would then surrender.

We have now considered three familiar slogans, each widely thought to name a constitutional right that enables Allan Bakke to stop programs of affirmative action no matter how effective or necessary these might be. When we inspect these slogans, we find that they can stand for no genuine principle except one. This is the important principle that no one in our society should suffer because he is a member of a group thought less worthy of respect, as a group, than other groups. We have different aspects of that principle in mind when we say that individuals should be judged on merit, that they should be judged as individuals, and that they should not suffer disadvantages because of their race. The spirit of that fundamental principle is the spirit of the goal that affirmative action is intended to serve. The principle furnishes no support for those who find, as Bakke does, that their own interests conflict with that goal.

It is regrettable when any citizen's expectations are defeated by new programs serving some more general concern. It is regrettable, for example, when established small businesses fail because new and superior roads are built; in that case people have invested more than Bakke has. And they have more reason to believe their businesses will continue than Bakke had to suppose he could have entered the Davis medical school at thirty-three, even without a task force program.

There is, of course, no suggestion in that program that Bakke shares in any collective or individual guilt for racial injustice in the United States; or that he is any less entitled to concern or respect than any black student accepted in the program. He has been disappointed, and he must have the sympathy due that disappointment, just as any other disappointed applicant—even one with much worse test scores who would not have been accepted in any event—must have sympathy. Each is disappointed because places in medical schools are scarce resources and must be used to provide what the more general society most needs. It is not Bakke's fault that racial justice is now a special need—but he has no right to prevent the most effective measures of securing that justice from being used.

What Did Bakke Really Decide?

Ronald Dworkin

The decision of the Supreme Court in *Bakke* was received by the press and much of the public with great relief, as an act of judicial statesmanship that gave to each party in the national debate what it seemed to want most. Such a sense of relief, however, hardly seems warranted, and it is important to explain why it does not.

Everyone knows something of the facts of the case. The University of California Davis School of Medicine administered a two-track admission procedure, in which sixteen of a hundred available places were in effect set aside for members of "minority" groups. Allan Bakke, a white applicant who had been rejected, sued. The California Supreme Court ordered the medical school to admit him, and forbade California universities to take race into account in their admissions decisions.

The United States Supreme Court's decision affirmed the California court's order that Bakke himself be admitted, but reversed that court's prohibition against taking race into account in any way. So opponents of affirmative action plans could point to Bakke's individual victory as vindication of their view that such plans often go too far; while proponents were relieved to find that the main goals of affirmative action could still be pursued, through plans more complex and subtle than the plan that Davis used and the Supreme Court rejected.

But it is far too early to conclude that the long-awaited *Bakke* decision will set even the main lines of a national compromise about affirmative action in higher education. The arithmetic of the opinions of various justices, and the narrow ground of the pivotal opinion of Mr. Justice Powell, mean that *Bakke* decided rather less than had been hoped, and left more, by way of general principle as well as detailed application, to later Supreme Court cases that are now inevitable.

Bakke's lawyers raised two questions against the Davis quota plan. They argued, first, that the plan was illegal under the words of the Civil Rights Act of 1964, which provides that no one shall "on the ground of race . . . be excluded from participation in, be denied the benefits of, or be subjected to discrimination under any program" receiving federal aid. (Davis, like all medical schools, receives such aid.) They argued, second, that the plan was unconstitutional because it denied Bakke the equal protection guaranteed by the Fourteenth Amendment.

Five out of nine justices—Justices Brennan, White, Marshall, Blackmun, and Powell—held that Bakke had no independent case on the first ground, the 1964 Civil Rights Act, and that the case therefore had to be decided on the second, the Constitution. They said that the language of the Civil Rights Act, properly interpreted, was meant to make illegal only practices that would be forbidden to the states by the equal protection clause itself. They decided, that is, that it is impossible to decide a case like *Bakke* on statutory grounds without reaching the constitutional issue, because the statute does not condemn the Davis program unless the Constitution does. The remaining four justices—Chief Justice Burger, and Justices Stewart, Rehnquist, and Stevens—thought that Bakke was right on the first ground, of the Civil Rights Act, and that they therefore did not have to consider the second, the Constitution itself, and they did not do so.

Of the five justices who considered the second, constitutional argument, four—Brennan, White, Marshall, and Blackmun—held that Bakke had no case under the Constitution either. Mr. Justice Powell held otherwise. He held that the equal protection clause forbids explicit quotas or reserved places unless the school in question can show that these means are necessary to achieve goals of compelling importance, and he held that Davis had not met that burden of proof. But he also held that universities may take race into account explicitly as one among several factors affecting admission decisions in particular cases, in order to achieve racial diversity in classes. (He cited the Harvard undergraduate admissions program as an example.) He said that the Constitution permits this use of race and, since the California Supreme Court had held otherwise, he voted to reverse that court on this point. So a majority of those considering the matter voted against Bakke on *both* of his arguments; but Bakke nevertheless won, because five justices thought he should win on some ground even though they disagreed on which ground.

What does all this mean for the future? The Supreme Court has now decided, by a vote of five to four, that the Civil Rights Act does not in and of itself bar affirmative action programs, even those, like Davis's, that use explicit quotas. It has decided, by a vote of five to none, that the Constitution permits affirmative action plans, like the Harvard undergraduate plan, that allow race to be taken into account, on an individual-by-individual basis, in order to achieve a reasonably diverse student body.

Both of these decisions are important. The Civil Rights Act issue was, in my opinion, not a difficult issue, but it is useful that it is now removed from the argument. The argument of the California Supreme Court—that racially conscious admissions programs are always unconstitutional—would have been disastrous for affirmative action had it prevailed in the United States Supreme Court, and it is therefore of great importance that it was rejected there. It is also important that at least five justices are agreed that a program like the Harvard undergraduate plan is constitutional. The Harvard model provides a standard; if the admissions officers of other universities are satisfied that their plan is like the Harvard plan in all pertinent respects, they can proceed in confidence.

It is equally important to emphasize, however, that the Supreme Court has *not* decided that only a program such as Harvard's is constitutional. It has not even decided that a program with a rigid quota such as the one Davis used is unconstitutional. Mr. Justice Powell drew the line that way in his opinion: he said that a quota-type program is unconstitutional, and his arguments suggest that only something very like the Harvard program is constitutional. But his opinion is only one opinion; no other justice agreed, and four other justices expressly disagreed with him on both points. So Powell's line will become the Supreme Court's line only if not a single one of the four justices who remained silent on the constitutional issue takes a position less restrictive than Powell's on that issue. In these circumstances it seems premature to treat Powell's opinion, and the distinction he drew, as the foundation of the constitutional settlement that will eventually emerge.

There seems little doubt that the four justices who remained silent on the constitutional issue will have to break that silence reasonably soon. For there are a variety of affirmative action cases likely to confront the Court soon in which no statute can provide a reason for avoiding the constitutional issue. The Court has now remanded a case, for example, which challenges the provision of the Public Works Employment Act of 1977 that at least 10 percent of funds disbursed under the act be applied to "minority" businesses. Since Congress enacted this statute, there can be no argument that its provisions violate congressional will, and the four justices will have to face the question of whether such quota provisions are unconstitutional when this case (or, if it is moot, when some similar case) finally arrives before them. Of course these will not be education cases, and Powell's opinion is carefully tailored to education cases. But the arguments of principle on which he relied, in taking a more restrictive view of what the equal protection clause permits than did the other justices who spoke to that issue, are equally applicable to employment and other cases.

Indeed, it is arguable that, in strict theory, the four justices who remained silent would have to speak to the constitutional issue even if another education case, like the *Bakke* case, were for some reason to come before the Court. Suppose (though this is incredible) that some university that administers a quota-type system like the Davis system were to refuse to dismantle it in favor of a more flexible system, and the Supreme Court were to review the inevitable challenge. Since *Bakke* decides that the Civil Rights Act is no more restrictive than the Constitution, the four justices might well consider this point foreclosed by that decision in any future case, in which event they would have to face the constitutional issue they avoided there.

(Anthony Lewis, in the *New York Times*, said that it was surprising that these justices did not give their opinion on the Constitution even in *Bakke*, since they knew that the Court as a whole rejected their argument that the case could be decided under the statute. Lewis speculates that one of the five justices who rejected the statutory argument might have held the contrary view until just before the decision was released, and so left the four little time to address the constitutional issue.

He may be right, but there is at least another possibility. Suppose at least one of the four believed that even the Davis quota-type plan was constitutional. If he had said so, but nevertheless voted in favor of Bakke on the statutory issue, then the Court would have ordered Bakke admitted even though a majority of the full Court, and not simply a majority of those speaking to each issue, was against Bakke on both grounds, and even though the Court would have been constrained, by precedent, to approve a quota-type program in the future. That would have been even more bizarre and confusing than the present decision. But all this is simply guesswork squared.)

Is there any point (other than as an academic exercise) in these speculations about the position that members of the silent four would take on the constitutional issue? Some practical lawyers have already said that the main goals of affirmative action programs, at least in university and professional school education, can be served by programs that fall comfortably within what Mr. Justice Powell expressly permitted. If that is so, then it might be wise to proceed as if the Powell opinion, even though the opinion of only one justice, states constitutional law for university educational programs, and then try to work out a similar settlement for other areas, like employment, in other cases. But I am not so sure that it is so, because the Powell opinion, at least until clarified by later decisions, is less coherent and may well be less permissive than it has widely been taken to be.

Powell expressly ruled out admissions programs, like the Davis program, that reserve certain places for minority members only. He approved programs, like the Harvard undergraduate program he cited, that do not even set target numbers for minority acceptance. Such programs are aimed at diversity in the student body. They recognize that racial diversity is as important as geographical diversity or diversity in extracurricular talents and career ambitions, and so take race into account in such a way that the fact that an applicant is black may tip the balance in his favor just as the fact that another applicant is an accomplished flutist may tip the balance in his.

But a great many affirmative action admissions programs fall between these two extremes. They do not expressly reserve a set number of places for which only minority applicants compete, but they nevertheless do set rough "target" figures representing a general decision about the proportion of the class that should on general principles be filled by minority applicants. The number of such applicants accepted will vary from year to year but will hover within a range that will be less varying than the proportion of accomplished musicians, for example, or of applicants from a particular section of the country. In most cases, the admissions committee will report the number of minority applicants selected to the faculty at large, as a separate statistic, and will attempt to explain a particularly low percentage in any particular year. Minority applications will in this way be treated very differently from applications of musicians or West Coast residents. Do such rough "targets," used in this way, make a program unconstitutional under the analysis Powell proposed?

The answer may depend on the goal or purpose of the "target." Powell considered a number of goals that affirmative action programs in a medical school might be expected to achieve, and he said that some goals were constitutionally permitted, while others were not. He rejected, in particular, "the purpose of helping certain groups whom the faculty . . . perceived as victims of 'societal discrimination.'" (He said that this goal must not be pursued by any classification that imposes disadvantages on others who had no responsibility for the earlier discrimination.) He accepted as permissible the goal of supplying more professional people for underserved communities, but denied that Davis had shown that a program "must prefer members of particular ethnic groups" in order to achieve that goal. He also accepted the goal of educational diversity, which in his opinion justified the flexible Harvard plan though not the Davis quota plan.

The constitutionality of an affirmative action plan therefore depends, according to Powell, on its purpose as well as its structure. It is not altogether plain how courts are to decide what the purpose of a racially conscious admissions program is. Perhaps they should not look behind an official institutional statement that the plan seeks educational diversity, if such a statement seems plausible.

But in the case of some professional schools it may not be plausible, and Powell says, in this connection, that "good faith" should be presumed only "absent a showing to the contrary." Perhaps the motives of individual members of the admissions committee or of the faculty as a whole are not relevant. It is nevertheless true that many faculty members, particularly of professional schools, support racially conscious admissions programs because they do believe that such programs are necessary to provide more professional people for the ghettos. Even more support them because they are anxious that their school help groups that have been disadvantaged by discrimination, by providing models of successful professional men and women from these groups, for example.

The leaders of many institutions are now on record, in fact, that these are their goals. (They may or may not also believe that the level of diversity in their classes that would be reached without racially conscious programs is unsatisfactory for purely educational reasons.) May disappointed applicants to such institutions now sue, placing in evidence statements faculty members have made about the purposes of racially conscious plans, or subpoenaing officers of admission to examine their motives under oath?

Powell's opinion raises these questions, but it does little to help answer them, even in principle, because the argumentative base of his opinion is weak. It does not supply a sound intellectual foundation for the compromise the public found so attractive. The compromise is appealing politically, but it does not follow that it reflects any important difference in principle, which is what a constitutional, as distinct from a political, settlement requires.

There are indeed important differences between the "quota" kind of affirmative action program—with places reserved for "minorities" only—and more flexible plans that make race a factor, but only one factor, in the competition for all places. But these differences are administrative and symbolic. A flexible program is likely to be more efficient, in the long run, because it will allow the institution to take less than the rough target number of minority applicants when the total group of such applicants is weaker, and more when it is stronger. It is certainly better symbolically, for a number of reasons. Reserving a special program for minority applicants—providing a separate door through which they and only they may enter—preserves the structure, though of course not the purpose, of classical forms of caste and apartheid systems, and seems to denigrate minority applicants while helping them. Flexible programs emphasize, on the other hand, that successful minority candidates have been judged overall more valuable, as students, than white applicants with whom they directly competed.

But the administrative and symbolic superiority of the flexible programs, however plain, cannot justify a constitutional distinction of the sort Powell makes. There should be no constitutional distinction unless a quota program violates or threatens the constitutional rights of white applicants *as individuals* in some way that the more flexible programs do not.

Powell does not show any such difference, and it is hard to imagine how he could. If race counts in a flexible program, then there will be some individual white applicant who loses a place but who would have gained one if race did not count. However that injury is described it is exactly the same injury—neither more nor less—that Bakke suffered. We cannot say that in a flexible system fewer whites lose places because race figures in the decision; that will depend on details of the flexible and quota programs being compared, on the nature of the applicants, and on other circumstances. But even if it could be shown that fewer whites would lose in a flexible plan, it would not follow that the rights of those individuals who did lose were different or differently treated.

Powell argues that in a flexible plan a marginal white applicant is at least in a position to try to show that, in spite of his race, he ought to be taken in preference to a black applicant because he has some special contribution that the black applicant does not. His race does not rule him out of even part of the competition automatically.

This argument may be based on an unrealistic picture of how admissions committees must deal with a vast volume of applications even under a flexible plan. An individual admissions officer will use informal cutoff lines, no matter how flexible the program is in principle, and a majority applicant with a low test score may be cut off from the entire competition with no further look to discover whether he is a good musician, for example, though he would have been rescued for a further look if he were black.

But even if Powell's sense of how a flexible plan works is realistic, his argument is still weak. An individual applicant has, at the start of the competition for places, a particular grade record, test score average, personality, talents, geographical background, and race. What matters, for a white applicant, is the chance these give him in the competition, and it does not make any difference to him in principle whether his race is a constant small handicap in the competition for all the places, or no handicap at all in the competition for a slightly smaller number of places. His fate depends on how much either the handicap or the exclusion reduces his overall chances of success; and there is no reason to assume, a priori, that the one will have a greater or lesser impact than the other. That will depend on the details of the plan—the degree of handicap or the proportion of exclusion—not which type of plan it is.

Powell sees an important difference between a handicap and a partial exclusion. He says that in the former case, but not the latter, an applicant is treated "as an individual" and his qualifications are "weighed fairly and competitively." (He chides Justices Brennan, White, Marshall, and Blackmun for not speaking to the importance of this "right to individualized consideration.") But this seems wrong. Whether an applicant competes for all or only part of the places, the privilege of calling attention to other qualifications does not in any degree lessen the burden of his handicap, or the unfairness of that handicap, if it is unfair at all. If the handicap does not violate his rights in a flexible plan, a partial exclusion does not violate his rights under a quota. The handicap and the partial exclusion are only different means of enforcing the same fundamental classifications. In principle, they affect a white applicant in exactly the same way—by reducing his overall chances—and neither is, in any important sense, more "individualized" than the other. The point is not (as Powell once suggests it is) that faculty administering a flexible system may covertly transform it into a quota plan. The point is rather that there is no difference, from the standpoint of individual rights, between the two systems at all.

There is a second serious problem in Powell's opinion which is more technical, but in the end more important. Both Powell and the other four justices who reached the constitutional issue discussed the question of whether racial classifications used in affirmative action programs for the benefit of minorities are "suspect" classifications which the Supreme Court should subject to "strict scrutiny." These are terms of art, and I must briefly state the doctrinal background.

Legislatures and other institutions that make political decisions must use general classifications in the rules they adopt. Whatever general classifications they use, certain individuals will suffer a disadvantage they would not have suffered if lines had been differently drawn, sometimes because the classifications treat them as having or lacking qualities they do not. State motor codes provide, for example, that no one under the age of sixteen is eligible to drive an automobile, even though some people under that age are just as competent as most over it. Ordinarily the Supreme Court will not hold such a general classification unconstitutional even though it believes that a different classification, which would place different people at a disadvantage, would be more reasonable or more efficient. It is enough if the classification the legislature makes is not irrational; that is, if it could conceivably serve a useful and proper social goal. That is a very easy test to meet, but if the Court used a more stringent test to judge all legislation, then it would be substituting its judgment on inherently controversial matters for the judgment reached by a democratic political process.

There is, however, an important exception to this rule. Certain classifications are said to be "suspect," and when a state legislature employs these classifications in legislation, the Supreme Court will hold the legislation unconstitutional unless it meets a much more demanding test which has come to be called the test of "strict scrutiny." It must be shown, not simply that the use of this classification is not irrational, but that it is "necessary" to achieve what the Court has called a "compelling" governmental interest. Obviously it is a crucial issue, in constitutional litigation, whether a particular classification is an ordinary classification, and so attracts only the relaxed ordinary scrutiny, or is a suspect classification which must endure strict scrutiny (or, as some justices have sometimes suggested, falls somewhere between these two standards of review).

Racial classifications that *disadvantage* a "minority" race are paradigm cases of suspect classifications. In the famous *Korematsu* case the Supreme Court said that "[All] legal restrictions which curtail the rights of a single racial group are immediately suspect. That is not to say that all such restrictions are unconstitutional. It is to say that courts must subject them to the most rigid scrutiny." But what about racial classifications that figure in a program designed to *benefit* a group of disadvantaged minorities? It had never been decided, prior to *Bakke*, whether such "benign" classifications are suspect.

The four justices who voted to uphold the Davis plan did not argue that "benign" racial classifications should be held only to the weak ordinary standard—that is, that it could conceivably serve a useful social goal. But neither did they think it appropriate to use the same high standard of strict scrutiny used to judge racial classifications that work against minorities. They suggested an intermediate standard, which is that remedial racial classifications "must serve important governmental objectives and must be substantially related to achievement of those objectives." They held that the Davis medical school's purpose of "remedying the effects of past societal discrimination" was sufficiently important, and that the racial classification Davis used was "substantially related" to that objective.

But Mr. Justice Powell disagreed. He held that "benign" racial classifications should be held to the same extremely strict scrutiny that is applied to racial classifications that disadvantage a minority. He therefore required that the Davis classification be "necessary" to a "compelling" purpose, and he held that it was not. He argued that no distinction should be made between the test applied to racial classifications that benefit and those that disadvantage an established minority for two reasons. First, because any such distinction would rest on judgments, like judgments about what groups are, in the relevant sense, minorities, and which classifications carry a "stigma," that Powell called "subjective" and "standardless." Second, because constitutionally important categories would then be constantly changing as social or economic conditions (or the perception of Supreme Court justices of such conditions) changed, so that yesterday's disadvantaged minority became a member of today's powerful majority, or yesterday's helping hand became today's stigma.

There is plainly some force in this argument. All else being equal, it is better when constitutional principles are such that reasonable lawyers will not disagree about their application. But often the political and moral rights of individuals do depend on considerations that different people will assess differently, and in that case the law would purchase certainty only at the price of crudeness and inevitable injustice. American law—particularly constitutional law—has refused to pay that price, and it has become in consequence the envy of more formalistic legal systems.

It is easy, moreover, to exaggerate the "subjectivity" of the distinctions in play here. Once the distinction is made between racial classifications that disadvantage an "insular" minority, like the detention of Japanese Americans in the *Korematsu* case, and those that are designed to benefit such a minority, then reasonable men cannot sincerely differ about where the racial classification of the Davis medical school falls. Nor is the social pattern of prejudice and discrimination the Davis program attacked either recent or transient. It is as old as the country, tragically, and will not disappear very soon.

My present point, however, is a different one. Powell's argument in favor of strict scrutiny of all racial classifications, which is that the putative distinction between benign and malignant classifications relies on "subjective" and "standardless" judgments, is not and cannot be consistent with the rest of his judgment, because his approval of flexible admissions programs, like the Harvard undergraduate program, presupposes exactly the same judgments. Powell begins his defense of flexible but racially conscious admissions programs with the following exceptionally broad statement of a constitutionally protected right of universities to choose their own educational strategies:

> Academic freedom, though not a specifically enumerated constitutional right, long has been viewed as a special concern of the First Amendment. The freedom of a university to make its own judgments as to education includes the selection of its student body. Mr. Justice Frankfurter summarized the "four essential freedoms" that comprise academic freedom: "It is an atmosphere in which there prevail the four essential freedoms of a university—to determine for itself on academic grounds who may teach, what may be taught, how it shall be taught, and who may be admitted to study."

Diversity is the "compelling" goal that Powell believes universities may seek through flexible (but not crude) racially conscious policies. But what if a law school faculty, in the exercise of its right to "determine for itself . . . who shall be admitted to study," decided to count the fact that an applicant is Jewish as a negative consideration, though not an absolute exclusion, in the competition for all its places? It might decide that it is injurious to "diversity" or to the "robust exchange of ideas" that Jews should form so large and disproportionate a part of law school classes as they now do. Or what if a Southern medical school one day found that a disproportionately large number of black applicants was being admitted on racially neutral tests, which threatened the diversity of its student body, to the detriment, as it determined, of its educational process? It might then count being white as a factor beneficial to admission, like being a musician or having an intention to practice medicine in a rural area.

The four justices who voted to uphold the Davis program as constitutional would have no trouble distinguishing these flexible programs that count being Jewish as a handicap or being white as a beneficial factor. Neither of these programs could be defended as helping to remedy "the effects of past societal discrimination." They could argue that, on the contrary, since these programs put at a disadvantage members of races that have been and remain the victims of systematic prejudice, the programs must for that reason be subject to "strict scrutiny" and disallowed unless positively shown to be both "necessary" and compelling.

Mr. Justice Powell did not, of course, have any such programs in mind when he wrote his opinion. He surely could not accept them as constitutional. But he, unlike the four justices, could not consistently distinguish such programs on their grounds, since the judgments I just described involve precisely the "subjective" and "standardless" judgments about "stigma" that he rejected as inappropriate to constitutional principles.

The point is, I think, a simple one. The difference between a general racial classification that causes further disadvantage to those who have suffered from prejudice, and a classification framed to help them, is morally significant, and cannot be consistently denied by a constitutional law that does not exclude the use of race altogether. If the nominal standard for testing racial classifications denies the difference, the difference will nevertheless reappear when the standard is applied because (as these unlikely hypothetical examples show) our sense of justice will insist on a distinction. If that is so, then the standard, however it is drafted, is not the same, and will not long be thought to be.

I raise these objections to Powell's opinion not simply because I disagree with his arguments, but to indicate why I believe that the compromise he fashioned, though immediately popular, may not be sufficiently strong in principle to furnish the basis for a coherent and lasting constitutional law of affirmative action. Later cases will, of course, try to absorb his opinion into a more general settlement, because it was the closest thing to an opinion of the Court in the famous *Bakke* case, and because it is the creditable practice of the Court to try to accommodate rather than to disown the early history of its own doctrine. But Powell's opinion suffers from fundamental weaknesses and, if the Court is to arrive at a coherent position, far more judicial work remains to be done than a relieved public yet realizes.

Equality, Diversity, and Good Faith

Carl Cohen

The *Bakke* decision has been both inappropriately praised and wrongly criticized. The opinion of Justice Powell especially has been commonly misrepresented, its force and ramifications widely misapprehended. I seek now to bring some clarity to the analysis of *Bakke* by doing the following things:

I.   Review briefly some common misconceptions of that Supreme Court decision

II. Explicate the role of Justice Powell's opinion in *Bakke*

III. Argue that Powell's opinion is not only pivotal but controlling

IV. Identify the principles that undergird Powell's opinion

V.   Respond to the objection that Powell's principles are not feasible

VI. Refute the objection that Powell's principles are fundamentally incoherent

VII. Expose a serious and widespread mistake in the interpretation of *Bakke*

VIII. Exhibit two important consequences of the *Bakke* decision that have gone largely unrecognized

IX. Specify one troubling aspect of the *Bakke* decision that deserves more attention than it has received

   I turn to each of these in the order given.

Reprinted from the *Wayne Law Review* 26, no. 4 (July 1980), by permission of the journal.

I

The *Bakke* decision has been praised as a masterful compromise, slicing the affimative action baby with "Solomonic" wisdom. In fact the decision is not a compromise at all, not a resolution agreed upon as the result of the conflicting parties giving and getting. Justice Powell's opinion, which occupies the central ground, may reasonably be thought controlling, but its dominance results from the configuration of the several opinions, not from his or anyone else's efforts to straddle the fence. One who reads the several opinions must quickly realize that no one of the nine justices was compromising. Strong convictions pervade each of the six opinions, and some, particularly those of Justices Marshall and Powell, are written with fervor. We should not wish it otherwise. The job of the Court is not to find a middle way that is politically palatable, but to determine, with intelligence and integrity, what the laws and the Constitution forbid and what they demand. That was done in *Bakke*. It is inappropriate to praise the Court for devising a political compromise that was neither its proper goal nor its actual product.

The decision has been criticized for being indecisive, inconclusive, and confused. It is certainly not indecisive; Allan Bakke won. He was admitted to the University of California Davis School of Medicine, which was the central object of his efforts. The special admissions program which, he argued, had denied him the equal protection of the laws has been eliminated by court order. The decision is not inconclusive with respect to the sphere of university admissions. Principles have been laid down by which college administrators and admissions officers may be firmly guided respecting the permissible uses of race and ethnicity in selecting among applicants for admission. Principles governing the uses of race in other spheres of American life—employment, or housing, for example—are of course not provided by the *Bakke* decision, the setting and scope of which is specifically academic. We should not want the Court to pontificate upon matters not germane to the issues essentially before it, and it would be wrong to criticize the justices for not doing, in this case, what they should not have done. Much more litigation over the uses of race in the public distribution of benefits and opportunities is inevitable; everyone understands that.[1]

Nor is the *Bakke* decision confused. It is complicated, yes; but its complexity may be taken as a mark both of deep division in the nation, and of sophistication within the Court. A decision that did not in any way reflect the agonizing conflicts created by the well-intentioned use of racial preference would be insensitive as well as simplistic. Some on both sides of the case hoped for a clarion call. Wise judges, however, resolve complicated matters with opinions refined enough to deal fairly with those complications, blowing clarions only when they must. We take pride in the Court's restrained effort to do justice rationally.

What is not confused may yet be confusing. The complications of the *Bakke* decision arise not only from the density of the issues, but also from the fact that the disagreements among the nine justices were of different kinds, resulting in the emergence of three groups, opposed yet overlapping in judgment. The central disagreement was on the question of the permissibility of the minority admissions program at the Davis medical school. A majority found it not permissible. On this issue Bakke plainly won.

There was also sharp division among the justices on the question of whether the uses of race in the Davis admissions system were forbidden by federal statute or by the Constitution.[2] On these issues there was no definitive outcome. Four of the five justices supporting Bakke's admission (Stevens, Stewart, Burger, and Rehnquist) relied exclusively on the statute. They deliberately refrained from addressing any constitutional issues because, they argued, it would be out of order to do so when the program in question was so plainly a violation of federal law. The fifth justice supporting Bakke, Powell, did so on constitutional grounds. The four justices holding against Bakke (Brennan, Marshall, Blackmun, and White) also grounded their opinions on the Constitution. The legal bases of the result are therefore mixed, but the central result itself is not.

II

In effect the opinion of Justice Powell decides the case. His opinion is but one of nine, and in itself has no more weight than that of any other member of the Court. Without his opinion, however, the Court is evenly divided: four justices (the Stevens group) support Bakke, condemn the Davis program, and find the Civil Rights Act dispositive; four (the Brennan group) support the regents, approve the Davis program, and find the Civil Rights Act not dispositive. Powell joins each of the two groups on different matters. On the substance of the central issue he agrees with the Stevens group; the Davis program is intolerable and Bakke must be admitted. But he does not agree that this result can be drawn from the Civil Rights Act by itself; on this issue he holds, with the Brennan group, that the case does raise constitutional questions demanding answers. Answering them, he finds the Davis program not merely unlawful, but also a violation of the equal protection clause.

III

Justice Powell's opinion is manifestly *pivotal*. Is it also *controlling*? Do the principles he formulates now govern the conduct of university admissions? I argue that they do, for three reasons.

First, the logic of decision making compels that result. Without Powell's opinion the remaining eight justices are in perfect deadlock, agreeing neither upon the result nor the legal ground. With his opinion the case at hand is resolved. It is no accident that in addition to his own opinion, Justice Powell was chosen to announce the formal judgment of the Court: that the racially preferential admissions program at Davis be struck down.

Each one of the five decisive votes counts equally, of course, and in that sense none is more entitled to control than any other. But the five votes of the majority differ in the following respect. Four strike down the Davis special admissions plan. They formulate no constitutional principles because for them the racial preference at issue was so patently a violation of federal law that no question of constitutional principle was raised by it. The fifth vote, Powell's, is carefully grounded on the Constitution. Powell also does not think the Davis plan lawful. But why it is unlawful or what the scope of the Civil Rights Act may be can only be determined, he contended, by referring to the equal protection clause.

Powell does not conclude that the Constitution requires admissions committees to be absolutely color-blind. He joins the Brennan four in reversing that portion of the California Supreme Court decision which held that race may never be considered in the college admissions process. But Powell also concludes that, to justify any such consideration of race, some constitutional value that can countervail the principle of equal protection of the laws must be adduced. He finds such a value in the First Amendment—guaranteeing freedom of speech and expression—which is greatly served by diversity in college and professional school classes. Powell's opinion restricts the uses of race in college admissions programs very tightly, yet is distinctly more permissive than the opinion of the Stevens four with whom he is allied in substance. To treat the Powell opinion as controlling, therefore—as prudent admissions officers will—is to read the majority view in its most liberal form, specifying most carefully what the Constitution permits.

Second, good authority strongly supports the conclusion that Powell's opinion is controlling. In choosing among competing interpretations of a complicated decision even the most objective scholars will have a natural inclination to select that interpretation most fully suiting their own larger theories or objectives. If, however, those least in sympathy with Powell, those whose larger purposes and general perspectives are sharply opposed to Powell's principles, nevertheless treat his opinion as controlling, or nearly so, one may be reasonably confident that that reading of the whole decision is fair. Such persons and institutions do so treat the Powell opinion.

The American Council on Education (ACE) and the Association of American Law Schools (AALS) are two large and influential institutions that bridle with evident pain against the restrictions upon the uses of race in the Powell opinion. Both submitted briefs, as interested third parties, in vigorous support of the Davis admissions system. Subsequent to the decision they prepared a lengthy joint report which, while struggling to give an accurate and balanced interpretation, is in large part devoted to the consideration of variant admissions systems that might be sustained within the frame of Powell's opinion, while incorporating as much racial preference as possible.[3] Doggedly they searched for a path that would do what the Davis program did, yet would also satisfy Justice Powell's demands that only diversity be the aim of race consciousness, and that no individual applicant be deprived, by race, of equal opportunity. Their efforts to achieve this reconciliation clearly show that in their judgment the Powell opinion is controlling.

Justice Powell's most thoughtful and most outspoken critic is Prof. Ronald Dworkin of Oxford University; he has attacked the opinion as incoherent and wrongheaded. He has argued at length not only that the Davis program should have been approved, but that Bakke had no case (see chapter 15).

Yet Dworkin comes at last to admit, with no pleasure, that if no one of the justices of the Stevens group takes a less restrictive position regarding the use of race, "Powell's line will become the Supreme Court's line" (chap. 16. p. 115).

Scholarly authority should be viewed with skepticism—but when scholars emerge with an interpretation unfavorable to their own aims their authority is the more trustworthy. That is the present case.

Finally, Powell's opinion does permit certain very narrow uses of race in college admissions. Beyond that, it is widely agreed, we may not now go. But why? A majority of the Supreme Court has not supported his precise restrictions. Indeed, four justices have come down on one side of him and another four, apparently, on the other side. What then obliges us, in now adjusting college admissions practices, to adhere closely to the restrictive side of a decision so nearly balanced?

The answer is rooted in the history of Supreme Court decisions pertaining to race and the equal protection of the laws. The case of Allan Bakke, after all, is but one of a long chain of cases in which the Court has grappled with the uses—evil and honorable—of racial classifications. Some classifications have been permitted under carefully specified circumstances. Most racial and other ethnic classifications used in the distribution of public benefits have been forbidden on the premise that, save in very special circumstances, classification by race is a nasty business, often malicious in intent and usually malignant in result. Our federal courts have therefore repeatedly insisted that certain classifications of persons, by race above all, are *suspect*. Such classifications, to be approved in any public context, must pass the test of *strict scrutiny:* they must be shown *necessary* to achieve a public purpose of *compelling* importance.

Whether the racially preferential admissions system at Davis met that test was the core of the argument in *Bakke*. Powell had no doubt that it did not. The

California Supreme Court, deciding earlier for Bakke on all counts (by a six-to-one majority) on constitutional grounds, also had no doubt that racial preference in university admissions fails that test.[4] The Washington Supreme Court, upholding (in a split decision) a racially preferential admissions system at the University of Washington Law School, did so because it believed that such uses of race did meet the appropriate standard of strict scrutiny.[5] That standard, and the need to apply it wherever programs are proposed that distribute goods by race, is the foundation of Justice Powell's opinion. He writes in a context in which all understand clearly that public bodies must act on the premise that racial classification is permissible only where its object has been proved *compelling*, and the racial instrument proved *necessary* to achieve it. Absent those proofs, racial classification may not be used.

This explains why those who had hoped *Bakke* would give approval to race-conscious admissions are pained by the Powell opinion, yet know themselves governed by it. Institutions do not have the same freedom of action on the two sides of the line Powell has drawn. Toward greater restrictiveness in the use of race there is room for choice; race may be considered in accordance with his restrictions, or we may elect not to consider it at all. Toward greater permissiveness we may not go. The state and its institutions may use race only when the strict scrutiny test has been passed. Race-conscious admissions systems (except to achieve diversity in the student body or to give remedy for injury unlawfully imposed by that school) do not pass that test; Powell makes that very clear.

Powell's opinion governs in this sphere, therefore, because it established constitutional limits. A university administrator may reasonably ask: If we think it wise to use race or national origin in choosing from among those who apply for admission, may we do so? Under what restrictions do we lie in doing so? Powell answered these questions clearly and firmly. He draws the line up to which the use of race in admissions is permitted. In that sense Justice Powell's opinion is controlling.

Speculation about the future path of the Supreme Court in this sphere is intriguing, but has no bearing on the present duties of university admissions officers. It is unsound to argue, as some do, that because the decision in *Bakke* is "fragile," university officials are justified in evading its demands for a while. When the Warren Court (by a five-to-four majority) established the *Miranda* rules, requiring that the rights of an accused be carefully explained to him before interrogation, some contended that the "fragility" of that decision might justify its temporary evasion by police officers. That fragility argument was unacceptable then, and is no less so now. The possibility of future changes in the interpretation of the equal protection clause by the Supreme Court is no excuse for present noncompliance with its present interpretation.

We know, without speculation, what the rules are now, and we have the obligation to comply with the principles of Justice Powell's pivotal opinion. He is, for the present, the gatekeeper for the uses of race in college admissions; no admissions program is permissible if it fails to meet the conditions he laid down.

IV

What conditions are these? They are specific prohibitions respecting both the *aims* of any uses of race in admission, and the *means* with which those aims are pursued.

One narrow purpose only, for Powell, justifies the use of race in college admissions—student diversity. Three other goals often advanced to justify such programs he explicitly rejected.[6]

1. He firmly rejects a university's use of race "to assure within its student body some specified percentage of a particular group merely because of its race or ethnic origin."[7] That is plain racial discrimination, he explains, and on its face is forbidden by the Constitution.

2. A university might conceivably use race in admissions to improve the professional services delivered to communities presently underserved, but only if it could prove that such use of race was necessary for that end—and that, Powell concludes, has not been shown at all.[8] Classification by race for preference in admission presently appears to have no significant effect upon health care delivery; until proved to have such an effect, that justification of racial preference must also be rejected.

3. Most important, universities may *not* consider race in admissions for the purpose of helping certain groups perceived as victims of societal discrimination. The end in that case may be honorable but, Powell insists, it "does not justify a classification that imposes disadvantages upon persons like respondent [Bakke], who bear no responsibility for whatever harm the beneficiaries of the special admissions program are thought to have suffered."[9]

A college has no business, Powell tells us, giving advantages to members of one race at the expense of disadvantaging members of another race, to compensate for damages that the college believes were done by society at large. Powell specifies that racial preference, as a remedy for injustice, may be given only where an institution has been found, by an appropriate authority, to have violated the laws or the Constitution to the harm of identifiable persons. Without that finding, publicly supported institutions have no adequate justification for inflicting the harm on those such as Bakke that racially preferential admissions programs do.[10] Universities do not have the authority to grant, at their pleasure, social remedies for some at the cost of injury to blameless third parties. College admissions committees are neither legislatures nor courts.

The one goal that may justify the use of race in admissions (but does not oblige that use) is "the attainment of a diverse student body,"[11] a First Amendment interest fitting for a university in view of its special functions. Colleges, Powell writes, have "the right to select those students who will contribute the most to 'the robust exchange of ideas',"[12] and they may consider ethnicity in admissions to advance that end—but only that end. It follows that attention to race is permissible only where a broad array of differing characteristics are, in fact, seriously and competitively weighed, "of which racial or ethnic origin is but a single though important element."[13] If the only diversity sought is among ethnic groups, that will not by itself satisfy the First Amendment value which alone may justify a consideration of race normally forbidden. Powell is specific. A college practice sensitive to the race of applicants must be concretely devised to achieve diversity on *many* dimensions. Nor may administrators say that since diversity has long been *one* of our objectives, business may go on as usual. Powell is emphatic. We are permitted attention to race for no reasons *other* than diversity; and our service to diversity, if race is involved, must be more than with our lips.

So much for the one *goal* that may justify the use of race in admissions. The *means* to achieve that goal are also narrowly restricted in the Powell opinion. Whatever system a university employs, it must guarantee that what applies to persons of one race applies equally to persons of every other race. Powell is unequivocal on this point. "The guarantee of equal protection cannot mean one thing when applied to one individual and something else when applied to a person of another color. If both are not accorded the same protection, then it is not equal."[14] Any program, therefore, that utilizes a double standard openly or covertly, or that excludes from the competition for any set of seats or benefits any persons because of their ethnic features fails this constitutional test. It is not saved by the good intentions of its authors. Any "system of allocating benefits and privileges on the basis of skin color and ethnic origin" manifests "inherent unfairness."[15] Applicants for admission must be treated as individuals; any special program dealing with applicants by race exhibits a "fatal flaw."[16] The bearing of these principles on present practice is much greater than has been generally realized. Virtually all special admissions programs have been, in Powell's sense, fatally flawed. Most have maintained double lists and double standards, have categorized by color and ethnic origin to set screening levels and procedures. Many still do exclude whites, or white males, from competition for certain places or other benefits. Most special admissions programs were deliberately devised to deal with people by race. Their objectives, moreover, have commonly been the very ones Powell rejects as impermissible. Most were frankly designed to "assure . . . some specified percentage of a particular group merely because of its race or ethnic origin."[17] Whether by "goal" or "quota" (a distinction Justice Powell dismisses as superficial) their targets have been racial or ethnic proportions, an aim Powell finds unconstitutional. Or they have been designed to compensate minorities for societal injury. Or they have been put forward as plans to compensate disadvantaged students, where "disadvantaged" commonly serves as a euphemism for black or brown in institutions embarrassed by plain racial discrimination. If Justice Powell's opinion is controlling, special admissions programs may no longer be defended on those grounds. If those are the grounds on which they rest, explicitly or tacitly, such programs, at least in state-supported institutions, are not in compliance with the law of the land.[18]

V

Objections to the Powell opinion are of two kinds. One concerns its merits—whether, after considering the many complexities of racially preferential admission systems, he would have been wiser to adopt some other interpretation of the equal protection clause. Some would wish the governing interpretation more restrictive, precluding all uses of race. Some would wish it less restrictive, permitting more uses of race. But as a matter of rule, that issue (until it comes before the Supreme Court, if ever, in another admissions case) is for the present closed.

A second set of objections deal not with the substantive merit of the opinion, but with its suitability as a set of governing principles for college admissions. Here the objections are of two subtypes, the first directed at the *feasibility* of the Powell principles, the second at their *coherence*. I deal with each of these in turn. Feasibility is a proper concern, even for those who do not quarrel with the authority of the principles outlined above. Can professional schools, in view of the enormous number of applicants for very few places, seriously hope to treat each applicant as an individual and not as a member of a group? Is the demand that ethnicity be no more than one of many dimensions on which all applicants are evaluated singly a realistic one? If not, the Powell principles, however right in theory, will be abandoned in practice, not out of defiance but out of practical necessity.

One who has experienced the complexity and burden of the admissions process at a fine college will appreciate the sincerity of this complaint. But it is entirely answerable. In the first place, most colleges and universities are troubled now not by excess of applicants, but by declining applications. Many institutions have faculties and residence halls larger than their present enrollments can justify. The decline is likely to continue. A number of private colleges are closing; some state colleges may follow suit. The problem of feasibility for the Powell principles seems greater than it is because of the general tendency to focus on a few premier colleges and professional schools where, indeed, applications outnumber places by twenty or thirty or more to one.

Even in these premier institutions the Powell principles can be applied by conscientious admissions officers. Objectives other than diversity for the use of race must be eliminated; there is no difficulty in that. But how can administrators achieve diversity without bundling applications in groups: rural and urban, out-of-state and in-state, male and female, over thirty and under thirty, black and brown and white, and so on? The identification of such characteristics will be entailed by a quest for diversity, but the process need not (and now must not) *center* upon the division of applicants into ethnic piles, and it must not be a process whose result is fashioned to reach certain numerical results with respect to those piles. Rather, the primary sorting will be by intellectual attainment or promise (or other characteristics reasonably linked to successful performance in the program in question) with subsidiary sortings by other characteristics that may reasonably be supposed to advance the aims of student diversity. Ethnicity may be one of these. The task is complicated. But the admissions process in such premier institutions must be complicated to be fair. There is nothing in the restrictions Powell lays down that cannot be readily incorporated in a just and rational admissions process.

Would that not impose a terrible burden of inconvenience and cost upon the college? No. Eliminating the double-standard system now commonly in use will effect substantial savings of time and energy. It will reduce the need to hide what is really going on. And treating ethnicity as but one of an array of subsidiary characteristics, most of which are already considered, will introduce no great additional complexity, and can be fitted readily into most race-neutral systems.

But the ultimate answer to the complaint that Powell's principles are burdensome is that, whatever the burden, it must be borne if ethnicity is to be weighed. The Supreme Court has laid down the ways in which race may be used in admissions *if it is to be used at all*. No college is obliged to consider race in admissions; a college may be well advised not to do so. But should it determine that diversity is essential, and that ethnic diversity is vital, the administrative costs in pursuing these goals lawfully may not serve to justify allegedly more convenient "two-class" systems that violate the equal protection guarantee of the Fourteenth Amendment. This judgment was explicitly confirmed by the federal court in *Hopwood v. Texas* in 1994: "*Bakke* gives no indication that the burden to a school in implementing a constitutionally valid program should be considered as a reason to diminish the need for individual comparison."

A related objection touches upon the genesis of Powell's principles, and his alleged misapplication of them. The critic contends that Justice Powell mistakenly supposes that admissions criteria arising in an undergraduate context and applicable chiefly to schools of liberal arts must be applied equally to professional schools. So he provides as a model for the consideration of race in a competitive medical school the admissions document from Harvard. Diversity may be an important consideration in undergraduate selection, but for the selection of future doctors or lawyers it has (says this critic) much reduced significance, perhaps none. To permit diversity as the only ground for the use of race in such professional contexts appears to exhibit a naive confusion.

But Powell is neither naive nor confused on this point. Those who register this criticism would do well to study this portion of his opinion more carefully.[19] Powell is fully aware that the need for diversity may vary with context. As former president of the American Bar Association, he may be supposed to have some understanding of the needs of the professional schools; he believes that diversity of students in the class is a desideratum as important in medical and legal education as in the liberal arts. Reasonable persons may differ on this question. Powell's point, however, is that *if* race is to be a factor in professional school admissions it may be a factor for no *other* reasons. Where diversity is believed a dimension of little import to medical or legal education, admissions officers are at liberty to ignore it. Powell, unlike some of his critics, is not searching for a handle with which racial preference can be saved. He is identifying a ground, the only one, upon which the consideration of race is permissible. Student diversity is that ground; ethnicity may enter the admissions process for no other reason.

VI

That Powell's principles do not make sense, that they cannot coherently achieve their aim, is a second subtype of complaint against them. Here also the thrust is practical, the spirit sometimes derisive. Everyone knows that under the language of the Harvard admissions program (appended by Powell to his opinion as an example of an admission system in which race enters only for the achievement of diversity), a college can do precisely what the Davis medical school did through open racial preference. "The cynical," wrote Justice Blackmun in his dissenting opinion, "may say that under a program such as Harvard's one may accomplish covertly what Davis concedes it does openly."[20] Justice Brennan wrote similarly:

> That the Harvard approach does not also make public the extent of the [racial] preference and the precise workings of the system, while the Davis program employs a specific, openly stated number, does not condemn the latter plan. . . . It may be that the Harvard plan is more acceptable to the public than is the Davis "quota." . . . But there is no basis for preferring a particular preference program simply because in achieving

the same goals that the Davis Medical School is pursuing it proceeds in a manner that is not immediately apparent to the public.[21]

This objection to the Powell principle is profoundly mistaken. Certainly some may cheat. Surely some may, under the cover of a set of approved words, engage in a pattern of action whose hidden principle, if exposed, would be found impermissible. Some say that Harvard itself is guilty of such duplicity. But the example Powell has given is not what Harvard *does*, but what Harvard *says* it does, which is, precisely, to consider race for the attainment of student diversity, and for that purpose only. If in truth a school considers race in admissions for reasons other than diversity it does wrong. We are all expected not to act so as to deceive the courts.

Between the Davis program and the Harvard program, Powell points out, there is this crucial difference: the former exhibits on its face an intent to discriminate by race, the latter does not. It is of course possible to adopt and present to the world language that reveals no discriminatory intent, and then, knowingly but covertly, to act with precisely the intention that is forbidden. The possibility of such subterfuge, although real, proves nothing. Frequent allusion to it suggests—unfairly in my view—that admissions officers are a breed specially prone to employ unlawful chicanery to achieve their ends.

If one college uses the Harvard language honestly, and another college uses the same language to cheat, there is between the two a most important distinction: the *intent* of their administrators. One can picture Justice Powell deliberately looking at us and saying emphatically, as he writes near the conclusion of his long and thoughtful opinion: "And a Court would not assume that a university, professing to employ a non-discriminatory admissions policy would operate it as a cover for the functional equivalent of a quota system. In short, good faith would be presumed."[22] All university officers must hear themselves addressed by these words.[23]

An objection to the Powell principles closely related to this one is presented by Ronald Dworkin, who reasons as follows: to reserve certain places in a medical school entering class for minority applicants only, while opening the remainder to all applicants through competition, is indeed to handicap the white, majority applicant in some degree (chap. 16, pp. 119–20). But to weigh the blackness or brownness of a minority applicant's skin as a plus factor in a quest for diversity is also to handicap the white, majority applicant to some degree. It cannot matter to the white applicants which way they are handicapped. What is important to them is the degree of the handicap. It may prove more to their advantage to be excluded from the competition for a few seats reserved for minorities than to have a crack at every seat yet be substantially handicapped by the "diversity" factor. Justice Powell thus draws a distinction without a real difference. He thinks that reserving places for minority applicants is unfair, while giving "plus points" for minority group membership is fair. But these are only two ways of doing the same thing. It is the size of the handicap imposed, the critic argues, not the mode of its imposition, that really counts. Dworkin writes:

> Whether an applicant competes for all or only part of the places, the privilege of calling attention to other qualifications does not in any degree lessen the burden of his handicap, or the unfairness of that handicap, if it is unfair at all. If the handicap does not violate his rights in a flexible plan [i.e., one pursuing only diversity], a partial exclusion does not violate his rights under a quota. The handicap and the partial exclusion are only different means of enforcing the same fundamental classifications. In principle, they affect a white applicant in exactly the same way—by reducing his overall chances—and neither is, in any important sense, more "individualized" than the other. The point is not (as Powell once suggests it is) that faculty administering a flexible system may covertly transform it into a quota plan. The point is rather that there is no difference, from the standpoint of individual rights, between the two systems at all. (chap. 16, pp. 119–20)

This complaint appears shrewd, but it rests upon a fundamental misunderstanding of Powell's distinction between the consideration of race as one factor in a quest for diversity (on the one hand) and plain racial preference (on the other). *If* our object were simply to favor nonwhite applicants by imposing a "handicap" on white applicants, there are many ways this could be accomplished. It can, of course, be accomplished by giving enough "plus points" for blackness or brownness to achieve the results desired. Any racial proportions antecedently chosen can be obtained by the manipulation of the diversity factor as well as by reserving places. But that use of diversity is fraudulent. To use diversity in that way is to do, under the cover of nondiscriminatory language, just what has been forbidden. Once we decide to *handicap* one racial group, the instrument is of no great consequence, save that some instruments are more detectable than others. But imposing a handicap on any ethnic group is precisely what is *not* permitted. Dworkin's reasoning reveals what *his* objective is: to save racial preference. But the intention to do that, *either* by reserving places or by manipulating the diversity factor, has been precluded by the Powell principles. Seeking diversity honestly is one thing; scheming under the name of diversity is another. Again, *intent* makes all the difference.

The critic may try to avoid this moral response by arguing that a handicap is simply a handicap—taken descriptively it involves no intent whatever. If minorities are advantaged in the quest for diversity because they are fewer, the majority is that far handicapped. That handicap (he may say) is intrinsically no different from one imposed deliberately by reserving places, irrespective of intent. If the degree of overall disadvantage is the same, intent makes no difference. The critic maintains that Powell is simply confused in believing that one system hurts the white majority unfairly while the other does not. Either both systems are unfair or neither is.

This version of the complaint is obtuse. An applicant is not treated unfairly when the characteristics that she or he does or does not in fact possess are weighed, along with those of all other applicants, in a system reasonably designed to choose the best entering class. If, in a medical school, diversity really is one consideration in the overall selection of the entering class, being in certain categories (having a rural background or indigent parents, being an experienced engineer or a Hawaiian, etc.) might reasonably be considered in one's favor, in small degree, after more fundamental intellectual characteristics had left some difficult choices before the admitting committee. When the unusual are favored, at the margins, the usual are disfavored that far. Everyone understands that, and the good reasons for it. No one, in that circumstance, is done injustice. But when the applicants are first categorized by race, and all members of one race are favored simply because of their race, while the members of other races or ethnic groups are disfavored by the same device, the matter is wholly different—as our courts have made very plain. That *is* unjust and is not to be tolerated.

In an honest quest for diversity one's race may be considered in one's favor as an applicant. But so also might one's family background be considered, or one's artistic accomplishments, or economic circumstances—or any other characteristics one possesses that may contribute to the larger goals that diversity itself serves. Each applicant is just what he or she is—exhibiting just his or her own degree of poise or poverty or whatever. There is all the difference in the world between disadvantage arising out of ordinariness, a marginal handicap every white male has the opportunity to overcome by exhibiting other features that enable him to contribute richly to the class, and disfavor flatly imposed because of one's race. Even if the degree of disadvantage were to prove the same (a most improbable outcome unless the diversity factor were being manipulated), the ground of the disadvantage matters a very great deal: racial preference is unfair in a way that advantage from unusualness is not.

Nor may it be argued that, although honestly seeking diversity, a scheme may be devised to consider only race because the other elements of diversity—sex, age, geographical origins, etc.—are incorporated without special attention. Diversity, this argument supposes, simply boils down to *racial* diversity. This objection will not do because, if diversity really is the honest aim of an individualized process, every applicant must have at least the equal opportunity to strengthen the case for his or her admission on the basis of diversity manifested in other ways. To provide that opportunity, a deliberate and conscious, not incidental, attention must be paid to at least a substantial range of applicant differences. The precise boundaries of the range may vary, but without explicit attention to manifold factors of which race is but one, diversity will not have been employed in such a way as to meet the demand of the Fourteenth Amendment—that no person, viewed as an individual, may be denied the equal protection of the laws.

Powell's principles are distinguished at bottom from attempted obfuscation or evasion by *intent*. He expects universities to act *in good faith*; this expectation cannot be emphasized too strongly. When explicit Supreme Court rules permit the use of race in admission only for certain purposes, and only in certain ways, institutions of higher learning have a powerful obligation to comply with the spirit of those rules. What we *intend* is part of the *act* governed by those principles.

In universities, of all places, intellectual integrity and civic responsibility must be sensitively and concretely honored. Devious schemes through which a college may satisfy the letter while evading the substance of its obligations are clearly not tolerable. Nor may a university respond to the law with procedures designed to obscure or mislead. Compliance must be unambiguous and forthright; for a university nothing less will be compliance in "good faith."

Universities that do not live up to this expectation will fail in their duty. They will also be acting imprudently. College officers who hide impermissible ends with hypocritical language may be obliged to answer for it. Admissions systems cannot be permanently shrouded in secrecy. Duplicity will not prove very hard to expose. Institutions that connive to avoid the law will bring upon themselves the policing of their intra-institutional processes by government in ways more painful than any our universities have yet experienced, to the serious detriment of their larger purposes.[24]

VII

A serious mistake about the *Bakke* decision has been very widely promoted by careless reporting—the belief that the *Bakke* decision, while striking down "rigid quotas," permits most university programs, giving minority preferences without quotas, to go on as usual. That, as we have seen in reviewing Powell's principles, is simply not the case.

State-supported racially preferential admissions systems, whether incorporating quotas, or goals, or using any other language, have been found impermissible. What was condemned by a majority of the Court in this case is not merely the use of quotas, but the system of favoritism by race of which it was the tool. Any tool having the same object is subject to the same condemnation.[25]

What explains this and other common distortions? Partly, perceptions are being colored by desire. When those doing the interpreting have themselves been long engaged in the practice now outlawed, they are tempted to construe critical court decisions very leniently. But the authority of persons who interpret a rule proscribing conduct in which they have been engaged is highly suspect. We should as well have court rulings protecting the rights of criminal defendants given their definitive interpretation by police chiefs and associations of prosecuting attorneys.

Is the *Bakke* decision, then, a serious blow to affirmative action in this sphere? That depends upon what one means by "affirmative action." If one means by it, as many now do, racial preference for minorities as such, the answer is yes. Everyone, minorities most of all, should give thanks for that. Institutionalized preference by race is not only unjust, but seriously damaging to those whom it purports to aid.

If by "affirmative action" we mean, however, what the phrase was originally intended to convey—the taking of positive steps to ensure that earlier discriminatory practices would be uprooted—the *Bakke* decision will advance, not deter, such action. To recruit from all sources fairly; to test fairly and without racial bias; to weight merits (intellectual or other) on an individual basis, with all handicap flowing from race scrupulously eliminated—these affirmative steps the *Bakke* decision supports without dissent. It was not affirmative action in this wholesome, impartial sense that was at issue in this case. Favor by race was the issue; it was here condemned.

VIII

The long-term ramifications of the *Bakke* decision have been underestimated. Two themes embodied in it will reverberate for many years to come, contributing substantially to our constitutional history.

The first of these bears chiefly upon colleges and universities. They are forbidden, by *Bakke*, from using admission standards to achieve societal objectives that are not properly in their sphere. Justice Powell writes:

> We have never approved a classification that aids persons perceived as members of relatively victimized groups at the expense of other innocent individuals in the absence of judicial, legislative or administrative findings of constitutional or statutory violations. . . . Without such findings of constitutional or statutory violations it cannot be said that the government has any greater interest in helping one individual than in refraining from harming another.
>
> Petitioner [the University of California] does not purport to have made, and is in no position to make, such findings. Its broad mission is education, not the formulation of any legislative policy or the adjudication of particular claims of illegality.[26]

By this firm restriction we—I speak for the academic world of which I am a member—are done a great service. Universities have repeatedly and rightly argued that legislatures should not seek to use us, deform us, to achieve political objectives foreign to our essential purposes. It is incumbent upon us to restrain ourselves from that same perversion. Restorative justice—taking from some and giving to others to right social wrong—is an enterprise universities and their admissions committees are not likely to be very good at. But even if our admissions officers were as well trained as judges, that is not our proper role. We are neither judges nor legislators. It is simply wrong for us to exercise our powers as though we were, conducting admissions policies not merely as a college function but as a device to correct social wrongs that we decide deserve remedy, at whatever costs to other parties we deem reasonable.

If we make it our business to set things right in the world, what may we expect from legislatures when we decline to serve as their political instrument in some other context they deem pressing? Shall we tell them then that ours is an educative mission, and that we ought not be made tools of social policy? Can we then expect to be taken seriously? Once the principle is accepted— indeed urged by us!—that we, the universities, are a proper court in equity, to take from X and give to Y to remedy historical social wrongs, we will face a host of moral and political claims, many entirely reasonable, to which we shall be obliged to respond. What a dreadful service that will be, both to education and to justice. Justice Powell, in forbidding this course to us, saves us from our overzealous selves. He takes the nonpolitical nature of higher education seriously, as we ought always do. His protection of the universities from self-assignment into political or juridical service is likely to prove, in the years ahead, a feature of the *Bakke* decision for which all will be grateful.

A second neglected aspect of *Bakke* is the understanding implicit in it throughout that persons like Allan Bakke, when displaced or disadvantaged by a racially preferential system, are *injured*. They are done *constitutional* injury in the being deprived of what they ordinarily would not have been deprived of under the Constitution.

All nine Supreme Court justices are in accord on this, not just the four justices of the Stevens group, not just they and Powell. The Brennan group, although approving the Davis plan, agrees throughout that Bakke was substantially hurt, and that his hurt was serious enough to require very solid justification. Justice Blackmun, one of the anti-Bakke four, writes in his separate opinion that he looks forward to the time when "persons will be regarded as persons and discrimination of the type we address today [i.e., against Bakke] will be an ugly feature of history . . . that is behind us."[27]

Reverse discrimination, in sum, is real and bad. In *Bakke*, for the first time, the Supreme Court recognized that reality explicitly, and made very clear to all that such discrimination, however well intended, is not to be taken lightly.

Until *Bakke* there were many who assumed that, so long as intentions were good, universities could act pretty much as they thought just, giving and taking as they pleased. Not so. There are those who believe that some reverse discrimination can be justified. But the lasting impact of the *Bakke* decision, practical and symbolic, is this: the advocates of racial discrimination face a mighty burden of proof. When, as in most contexts, that burden cannot be met in court, colleges and universities are well advised to avoid scrupulously all preference by race.

IX

Finally, there is one troubling aspect of the *Bakke* decision that flows directly from the Powell principles. It may be taken to proffer an invitation that could lead to most unhappy practices. We are told that the Constitution permits the consideration of race in admissions for the sake of diversity to further the First Amendment interest in free expression. That being so, it would appear that other suspect classifications—by political affiliation or by religion—may also be used for the sake of diversity. This is a disquieting result. Should the fact that one is a Republican or a Socialist, Catholic or Jew, be allowed to count in the distribution of opportunities? Even if by invoking such considerations we could increase diversity in some contexts, they surely ought never be factors in the apportionment of any public goods. History gives us strong reasons to conclude that the uses of such classifications, even for putatively honorable goals, invite disaster. We forswear them. For the same reasons, even if *Bakke* permits us to promote diversity in a student body, it will be the part of wisdom to forswear the use of race as well.

Notes

1. A precise formulation of the standard by which the uses of racial classifications are to be judged in general was later provided by the Supreme Court in *Wygant v. Jackson Board of Education*, 476 U.S. 267 (1986). That standard is discussed in detail below.
2. Title VI of the Civil Rights Act of 1964 § 601, 42 U.S.C. § 200d (1970) provides: "No person in the United States shall, on the grounds of race, color, or national origin, be excluded from participation in, be denied the benefits of, or be subjected to discrimination under any program or activity receiving Federal financial assistance." The U.S. Constitution, Amendment XIV, provides in part: "No State shall . . . deny to any person within its jurisdiction the equal protection of the laws."
3. American Council on Education and Association of American Law Schools, "The Bakke Decision: Implication for Higher Education Admissions" (1978).
4. *Bakke v. Regents of the Univ. of Cal.*, 553 P. 2d 1152 (1976).
5. *DeFunis v. Odegaard*, 507 P. 2d 1169 (1973).
6. 438 U.S. at 305–11.
7. Ibid., p. 307.

8. Ibid., pp. 310–11.
9. Ibid., p. 310.
10. Ibid., pp. 307–309.
11. Ibid., p. 311.
12. Ibid., p. 313.
13. Ibid., p. 315.
14. Ibid., pp. 289–90.
15. Ibid., p. 294 n. 34.
16. Ibid., p. 320.
17. Ibid., p. 307.
18. *Bakke* still governs. In 1994 a federal court struck down a racially preferential admissions program at the law school of the University of Texas, under which minority and nonminority applicants were evaluated separately, minority applicants competing only against other minority applicants, very much as had been done at the Davis medical school twenty years before. The Court wrote: "Two wrongs do not make a right; nor does blatant discrimination cure the ills of past discrimination. Indeed, affirmative action that ignores the importance of individual rights may further widen the gap between the races . . . and create racial hostility. The only proper means of assuring that all important societal interests are met, whether in the context of creating diversity or redressing the ill effects of past wrongs, is to provide a procedure or method by which the qualifications of each individual are evaluated and compared to those of all other individuals in the pool, whether minority or nonminority" (*Cheryl Hopwood et al. v. State of Texas*, U.S. District Court, Western District of Texas; Memorandum Opinion, p. 64, 13 August 1994).
19. 438 U.S. 265, at 311–19.
20. Ibid., p. 406.
21. Ibid., p. 379.
22. Ibid., pp. 318–19.
23. This passage has been grossly misinterpreted by some as an invitation to colleges to go underground, through an indirect assurance that the courts will not inspect their processes. The central holding of *Bakke* is *not* (as one anonymous attorney suggested) that schools are supposed to lie about what they are doing with respect to minority admissions. Many do lie. But nothing could be further from the spirit of Justice Powell's opinion than that. One who reads deviousness into a passage designed to warn against deviousness reveals the nature of his or her own intentions.
24. The accountability to which college administrators would be subject was greatly overestimated at the time this was written. In fact, duplicity and secrecy have pervaded affirmative action programs in the years since *Bakke*. Powell's principles, clearly formulated as part of the law of the land, have been defied, or knowingly ignored, by admissions officers and their superiors contending with immediate political pressures. College officers ought to have been held accountable for widespread deception and occasional dishonesty, but generally that has not happened. At least, it has not happened yet.
25. Some accounts of the outcome in *Bakke* are dumbfounding. Here is one example from the work of a prominent Harvard professor of law, Lawrence Tribe, an ardent supporter of racial preference in admissions. Of the *Bakke* decision, he wrote, "The Court thus approved the kind of affirmative action used by most American colleges and universities, while striking down only the unusually mechanical approach taken by the Medical School of the University of California at Davis" [L. Tribe, *American Constitutional Law* 88 (Supp. 1979)].
26. 438 U.S. at 307–309.
27. Ibid., p. 403.

Diversity

In Defense of Affirmative Action

Barbara R. Bergmann

When Bill Clinton was campaigning for the presidency in 1992 as the candidate of the Democratic Party, he promised to appoint a cabinet that "looks like America." At the time Clinton made his rather poetic promise, nobody, including his political enemies, spoke out against it. Nobody said that attempting to fulfill that promise would be a bad idea.

A cabinet that really looks like the American labor force would have six of its fourteen seats filled by white and minority women and two of its seats filled by minority men. As Clinton's cabinet selection process was approaching its end in early 1993, only two of the appointments had gone to women. Feminist organizations, concerned that women would again be restricted to the marginal role they had played in all previous administrations, urged publicly that more women be appointed. Women reporters at Clinton's news conferences kept asking him about it.

This pressure provoked an angry outburst from Clinton. He said that those pressing him to appoint more women were "playing quota games" with the selection process, implying in his response that he himself disapproved of quotas. The truth, however, was that Clinton did want to appoint more women than his predecessors had, and he had apparently decided that three was the number he wanted. Many reasonable people would call that "setting up a quota," since Clinton was trying to appoint women to a predetermined number of slots. At that point, with few vacancies left, the simplest and most

Reprinted from *In Defense of Affirmative Action* (New York: Basic Books, 1996) by permission of the publisher.

practical way to ensure the appointment of a third woman was to earmark one of the remaining slots for a woman. That Clinton had done so became nakedly obvious when his first female candidate for the office of attorney general ran into trouble. He then put forward a second woman for the job and discarded her in turn when a problem arose. His third woman candidate was appointed and confirmed. She, like the other two, was obviously capable, qualified, and experienced. But by that time it was clear that Clinton had not been looking for the "best person" for the post of attorney general without regard to sex or race—he had been looking for the "best woman."

The Clinton cabinet episode raises questions that always arise when attempts are made to increase the gender and racial diversity in any group of employees. One fundamental question is whether diversity of sex or race or ethnicity in the cabinet was a worthy and important goal. How much harm would have been done if Clinton had appointed a cabinet consisting entirely or almost entirely of white males? He might simply have explained that each cabinet officer he appointed was, in his honest opinion, the best he could select from the wide range of candidates of both sexes and all ethnic and racial groups that he had considered. Would real harm have been done to the country's interests?

In thinking about that, we can note that presidents have always taken care to see that all geographic regions are well represented in the cabinet. Seeking that kind of diversity is not considered wrong; it is thought of as just being fair to all sections of the country. People in the West would be surprised and suspicious and hurt if the cabinet turned out to contain only people from east of the Mississippi. Clinton's selection of a cabinet that was markedly short of women and minorities would have done something far worse—it would have dealt a major setback to the pride and status of people in those groups. It would have strengthened the hand of those who think women, blacks, and other minorities do best in the jobs they have traditionally held and should stay there.

A second question is whether Clinton could have succeeded in assembling a reasonably diverse cabinet without setting up numerical goals by race and sex. Could he have avoided a cabinet that was completely or almost completely composed of white males without paying attention to the race and sex of the candidates as he made his appointments? There are good reasons to think that the answer is no. Dozens of superbly qualified and well-connected white males were available and competing for each cabinet position. A white male president can be expected to be most comfortable with advisers who are white males. Unless he disciplines himself by using a system of hiring goals for women and minorities, he may do the most comfortable thing and appoint only white males. President Clinton showed his leanings in this regard when he appointed his key White House staffers. They were chosen without publicity, and apparently without any effort at affirmative action. They all turned out to be white males, with one exception—a woman who was later replaced by a white male.[1]

Suppose, in appointing the cabinet, Clinton had chosen, one at a time, the person who appeared to him to be the best for each post, taking no special measures to find and include women and minorities and not worrying about appointing "too many" white males. How likely is it that there would have been much if any diversity by sex or race in his cabinet? Clinton really did have to mark out a seat for a woman if he was to shoehorn that third woman into the cabinet. The need to resort to such a potentially embarrassing method testifies to the low chance of achieving the degree of diversity he wanted without it. . . .

Diversity has positive value in many situations, but in some its value is crucial. To give an obvious example, a racially diverse community needs a racially diverse police force if the police are to gain the trust of all parts of the community and if one part of the community is not to feel dominated by the other part. While education and physical fitness are certainly aspects of "merit" in police officers, and while an appropriate floor on merit needs to be set and adhered to, efforts to get a corps of officers who are as educated and fit as possible should not be allowed to produce a police force that fails to include significant parts of its community. In such cases, it is legitimate to take account of what a candidate contributes to diversity. . . .

I have already noted the benefits of diversity in the president's cabinet and in police forces that serve racially diverse populations. Diversity prevents power from being concentrated in any one group and promises sympathetic and fair treatment to all sections of the public. Besides government officials and police officers, other examples of occupations in which diversity is especially important include journalists and others working in media, physicians, social workers, models in mail-order catalogs, judges (and therefore lawyers), managers and other people in authority, and politicians and other government employees. One of the major benefits of diversity is that it makes visible an organization's adherence to the principle that no type of person is excluded from performing any function, including responsible, important, and prestigious ones.

Another benefit of diversity is the differing points of view, insights, values, and knowledge of the world that members of various groups bring to their roles. Examples of the harmfulness of lack of diversity are easy to find. In the United States, medical researchers have repeatedly studied large groups of subjects consisting entirely of males and done no corresponding studies on groups of female subjects. The result has been that we know a lot more about men's health than about women's. Women in Congress and women medical researchers, newly increased in numbers and power, have lately challenged that practice. In decades of research on poverty, the economics profession, dominated by white males, ignored the concentration of poverty among female single parents and the problems they faced with sex discrimination in the labor market, with child care costs, and with child support enforcement. Researchers also largely ignored racial discrimination as a leading cause of poverty.

Diversity is especially important in some situations, but it might be argued that in a racially diverse society there is some positive value to having diversity in any sizable work group, regardless of its function. Leading a segregated life on the job makes workers less fit for life in a community where respect for all groups is supposed to be the rule. All-male crews sometimes aggravate the misogyny of those who serve in them, and all-white crews sometimes aggravate racism. In all-male and all-white groups, disparaging remarks about those not represented are likely to be uncontradicted, and attitudes harden.

Perhaps the most important reason for valuing the introduction of diversity into workplaces is that it helps dismantle two caste systems—one based on race and another based on gender—that have been responsible for a great deal of misery. A caste system dictates that your social status forever be that which you were born into, limits your choice of occupations, regardless of your talents and taste, and visits automatic disrespect on those at the bottom of the caste pecking order. The fate of many of those at the bottom of the race caste system is poverty. The fate of many of those at the bottom of the sex caste system is a choice between poverty and dependency. Our caste systems based on race and sex were in full flower until quite recently, and the remnants of them are still very much with us. . . .

The major justification for affirmative action in the workplace is its use as a systematic method of breaking down the current discrimination against African Americans and women. The desirability of diversity provides the strongest justification for affirmative action in college admissions. At a university, young people are trained for leadership roles in the professions and in public life. If we are to erase the deep racial cleavages that currently trouble us anytime soon, we cannot have campuses where black and Hispanic young people are rare or nonexistent. We cannot have white leaders who spent their college years in segregated institutions and never interacted with African Americans or heard their point of view.

Our campuses are in many ways the best parts of our country. For all their faults, they are places where people of intelligence gather to interact, to enjoy our literary and artistic inheritance, to enlarge their vision, to hone their critical sense, and to understand their place in life and their own potentialities. It would be tragic if on some campuses, and in some programs on our campuses, those African Americans who could perform there creditably were to be absent. A scientist who teaches at Brown says this about the talents and efforts of such students:

In twenty years of teaching at the university level, I have taught, advised and mentored a good many affirmative action admission students and not one of them could by any stretch of the imagination have been called an "underachiever." Most, in fact, were clearly overachievers who had made great strides despite the many obstacles that society and chance had placed in their paths. No, affirmative action doesn't allow anyone to get by on the color of his/her skin—we don't give affirmative action grades (except to athletes) no matter how the student got in. Affirmative action partly redresses a history of wrongs. We won't need it anymore once we have eliminated those wrongs.[2]

Campuses are also, of course, the places where the training and certification for the most prestigious, conspicuous, interesting, and lucrative careers take place. There is an obvious connection between the desegregation of higher education and the desegregation of the workplace: certain occupations cannot be entered without a credential from a college or university. Furthermore, there are important niches in certain occupations that anyone who has not passed through an elite university finds much more difficult to occupy. So the elite institutions, along with all of the others, cannot remain segregated if we are to fully desegregate the country's jobs and to get black and female faces into all professional ranks, up to the highest.

It might be argued that achieving integration through affirmative action is appropriate in those parts of the labor market where outright discrimination still occurs but not in higher education, where discrimination in student admissions is no longer a problem. If affirmative action succeeds in the workplace, perhaps in the future a greater proportion of the sons and daughters (or grandsons and granddaughters) of the currently disadvantaged groups will have attended better elementary and high schools, grown up in better neighborhoods, and developed the hopes and sense of self-worth that will enable them to apply themselves in school and achieve admission to colleges and universities in greater numbers on a "fair" basis—on the same basis as whites and Asians.

In a sense, affirmative action programs on campus are a way to jump-start or accelerate the process of reducing racial disparities—by getting more members of the current generation of minority young people into higher education and not waiting for the better academic and psychological preparation of future generations that may follow when blacks gain a better position in the job market. Affirmative action in higher education admissions speeds the arrival of the day when racial disparities in status and economic success will have been greatly reduced. It makes allowances for something that admittedly is not the fault of black teenagers: the relatively poor preparation of many of them for higher education.

The major argument against affirmative action in higher education admissions is that it is unfair to those candidates with better test scores who are displaced to make room for the African American and Hispanic students. For those who urge this point of view in university admissions, the nation's need to erase the effects of a shameful caste system count for nothing.

In fact, colleges and universities allow many considerations besides academic promise to affect admissions. Across the country, selective colleges and universities, which turn away many highly qualified students, admit several hundred athletes of low or nonexistent academic promise each year. These athletes, some black and some white, displace applicants—including black applicants—who have better test scores and better grades. Besides football and basketball players, schools give preference to runners, soccer players, baseball players, swimmers, and lacrosse players; the school must have them in order for their football and men's basketball teams to be allowed to compete in events sponsored by the National Collegiate Athletic Association (NCAA). It is sometimes said that one benefit of sports is to increase the number of blacks on campuses, that athletics constitutes a kind of affirmative action program that everyone can get behind—a two-for-one bargain. But many athletes have no interest in their studies, and no time or energy for them, and take the places of more academically motivated white and black students.

Many schools allow for regional diversity in their admissions process, giving preference to students from regions in which applicants are scarce. At Princeton or Yale, an applicant from Nebraska may be put ahead of an applicant from the East Coast with higher grades and test scores. Other applicants who are given special treatment in selective institutions are children of alumni. In 1988, 280 of 1,602 Harvard freshmen had fathers who had attended Harvard.[3] Of alumni children who apply, about 40 percent are admitted each year, while only 14 percent of non-alumni children are admitted. It is estimated that 240 more alumni offspring are admitted each year than would be the case if the parents' alumni status were not taken into consideration. Again, these 240 alumni children displace applicants with better grades and test scores. The Harvard Medical School announces in its application material that it gives preference to applicants who are the children of its graduates.

Applicants who are connected to influential or wealthy people—movie stars, other celebrities, multimillionaires—are also routinely given special preference. In addition, a university's administrative officers are known to ask for and to get special consideration for children of personal friends. The medical school dean's friends' children displace people with superior academic qualifications.[4]

Of course, two wrongs do not make a right. Preferential admissions of athletes, Nebraskans, offspring of alumni, and offspring of friends of the dean, if they are harmful, do not justify whatever harm affirmative action does. In fact, all such admissions do the same kind of harm—they displace candidates with better cognitive credentials, those whose talents run to academic pursuits rather than cross-country running or basketball. But just as affirmative action programs have benefits, these other special admissions practices have benefits too.

We can look at the benefits of each of these kinds of special admissions and see how they compare in value. The extra alumni children are presumably admitted to reward the alumni for making financial contributions. (Have their places been bought, in a sense?) The children of friends of the dean are there to give a nice perk to the dean: they are one of the dean's fringe benefits, so to speak. The athletes (or at least a few of them) provide entertainment, boost school spirit, and in some rare cases, bring fame to the school. If, however, the school is highly selective, it does not need extra fame, since it has plenty of good applicants. By the laws of mathematics, only half of the collegiate teams can win more games than they lose in any season, and a much smaller proportion can have an outstanding number of wins. So the special admission of the talented football and basketball players fails its ostensible purpose a good part of the time for almost all schools. The assumption that sports teams generate revenue for schools is unfounded in most cases.[5]

How do the reasons for affirmative action stack up against the reasons for the other admissions? The reasons for affirmative action are far more compelling: helping to cure this country's racial cleavage, improving the parity of blacks in the job market, encouraging blacks and whites to know each other on campus, and giving a hand to the many young black people who grow up in bad environments.

If we are going to eliminate special admissions to selective schools, we should start with those special admissions that have the weakest justification. Those who think that the special admission of alumni children and the other special admissions are more justified than the special admission of African Americans should express that belief openly. If, on the other hand, they have merely overlooked the traditional beneficiaries of special admissions, they should redirect their drive for fairness in admissions to these higher-priority targets. After they have succeeded in eliminating special admissions for alumni children, athletes, Nebraskans, the wealthy, the well connected, and friends of the dean, they will have acquired the moral standing to raise their voices against affirmative action.

Notes

1. Dee Dee Myers was Clinton's first spokesperson. For the list as of 1995, see Todd S. Purdum, "Desperately in Need of Winning Streak, Clinton Finds One," *New York Times*, May 7, 1995, p. 1.

2. David F. Duncan, Division of Biology and Medicine, Brown University, e-mail message to FEMECON-L network, May 5, 1994.
3. Jerome Karabel and David Karen, "Go to Harvard, Give Your Kid a Break," *New York Times*, December 8, 1990, p. 25.
4. The dean of the University of California Medical School—which figured in Allan Bakke's reverse discrimination case that went to the Supreme Court—intervened each year in the admissions process on behalf of the children of friends and acquaintances.
5. See Barbara R. Bergmann, "Do Sports Really Make Money for the University?" *Academe* (January–February 1991): 28–30; and Murray Sperber, *College Sports Inc.: The Athletic Department vs. the University* (New York: Henry Holt and Co., 1990).

The Role Model Argument and Faculty Diversity

Anita L. Allen

Introduction

Proponents of faculty diversity in higher education sometimes advance the "role model" argument.[1] The argument is a familiar player in confrontations over race, gender, and the allocation of employment opportunities. In these contexts, the role model argument asserts that colleges and universities ought to hire females of all races and male members of minority groups to ensure that undergraduate, graduate, and professional school students will have appropriate role models among their teachers.[2] The role model argument is popular because the belief that young people need role models is pervasive. In words so familiar that they bear the stigma of cliché, many say that if students are to realize their full potential as responsible adults, they need others in their lives whom they can emulate and by whom they will be motivated to do their best work.

Academic philosophers have seldom shown signs of taking the popular role model argument seriously. To be sure, philosophers who wrote about the moral foundations of civil rights policy in the 1970s and '80s invariably mentioned the argument.[3] But they mentioned it in passing as an argument—though not the most powerful or interesting argument—for a permissive, liberal stance toward policies they labeled "affirmative action," "preferential treatment," "reverse discrimination," or "quotas." Even philosophers like Bernard Boxill, who defended liberal, race-conscious policies for minority and female inclusion,

Reprinted from the *Philosophical Forum* 24 (1992–93) by permission of the journal.

gave the role model argument cursory treatment.[4] Everyone seemed content to regard the role model argument as ancillary to more powerful and interesting arguments for distributive and reparative justice. By the 1990s an apparent consensus had been reached in philosophical circles: the role model argument may reflect legitimate utilitarian concerns, but it does not deserve to be taken seriously as an independent argument for recruiting traditionally excluded minorities and white women.[5]

The persistent popularity of the role model argument in rationales for diversity and affirmative action has made it increasingly important to rethink the consensus. Accordingly, I will examine the power and limitations of the role model argument here. My focus will be the case for black female law teachers as role models for black female law students. The high standing of lawyers in American society justifies close attention to issues within *legal* education. I focus on *black women* in legal education for three reasons. First, black women are one of several groups in higher education still described as excluded or underrepresented. Second, according to one study, black and other minority women who manage to enter law teaching are "at the bottom" of their profession, "hindered by their sex rather than aided by it" when it comes to tenured teaching positions at the nation's law schools.[6] Third, recent events at Harvard University called the nation's attention to black women law teachers and to a particularly strong version of the role model argument made on behalf of black women law students. The events at Harvard prompted a number of minority scholars to assess the logic and politics of the role model argument.[7]

In the spring of 1990, protests by Harvard Law School students demanding faculty diversity culminated in a "sit-in" demonstration outside the office of Dean Robert Clark. Professor Derrick Bell, Harvard's first and most senior black law professor, stated publicly that he would take an unpaid leave of absence until the law school tenured a black woman. Two years later, Harvard had tenured no black woman, students again demonstrated at the dean's office, and Bell made plans to be away from the law school for a third year.

Bell's actions were praised in some quarters, criticized in others. Critics charged that Bell's demand for a woman of color on the faculty was unreasonable, in view of the limited pool of qualified minority candidates. Bell replied that the pool of qualified black women candidates appears prohibitively small only because Harvard is determined to perpetuate narrow, self-serving criteria of qualification. Bell's critics also stressed that Harvard's law faculty of about seventy already included six black men, three of whom were tenured, and five tenured white women. To this, Bell responded that the presence of white women and black men on the teaching staff did not answer the full demand for diversity: black women law students, he said, need black women law teachers.

One man's sacrifice in the name of black female role models for black female students drew the attention of the national media. In the wake of publicity, one organization approvingly named Bell "Feminist of the Year." Belittling Bell's efforts in an editorial praising Harvard for offering tenure to four white men, a journalist quipped that "[o]nly in the curious world of university campuses could anyone argue that professors should be judged by their skin color, gender or sexual practices instead of their merit as teachers."[8] Some members of the general public took umbrage at the idea that a school might be pressured by politics to favor a black woman over outstanding white teachers. For them, Bell's demand symbolized the demise of excellence and the excesses of preferential affirmative action policies. Yet, as affirmative action entered its third decade, black women remained largely absent in most fields as higher education teachers. The population of black women tenured as professors of philosophy, mathematics, economics, and the natural sciences is exceedingly small.

From the point of view of Professor Bell and the law students of all races who have risked arrest in the name of faculty diversity, being and providing role models is a distinct moral imperative for faculty and administrators in American higher education. More precisely, being and providing *same-kind* role models is often a moral imperative: black men for black men, black women for black women. Some who oppose the political tactics employed by Bell and the Harvard law students nevertheless share their perspective on the importance of same-kind role models. Indeed, as elaborated below, I share the perspective that minority students need same-kind faculty role models. The demand for same-kind role models is not illegitimate in principle.

The stance that institutions and appropriate individuals ought to provide same-kind role models does not, however, translate into unqualified endorsement of the role model argument for faculty appointments. On the contrary, one might believe, as I will argue here, that when it is used as the centerpiece of the case for minority faculty appointments, the role model argument is profoundly problematic. Obscuring both the varied talents of minority teachers and the varied tasks their institutions expect them to perform, "centerpiece" uses of the role model argument impede fairness and honesty in the faculty appointments process.

Against the Role Model Argument

Who Is a Role Model?

I maintain that, despite the very real value to students of faculty role models, we should abandon the minority role model argument heard today in the context of faculty appointments. However, before turning to the case for outright abandonment, I want to make the case for a weaker claim—that greater care should be taken in the phrasing of the role model argument.

The role model argument tolerates an intolerable degree of ambiguity about what it means to be a "role model." Judith Thomson, George Sher, and other philosophers who have attempted to assess the role model argument for race-based and gender-based preferences have not grappled with the ambiguity of the concept (see Thomson, chap. 9; Sher, chap. 11). Thomson's admirable defense of the role model argument was undercut by ambiguity about precisely what she understood a role model to be.

Not everyone means the same thing when they refer to themselves or others as "role models." For example, one academic dean may describe excellent classroom teachers who rarely counsel students outside of class as role models. Another dean may reserve the term for teachers who also counsel students outside of class about career and personal concerns. Different individuals may define "role model" differently; but also, the same individual may define it differently in different settings. A university provost may on one occasion employ "role model" as a term applicable to all faculty members and administrators, yet on another occasion employ it as a term of special approbation for outstanding faculty and administrators.

The ambiguity of the expression "role model" is not so fundamental that moral claims about the importance of role models cannot be sustained. However, it is incumbent upon those who rely upon the term to get beyond the initial ambiguity of "role model." It is helpful to begin by distinguishing the three most common senses in which educators currently employ the term. When we say that a teacher is a "role model," we generally mean that that individual serves as one or more of these:

(1) an *ethical template* for the exercise of adult responsibilities;

(2) a *symbol* of special achievement;

(3) a *nurturer* providing special educational services.

Philosophers must hope in vain to alter by fiat the ordinary language practices of the general public. However, it would greatly clarify academic debates about the value of role models and the role model argument were the academic community always to specify whether the role models at issue in a given instance are supposed to be templates, symbols, or nurturers.

All teachers are ethical templates, but only some significantly function as symbols and nurturers. When teachers teach, they model the role of teacher. They are ethical templates, men and women whose conduct sets standards for the exercise of responsibilities. Like other teachers, law school teachers are role models in the ethical template sense. The manner in which faculty members exercise their responsibilities as teachers sets standards for how those responsibilities ought to be exercised. How law school teachers speak and behave will suggest something to their students about how law school teachers ought to speak and behave. Because most law professors are also members of the bar or bench, the conduct of law professors also carries general messages about the exercise of responsibility in adult roles other than teaching, especially the roles of attorney and judge.

As ethical templates, teachers can set high standards or low. An alcoholic teacher who routinely teaches classes in a state of intoxication would set an arguably low standard. Even if the content of an inebriated teacher's lectures were otherwise adequate, one could still argue that the lecturer was a poor role model. An arguably praiseworthy role model who set a high standard may not be viewed as such by students. When visiting professor Patricia Williams taught a commercial law course at a prestigious law school several years ago, students quickly devalued her modeling of the commercial law professor role.[9] As a black female professor attempting to advance original scholarly perspectives, Williams represented a new kind of template. Many students admired her teaching and some said they admired her clothes; but a number wanted a traditional professor's perspective and complained about Williams's teaching to the dean.

All teachers are ethical templates, but only some are symbols of special achievement. The "symbol" is the kind of role model philosophers most commonly acknowledge. As explained by Thomson and Sher, "role models" are individuals who inspire others to believe that they, too, may be capable of high accomplishment.[10] Kent Greenawalt had this same understanding in mind when he described the utilitarian, "role models for those in the minority community" argument for racial preferences:

> If blacks and other members of minority groups are to strive to become doctors and lawyers, it is important that they see members of their own groups in those roles. Otherwise they are likely to accept their consignment to less prestigious, less demanding roles in society. Thus an important aspect of improving the motivations and education of black youths is to help put blacks into positions where blacks are not often now found so that they can serve as effective role models.[11]

Like members of racial minority groups and white women, white men can also be symbols of special achievement. A criminally delinquent white juvenile who reformed himself and became a respected professional could serve as a role model for others of his same background.

If an individual is to serve as a symbol of special achievement for a group, group members must recognize the individual as belonging to their group. A recognizability requirement thus constrains would-be role models. With this in mind, some have occasionally argued that institutions seeking to hire blacks as role models should hire blacks who "look black" rather than blacks who "look white." But such a requirement does not follow from the recognizability imperative. Physical appearance is only one basis for racial recognition. Outward appearance has never been the only basis of racial identification, not under American race law and not under prevailing American custom. For African

Americans, Native Americans, and Hispanic Americans who look—or look to some—like Caucasians, recognition by strangers as members of minority groups may require deliberate verbal disclosure.

Disclosure is essential for the identification of members of a number of minority groups. The faculty diversity movement at Harvard included a demand for openly gay and lesbian law teachers. One cannot be a gay or lesbian role model if no one knows one is gay or lesbian. Serving as a symbol of gay achievement depends upon first disclosing that one is gay. The situation is somewhat analogous for blacks, Native Americans, and Hispanics who "look white." The mere fact that a person is not visually recognizable to strangers as a member of a racial minority group does not mean that such a person will not eventually disclose their racial affiliation and become an effective symbol of special minority achievement. A light-skinned person with African ancestors and a black cultural self-understanding can be as effective as a dark-skinned person with African ancestors and a black cultural self-understanding. Throughout American history black communities have embraced high-achieving blacks of whatever hue as symbols of special achievement for the race, where a black racial heritage was discernable either through appearance, family history, or credible self-disclosures. Indeed, a number of historically important black political leaders have been men of mixed race ancestry who "looked white," but opted against "passing."[12]

Teachers who directly engage students through mentoring, tutoring, counseling, and special cultural or scholarly events are role models in a final sense. They are nurturers. Educators sometimes assume nurturing roles as personal, supererogatory commitments to students they believe would not be adequately served by mere templates and symbols.

The roles of template, symbol, and nurturer are typically conflated in the role model argument for including minorities in higher education. Yet, being a minority group member is neither a necessary nor a sufficient condition for being a "role model" for minority students in every sense identified. For example, a black woman's mere presence in an institution can help to reshape conceptions of who can be a law teacher. Her style and perspectives can perhaps reshape conceptions of what is appropriate for law teachers to do and say.

But only some black women teachers are role models in the sense of "symbols" of special achievement and "nurturers" of students' special needs. Blacks nominally hired as symbols may turn out to be nurturers. In this vein, Robert K. Fullinwider once hinted that implicit in the rationale for placing blacks in "visible and desirable positions" is the possibility that individual blacks will provide "better services to the black community."[13]

However, some black women "symbols" do not give a "nurturer's" priority to the advancement of the interests of black students and wider black communities. These women would understandably resent students and colleagues who assume on the basis of their race and gender that they are willing to add nurturing to a long list of tasks that include teaching, writing for publication, and committee assignments. In arguments for academic role models for black women, a high degree of clarity requires specification of the tasks one expects the role model to perform. Not every black woman will be willing or able to perform every task.

The Cost to Integrity and Well-Being

We can continue to speak ambiguously about role models and breed misunderstanding. Or, we can begin to speak less ambiguously, as I suggest, about templates, symbols, and nurturers. But the ambiguity of the expression "role model" is only a small part of what makes the role model argument problematic. Even after conceptual clarity is achieved about what "role model" denotes, premising minority recruitment centrally on the capacity to serve as role models proves too costly.

One cost is that reliance upon the role model argument helps to sustain the widespread prejudice that African Americans, Hispanics, and members of certain other minority groups are intellectually inferior to whites. Faculties typically use the role model argument for minority appointments in situations in which they would rarely think to cite role modeling capacities as a reason for hiring whites. They hire white men on the expectation that they will excel as teachers, scholars, or administrators. They hire minorities, notwithstanding a presumption of lesser talent, on the expectation that they will serve as minority role models. The role model argument therefore functions as an excuse for employing someone regarded as lacking full merit.

Believing that they are better than prejudiced colleagues assume they are, and knowing that they will in fact serve as templates, symbols, or nurturers, some minority job candidates may be content to secure academic employment on grounds that imply inferiority. This is why conservative efforts to shame minorities out of accepting affirmative action appointments have largely failed. Minorities understand how valuable they are to their institutions, even if conservative opponents to minority recruitment do not. Yet to escape the degradation of fair process that role model–based recruitment represents, higher education has two choices consistent with integrity. It can limit minority recruitment to individuals who satisfy the traditional, narrow conceptions of merit purportedly applied to white men. Or, it can premise recruitment on revised, broader conceptions of merit proposed by progressives who aggressively contest tradition.

A second cost of the role model argument relates to the first. It perpetuates institutional bad faith. The role model argument mires those who rely upon it in self-deception. The role model argument dishonestly understates the actual contributions of minority faculty. Like nonminority colleagues, minority faculty must prepare and teach courses, supervise student projects, write for publication, and serve on committees. The role model argument obscures these typical responsibilities. Blacks retain posts as pilots, not because they are role models, but because they are skilled at keeping their aircraft aloft. By analogy, black college and university professors ultimately receive tenure not because they are symbols and nurturers, but because they provide essential services. Colleges and universities should not be permitted to pretend that the only valuable service performed by minority faculty is role modeling.

The role model argument has a third cost. Reliance on the role model argument can easily result in the search for someone's stereotype of the best or the most "positive" minority. Those charged with making judgments about who is and is not a positive minority role model can easily run amok. Blacks and other minorities who look, sound, or think like upper-middle-class whites may be overvalued by decision makers who are not at ease with cultural diversity. Those with the power to appoint faculty may interpret traits of ethnic differences as indicia of lesser competence.

But by the same token, minorities with "white" attributes may be undervalued by decision makers who see no point to hiring minorities who are not discernably ethnic in appearance, speech, or perspective. At Harvard Law School, Professor Bell and the student diversity activists expressed a preference for minority faculty with culturally distinct perspectives, significant ties to the minority community, and an express willingness to nurture.

The knowledge that they are hired as minority role models in an atmosphere penetrated by stereotypes of race and gender can impose undue psychological burdens on affected faculty. The burden in question is the burden of measuring up to an unreasonable number of externally imposed standards as a condition for community approval. It can make a black woman feel that she must be perfectly black, not just black; perfectly female, not just female. Even an enthusiastic role model can tire of the extraordinary service she is expected to give her school. She can grow weary under the weight of having to wear her racial commitment and feminism always on her sleeve.

A final cost of the role model argument is that it can signal to white male faculty that they do not have role-modeling obligations toward minority students. The possibility that white faculty may regard minority students as unreachable and thus, to an extent, unteachable, is an alarming one. Even today, white males are the predominant group in most departments in most institutions in the United States. It is from white men that black women, for example, are required to learn most of what they need to know. Race-related faculty indifference is a commonly heard student complaint. Appointing a quota of same-kind role models in response to such complaints may strike some whites as all they need to do to address the special needs of minority students. Minority students can greatly benefit from same-kind minority role models. But it does not follow that black role models on campus leave white faculty with less than equal educational obligations toward minority and nonminority students.

Affirmative Action

I support many of the goals and practices of affirmative action in faculty appointments, especially the practice of relying upon broad criteria of merit that encompass a range of talents and methods. Yet one could easily mistake my criticism of the role model argument for a criticism of affirmative action in faculty appointments. This is because, in the political realm, the role model argument is closely associated with the case for affirmative action. The role model argument ties the case for affirmative action in student admissions to the case for affirmative action in faculty appointments in the following way. Once historically white institutions begin to admit minority group members in large numbers, they create a need for minority teachers to teach, inspire, and mentor. The role model argument acknowledges the needs of affirmative action students for affirmative action to supply appropriate faculty.

However, the logical relationship between the affirmative action and role model argument is less snug than first appearances might suggest. In theory, a staunch opponent of affirmative action could advocate hiring minority role models to improve the educational experiences of "wrongly" admitted, "unqualified" affirmative action students. To put it starkly, even a racist or sexist could advance the role model argument.

The soundness of the role model argument does not entail or presuppose the soundness of all of the liberal egalitarian arguments for affirmative action found in the philosophical literature.[14] In fact, because what I am calling the role model argument defends minority faculty recruitment on utilitarian grounds referring to student and institutional need, rather than on grounds referring to compensatory justice, reparative justice, or moral desert, the role model argument is neutral as among affirmative action's possible forward- and backward-looking rationales. Possibly some of the best reasons for providing minority students with same-kind teachers relate narrowly to educational necessity rather than broadly to the moral necessity of redressing slavery or addressing current economic injustices in the wider society.

In light of the foregoing, the logical linkage between the role model argument and the case for affirmative action is attenuated. Nevertheless, some for whom the end of increasing the number of minority faculty is paramount may object on practical grounds to my call for the abandonment of the role model argument. "Sure, the role model argument has the drawbacks you identify; but it works to get minorities onto faculties; it therefore has strategic value for minority inclusion and empowerment."

This strategic defense of the role model argument is ultimately unpersuasive. To counteract myths of minority inferiority, while avoiding stereotyping and institutional self-deception, minority appointments must be made on grounds that yield to or aggressively contest traditional notions of merit. It is tempting to view the presence of institutionally designated minority role models as necessarily a step toward satisfying the need for better representation and resources for minority communities. But it is unrealistic to suppose that an isolated black woman law teacher or Latina mathematician represents meaningful gains in minority power. Minority professors are sometimes disaffected by their labors and marginalized by their colleagues. The presence of minority faculty does not guarantee that minorities share power in the simplistic cause-and-effect fashion suggested by defenders of strategic approval of the role model argument.

The Need for Same-Kind Role Models

The claim Professor Bell made for a black female law professor for black female students at Harvard Law School struck many as untenable. I would conjecture that most in higher education greet the claims made for same-kind role models with frank skepticism. Would law students of any race or status be better off if schools provided more same-kind faculty role models? There appears to be evidence to the contrary. Blacks who attend historically black colleges, where black faculty role models abound, receive lower scores on average on the law school admissions test than blacks who attend historically white schools.[15]

Some critics dismiss the claim for same-kind role models as just so much political rhetoric. Black "role models," they argue, have political, not educational importance. Mere politics should not, the argument continues reductio ad absurdum, lead schools to invest in endless searches for black females, handicapped lesbians, and every other minority group that might claim special needs.

To get beyond this skepticism, some insight is needed into the experiences of persons from traditionally excluded minority groups, such as black women. Until recently, little was known about the experiences of black women in legal education. The number of black women law teachers and students was small and their misfortunes were their closely guarded secrets.

First as a student and professor in the field of philosophy, and later as a student and professor in the field of law, I have had numerous experiences that point toward the need for faculty diversity and same-kind role models. My experiences, sketched below in illustrative examples, suggest why so many minority group members and their supporters strongly believe in the need for minority templates, symbols, and nurturers. As the dates of each of my examples suggest, there may be as much old-fashioned prejudice and insensitivity to contend with in the 1990s as there was in the infancy of the civil rights and women's movements, over two decades ago.

Perhaps the most important rationale for same-kind role models is this. White men, who predominate in higher education, have frequently failed to communicate confidence in the possibility of minority achievement. Snap judgments made on the basis of skin color alone are not uncommon; nor are begrudging affirmative action appointments. Black women have been made to feel inferior and out of place in higher education:

(1) In 1971, a white male classics professor to a black female student: "Why don't you forget about college and become an airline stewardess?"

(2) In 1976, a white male undergraduate to his black female teaching fellow in philosophy on the first day of class: "What gives you the right to teach this class?"

(3) In 1978, the white chairman of a philosophy department to a black female candidate for an assistant professorship: "You don't have the kind of power we are looking for, but I am personally committed to affirmative action."

Increasing the number of minority faculty could increase the chances that minority group members will find peers and role models in the ivory tower capable of believing sincerely in their competence. Moreover, a flourishing minority community within an institution could reduce the tendency to stereotype nontraditional students and faculty members as third-rate intellects.

White male professors have often defined agendas that ignore the intellectual needs of minority students. This can happen when "traditional" faculty take narrowly Western perspectives or exclude from their courses issues affecting minority communities. It can also happen, however, when "progressive" faculty view their classrooms as opportunities to convert conservative students into radicals:

(4) In 1982, a white male law professor to a black female law student: "I'm not aiming this class at people like you, I'm aiming it at the conservative white males headed for Wall Street."

In law schools, one problematic side effect of white professors ignoring the intellectual needs of minority students is that students come to believe that whites teach an established "white" version of the law, and blacks teach a different "black" version:

(5) In 1987, a black male law student to a black female professor: "I'm not taking any courses from blacks; I want to learn the same thing the white boys are learning."

In a different vein, white professors' racial slights can seriously undercut professional relationships based on mutual respect:

(6) In 1981, a distinguished white male philosophy professor to a black female, now a professional colleague: "You look like the maid my family once had."

(7) In 1990, a white colleague to a black female colleague with curly hair tied back with a bandanna: "You look like Buckwheat."

Sexual harassment, including unique, race-related forms of sexual harassment, can also undercut professional relationships:

(8) In 1977, a white male professor to a black female former student who dropped him as an advisor after an uninvited kiss: "I thought you were my student; I was surprised to learn you'd completed your dissertation under someone else."

(9) In 1990, a white male college professor to a black female law professor at a conference panel on discriminatory harassment on campus: "You should-n't mind being called a jungle bunny; bunnies are cute and so are you."

Painful, demoralizing experiences such as these lead black women to develop personal skills, social perspectives, and concerns to which their students are beneficially exposed throughout the course of formal education. It can teach a black female student a great deal to have access to black women teachers who have negotiated the gauntlet of racism and sexism that she, too, must negotiate.

It is important for minorities training to be professionals to know how to maintain composure and self-respect in situations like these:

(10) In 1983, a white female undergraduate in a class on the subject of affirmative action taught by a black female: "There are no intelligent black people in Oklahoma."

(11) In 1983, a partner at a prestigious law firm to a black woman law student working as his summer intern: "Write a memo explaining why legislation requiring private eating clubs to admit minorities and women would be unconstitutional."

(12) In 1990, a white female law student to an Hispanic student in the presence of a black woman law professor: "Forget about trying to improve this school's loan forgiveness program for public interest lawyers. If you ever have any problems paying back your student loans you can always contact me, a person of privilege and increasing privilege, for help."

Those who disparage the demands for same-kind role models must try to understand the kinds of life experiences that prompt them. Behind the demands for same-kind black female faculty role models for black female students lies a fundamental sense of abandonment. As undergraduate, graduate, and professional school students, black women often feel that their institutions have abandoned them to racism, prejudice, and indifferent or hostile teachers.

This feeling of abandonment increases the alienation and hostility of minority students. It may correlate with underachievement among black women who attend even the best predominantly white schools; and it may help to explain the high rate of minority undergraduate attrition. Quite possibly, good black female students would do even better if "same-kind" role models were available to serve as examples (ethical templates), motivators (symbols of special achievements), and attention givers (nurturers).

Although white males, black males, and other categories of teachers could serve black women in these ways, the fact of the matter is they do not, they have not, and, to some extent, they cannot in the current social and political climate. The demand for same-kind role models heard today underscores the diversity of student needs that results from the diversity of Americans' social experiences.

Conclusion

My thesis has the flavor of a paradox. I argue for role models, but against the role model argument. But it is no paradox to say that we should praise faculty role models who take seriously their power and responsibilities as templates, symbols, and nurturers—but condemn uses of the role model argument that treat minorities like inferiors. Nor is it a contradiction to say that we should praise the minority and white female faculty who are willing to accept jobs others believe they are not qualified to hold, but condemn those who offer jobs to minorities and white women whose professional equality they are not prepared to admit.

After twenty years in higher education as a student and teacher, I have come to accept as true empirical claims commonly made by friends of the argument for same-kind role models: minority students have special role model needs that minority faculty are uniquely placed to service. The same decades of experience point toward the need for an egalitarian and empowered vision of minority teachers, scholars, and administrators. The "role model" argument for minority appointments simply obstructs such a vision.

Higher education has taken on the education of students from all segments of the community. In doing so, it has assumed an obligation to provide role models for students who need them. To meet this obligation, colleges and universities will have to diversify their faculties to include men and women of varied backgrounds. The goal of faculty diversification is distorted when the search for minority candidates—and not others—is understood principally as a search for role models rather than as a search for talent in its many and diverse forms.

Faculties will have to diversify their talent, but diversification is not enough to satisfy the need for role models. Schools will have to encourage their faculties to be more responsive and respectful than ever before.

Notes

1. Portions of this paper are adapted from a longer essay. See Anita L. Allen, "On Being a Role Model," *Berkeley Women's Law Journal* 6 (1990–91): 22.
2. Bernard Boxill has suggested that even if affirmative action "sins against a present equality of opportunity, [it may be acceptable because it] promotes a future equality of opportunity by providing blacks with their own successful "role models." See Bernard Boxill, *Blacks and Social Justice* (Totowa, NJ: Rowman and Allenheld, 1984), p. 171.
3. See Robert Fullinwider, *The Reverse Discrimination Controversy: A Moral and Legal Analysis* (Totowa, NJ: Rowman and Littlefield, 1980); M. Cohen, T. Nagel, T. Scanlon, eds., *Equality and Preferential Treatment* (Princeton, NJ: Princeton University Press, 1977); Kent Greenawalt, *Discrimination and Reverse Discrimination* (New York: Alfred Knopf, 1983); Boxill, *Blacks and Social Justice*, pp. 147–72.
4. See Boxill, *Blacks and Social Justice*, p. 171.
5. See Gertrude Ezorsky, *Racism and Justice: The Case for Affirmative Action* (Ithaca, NY: Cornell University Press, 1991). Ezorsky does not name the need for role models as an argument for affirmative action. See pp. 73–94.
6. "Minority Women at the Bottom of Law Faculty," *New York Times*, April 3, 1992.
7. See, for example, Linda Greene, "Tokens, Role Models, and Pedagogical Politics: Lamentations of an African American Female Law Professor," *Berkeley Women's Law Journal* 6 (1990–91): 81. Professor Greene's essay was part of a symposium issue of the *Berkeley Women's Law Journal* titled "Black Women Law Professors: Building a Community at the Intersection of Race and Gender," consisting of fifteen essays by black women law teachers.
8. L. Gordon Crovitz, "Harvard Law School Finds Its Counterrevolutionary," *Wall Street Journal*, March 25, 1992.
9. Cf. Patricia Williams, *The Alchemy of Race and Rights* (Cambridge, MA: Harvard University Press, 1991), p. 95.
10. According to Thomson,

> What is wanted is *role models*. The proportion of black and women faculty members in the larger universities (particularly as one moves up the ladder of rank) is very much smaller than the proportion of . . . them amongst recipients of Ph.D. degrees from those very same universities. Black and women students suffer a constricting of ambition because of this. They need to see members of their race or sex who are accepted, successful professionals. They need concrete evidence that those of their race or sex *can* become accepted, successful professionals. (chap. 9, p. 37)

Sher considered the argument that

> Past discrimination in hiring has led to a scarcity of female "role models" of suitably high achievement. This lack, together with a culture which . . . inculcates the idea that women should not or cannot do the jobs that men

do, has in turn made women psychologically less able to do these jobs. . . .
[T]here is surely the same dearth of role models . . . for blacks as for
women. (chap. 11, p. 64–65)

11. Greenawalt, *Discrimination and Reverse Discrimination*, p. 64.
12. Their stories are told in F. James Davis, *Who Is Black? One Nation's Definition* (State College: Pennsylvania State University Press, 1991).
13. Fullinwider, *The Reverse Discrimination Controversy*, p. 18.
14. For a recent survey of the arguments generally, see Ezorsky, *Racism and Justice*.
15. Of course, the racial composition of their faculties is not the only respect in which white and black colleges differ.

Proportional Representation of Women and Minorities

Celia Wolf-Devine

I begin by asking a question, an affirmative answer to which seems presupposed by the current debate on affirmative action:[1] Is there necessarily something wrong if there is a low percentage of African Americans or women or Hispanics, et cetera, in the field of college teaching relative to their proportion in the population at large? Why is this a goal we should aim at? I do not mean to deny that women and racial and ethnic minorities have been victims of discrimination in academia (although this is by no means limited to blacks, Asians, Hispanics, and Native Americans—consider, for example, Polish, Lebanese, or Portuguese Americans) or that some discrimination still persists. Such discrimination is bad and should be eliminated; in fact, we ought to put more resources into enforcing antidiscrimination laws. My argument here is that there is no reason to believe that proportional representation of minorities and women among the professoriate is a requirement of justice or that a situation where such proportional representation obtained would necessarily be better than one in which it did not.[2]

Arguments that might be advanced in favor of the claim that something is wrong if women and minorities are not proportionally represented fall into two general categories: those that take the existence of such statistical disparities to be evidence of discrimination or injustice, and those based on the value of

Reprinted with minor omissions from *Affirmative Action and the University: A Philosophical Inquiry,* ed. Steven M. Cahn (Philadelphia: Temple University Press, 1993), by permission of the publisher and the author.

diversity. These two types of arguments differ in that those based on the need for diversity would not prove that universities are required as a matter of justice to appoint more women and minorities, but merely that it would be educationally desirable were they to do so. But if it could be shown that the lack of proportional representation of minority groups among the professoriate either itself constituted an injustice or provided adequate evidence of the existence of ongoing injustice, then the case for involvement of the federal government to correct this becomes stronger.[3]

Is Proportional Representation a Requirement of Justice?

Does the lack of proportional representation of women and minorities among the professoriate constitute an injustice? Or is it necessarily evidence of discrimination or injustice of any sort? It would be evidence of injustice or discrimination only if it is reasonable to believe that, in the absence of discrimination and injustice, women and all racial and ethnic minorities would be proportionately represented in college teaching (and other professions). But *is* it reasonable to believe this?

The important issue here philosophically is where we place the burden of proof. Should we assume that the statistics reflect some sort of discrimination or injustice unless we have evidence to the contrary? But why put the burden of proof here? While it is legitimate to put the burden of proof on the employer in cases where the proportion of women and minorities hired is radically lower than their proportion *in the applicant pool*, the case is totally different when we are comparing the proportion of women and minorities in the professoriate with their proportion in the population as a whole.

Looking first at racial and ethnic groups, there is no prima facie reason to suppose that members of different racial and ethnic minorities would be equally likely to want to go into the professoriate and, on the contrary, many reasons to expect that they would not. To the extent that ethnic and racial groups form at least partially self-contained communities (and they do), members of one community will value different sorts of character traits, encourage the acquisition of different skills, and have different ideas about what sorts of jobs carry the most prestige.[4] Most arguments in favor of affirmative action in fact suppose that racial and ethnic groups differ in these sorts of ways; if they did not, then bringing in a wider variety of such groups would not contribute to diversity.

In one culture, scientists might be particularly respected, while in another being a media personality might be viewed as the height of success. Sometimes traditional patterns in a culture predispose members toward certain professions, as the great respect for Torah scholars in Jewish culture fits very naturally with aspirations for careers as scholars or lawyers. Cultures that are highly verbal might be expected to produce more teachers than others. In addition, of course, as some members of a community go into a particular field, others aspire to go into it also since they already know something about it from their friends and relatives and have contacts in the field.[5]

So even if equal percentages of the members of all racial and ethnic groups might desire some sort of prestigious job, there is no reason to suppose that all of them would regard the same jobs as prestigious. Or to put the point more bluntly, not everyone would regard being a professor as prestigious. And there are special reasons why college teaching might be less attractive than other professions to those (for example, blacks and Hispanics) who are trying to struggle out of poverty. Due to its low salaries relative to the amount of training required, college teaching has long tended to attract people brought up in relatively secure financial conditions, plus a few other individuals who feel a strong calling to the intellectual life.

To put the dialogue about affirmative action in academia in the proper perspective, we need to keep in mind some background facts. Certainly there are some prestigious research institutions where professors make excellent salaries, and in business or technical fields professors can often make good money consulting and exercise some power in the larger society. But the salary of the average academic has not kept pace with salaries in other fields; nonacademics I meet are universally shocked to learn how little professors are paid. An associate professor I know is forced to teach an extra night course each term, to teach both summer sessions, and on top of that to sell suits at a men's store during the Christmas season in order to be able to support a wife and two children and to meet mortgage payments on a house in an area that is adequate but by no means fancy.

In addition, the social status of professors (particularly in the humanities) has declined significantly from what it was in the 1950s and 1960s. (And if affirmative action is stronger in academia than elsewhere, this might lower the status of professors still more, since they would be perceived as being appointed because of their sex or race.) These problems, together with a widespread loss of a sense of purpose among academics, have led to a lot of demoralization among faculty. Ambitious young members of minority groups may quite reasonably prefer careers in law, politics, industry, or the media. Indeed, the problem of how to attract bright young people of *any* racial or ethnic group into college teaching is becoming increasingly severe. Even students who feel strongly drawn to the intellectual life are often deterred from pursuing academic careers by poor salaries and by what they hear about academic politics.

If I am right, then, one important reason why racial and ethnic minorities are not proportionately represented in the professoriate is because those who are in a position to acquire the credentials are going into other professions. Bright, ambitious members of such groups who have B.A.s often find careers in other areas more attractive than college teaching. This is partly a function of their cultures, which may not accord high prestige to professors relative to other professions, and partly a result of low salaries and demoralization among many (although certainly not all) professors. And in order to attract them into the professoriate, it is essential to begin by improving the situation of those already in the field in a number of ways (and not just salary, although that is important). We should then make it clear to minority members that they are genuinely welcome in academia and will receive fair consideration.

Another reason why racial and ethnic minorities are not proportionally represented in the professoriate is because large numbers of them have been deeply scarred by poverty (and often racism) and do not enter college. They are therefore not even in the running for becoming college teachers or for pursuing most careers with high status and pay. The difficulties involved in remedying this situation are massive, and the universities can play only a limited role. Universities could, for example, set up tutorial programs aimed at helping disadvantaged students (and staffed by faculty and student volunteers). Or they could offer scholarships for college and graduate school to talented disadvantaged students or have need-blind admissions if they can afford to do so. Since such programs are costly, government assistance would probably be necessary.

The big question that arises at this point is to what extent such remedial programs should be directed at racial and ethnic minorities. At this point I believe another background fact becomes relevant—one that is too often overlooked by supporters of affirmative action. During the Reagan years, American society underwent a marked polarization between rich and poor. We have, in fact, the most extreme polarization of any industrialized country (measured by the gap between the wealth of the upper fifth of society and that of the lower fifth). And it is arguable that affirmative action has contributed to this polarization (at least it has done nothing to prevent it), since those women and blacks who were in a position to take advantage of it (i.e., those who had suffered less discrimination) did so, leaving the really poor no better off and simply displacing other groups and pushing them down into poverty.[6]

The problem of the widening gap of rich and poor should be confronted directly, rather than gearing remedial programs too closely to race and ethnic group (as affirmative action does). In addition to making people more rather than less race conscious and generating resentments along racial and ethnic lines, such programs are not radical enough, because they lead people to think that by appointing middle-class blacks, Hispanics, or Asians that they have thereby really helped the poor.

The poor need direct assistance, and it is not only minority members who are poor. There are enormous numbers of white poor, particularly in rural areas of the South. Many ethnic groups are impoverished and have suffered discrimination at least as severe as that against Hispanics and Asians. The children of single mothers of all races and ethnic groups have been pushed down into severe poverty, and many blue-collar workers have been impoverished (e.g., small farmers or residents of the Minnesota Iron Range). Programs targeted at the economically disadvantaged should perhaps be supplemented by special compensatory programs aimed at blacks and Native Americans (since most Hispanics and Asians are recent immigrants, compensatory arguments do not carry the same force in their case). I do not here take a position on this thorny issue, except to say that not all scholarships and special assistance programs should be earmarked for such groups, but a significant proportion should be awarded on the basis of merit and financial need alone.

The more poor people are brought up into the middle class, the more of them will obtain B.A.s and be in a position to consider college teaching as a career. We will still need to improve the situation of the professoriate if we are to be able to attract good Ph.D. candidates. But at least more people will have a chance to enter the profession, especially if graduate school scholarships are available to talented students who need them. The poor who are not upwardly mobile (e.g., the retired, the chronically ill, the mentally retarded, etc.) will still need direct financial and medical assistance.

The situation of women in academia is somewhat different from that of ethnic and racial minorities, in that they are closer to being proportionally represented, at least in the humanities, although they tend still to be absent from some scientific and technical fields and from the most prestigious positions. Does this prove they are being discriminated against? Certainly in some cases they have been and still are discriminated against (especially in promotion and pay), and these abuses should be corrected. But here also the statistics alone do not establish discrimination. Their own choices to spend more time with their children may account for their failure to advance as far or as quickly as their male colleagues and for the fact that they hold part-time positions more frequently. Certainly not all women make these sorts of choices, but enough do to affect the statistics. (It could, of course, be argued to be unjust that women take on a larger share of child care, but we should beware of paternalistically telling people what choices they ought to make.)

In order to establish the presence of injustice or discrimination, we need to know more about the actual preferences of the women in question, and not just adopt a bureaucratic approach of trying to get the numbers to come out right. Suppose an academic couple who wish to combine career and family decide between themselves that he will work full time and she will work part time in order to spend time with the children. Then suppose that due to affirmative action he is unable to get a full-time job and she is forced to take full-time work to support the family. The statistics may look better, but both people are less happy than they would have been without affirmative action.

Proportional representation of women and of blacks, Hispanics, Native Americans, and Asians in the professoriate, then, is not a requirement of justice, and a situation where such proportional representation is present is not necessarily more just than one where it is not—for example, if it was obtained by overriding the preferences of those concerned without some reason other than a desire to get the statistics to come out right.[7] Furthermore, a society where such proportional representation was present along with a vast and unbridgeable gap between rich and poor would be less just than one with a more equitable distribution of wealth and opportunities for advancement but which lacked proportional representation of women and minorities in some professions.

Promoting Diversity

Affirmative action is often defended as a means to greater diversity on college faculties, and a faculty that does not have proportional representation of women and minorities is regarded as not diverse enough. Diversity, unfortunately, has become something of a buzzword these days, and it is necessary to give thought to what sorts of diversity should be promoted and why. And this requires some reflection about what the purposes of the university are. Diversity of opinion is not enough, but neither is diversity of methodology. Not all methodologies deserve representation. Consider, for example, astrology, or the systematic vilification of one's opponents.

If one agrees that encouraging intelligent dialogue about important issues is one of the purposes of the university (and I do), then this has at least some implications for the sort of diversity we want. If dialogue is of central importance, then it is desirable to have intellectual diversity. But limitless intellectual diversity is not good; the value of diversity must be weighed against the value of community. Certainly, there can be communities that are too ingrown and homogenous. If a psychology department appoints only behaviorists, then students are deprived of exposure to other quite legitimate traditions of thought within their discipline. And the same is true if an economics department appoints only followers of Milton Friedman, or a philosophy department appoints only Thomists or only phenomenologists. But on the other hand, too much diversity leads to the breakdown of communication between groups. If this occurs, faculty become unable to talk with each other and work within totally different conceptual frameworks, making no attempts to respond to positions other than their own. Students, then, tend to become hopelessly confused, give up even trying to develop coherent beliefs of their own, and retreat into just giving each professor what he or she wants. Maintaining community is, thus, just as important for education as introducing intellectual diversity.

Suppose, then, we are agreed that intellectual diversity, per se, is not simply a good to be maximized (and in real life, no one, not even the defenders of affirmative action, believes in the value of limitless diversity); we then must specify what sorts of diversity will contribute to stimulating intelligent dialogue and learning on college campuses. And I see no reason why proportional representation of groups now officially recognized as protected minorities should be expected to produce the right sort of diversity. First of all, diversity of skin color is quite consistent with total ideological conformity and therefore need not conduce to dialogue at all.

Furthermore, as people like Stephen Carter have been pointing out lately, we ought not to suppose that because a person is black or Hispanic that he or she will have some particular set of beliefs or espouse a particular methodology.[8] This expectation is a form of racial stereotyping and as such is demeaning to the person. Pressures toward ideological conformity among members of minority groups are increased by this sort of dishonest attempt to smuggle in one's ideological agendas under the guise of affirmative action. A Hispanic who is a Republican is no less a Hispanic, and a woman who is not a feminist is no less a woman.

There is, then, no good reason to suppose that proportional representation of the minority groups now officially recognized will yield the right sort of intellectual diversity. And the same sorts of arguments developed above could be applied to cultural diversity as well as to intellectual diversity. People from the same cultural background share common prereflective attitudes, patterns of feeling and imagination, ways of talking, and styles of behavior. But although it is educationally valuable for students to be exposed to people from different cultures, limitless cultural diversity is not a good thing (for the same reasons that limitless intellectual diversity is not), and skin color is not a reliable guide to culture. An enormous amount of cultural diversity exists, for example, among blacks and Hispanics. Poor rural Southern blacks, for example, may be culturally more similar to poor rural Southern whites than they are to Northern middle-class urban blacks.

In short, one cannot generate the right sort of diversity (intellectual or cultural) by simply pursuing neatly measurable goals like proportional representation of women, blacks, Hispanics, Asians, and Native Americans. In addition, the sort of diversity needed at a given school will itself be a function of a number of factors, such as the character of the faculty already there, the student body, and the sorts of vocations for which students are preparing. A school preparing students for careers in international business or diplomacy might find that the sort of diversity introduced by appointing foreign nationals to their faculty is particularly valuable, for example. These sorts of judgments involve a great many complex considerations and cannot be made mechanically by trying to get statistics to meet some target percentages (comforting though it would be if things were so simple).[9]

Notes

1. By affirmative action, I mean preferential treatment and not just things like announcing openings and encouraging women and minorities to apply. And tie-breaking affirmative action might, I believe, be justified in some cases on the basis of the role model argument. The reason the role model argument does not support preferential appointments in order to attain proportional representation is that a minority member can only function as a model for excellence if he or she is perceived as having been appointed because of qualifications rather than race or sex. One really good minority faculty member is a more effective and inspiring role model than ten mediocre ones.

2. Note, again, that I am speaking of proportional representation relative to their percentage in the population at large.

3. I do not consider here compensatory arguments. That institutions should make compensation to individuals they have discriminated against is self-evident, but problems arise when those receiving compensation are not the persons who were wronged. For example, how are older women who have suffered discrimination in any way made whole from their injury by the appointment of younger women unrelated to them? In any case, there is no clear way compensatory arguments could tell us what proportion of minority groups should be on university faculties. How can we tell what proportion of Hispanics would have become professors in the absence of discrimination? Or, in the absence of slavery, that the number of blacks teaching in American universities would be no higher than it is now. An additional problem with compensatory arguments is that, like redistributive arguments, they treat teaching appointments as plums to be distributed instead of as focusing on the responsibilities that such positions involve.

4. Perhaps instead of conceptualizing society as a pyramid with one top, we should think of it as a group of hills with many different peaks; people may choose different paths to wealth, power, and prestige.

5. This is called the "cousinhood advantage." While in academia it operates in favor of WASPs and Jews, this is not the case everywhere. Although building contractors frequently make very good money, a WASP would be at a great disadvantage in this field in many parts of the country where the building trades are heavily dominated by certain ethnic groups.

6. See Kevin Phillips, *The Politics of Rich and Poor* (New York: Random House, 1990), pp. 18, 203, 207.

7. People should, I believe, be free to enter the occupation of their choice (subject, of course, to certain broad constraints based on the common good—such as that if everyone wanted to be lawyers and no one wanted to grow crops, some adjustments would be necessary) and make other career decisions as they see fit, even though we might think (rightly even) that it would be better for them to choose otherwise.

8. Stephen Carter, *Reflections of an Affirmative Action Baby* (New York: Basic Books, 1991).

9. I am indebted to my husband, Phil Devine, for many valuable discussions of the ideas in this article and for reading and commenting on the manuscript. I have also profited from discussions with Beth Soll, John McGrath, Joseph Ryshpan, and my colleagues Richard Capobianco, Soo Tan, and Richard Velkely.

The Meaning of "Merit"

William G. Bowen and Derek Bok

"Merit," like "preference" and "discrimination," is a word that has taken on so much baggage we may have to re-invent it or find a substitute.

Still, it is an important and potentially valuable concept because it reminds us that we certainly do not want institutions to admit candidates who *lack* merit, however the term is defined. Most people would agree that rank favoritism (admitting a personal friend of the admissions officer, say) is inconsistent with admission "on the merits," that no one should be admitted who cannot take advantage of the educational opportunities being offered, and that using a lottery or some similar random numbers scheme to choose among applicants who are over the academic threshold is too crude an approach.

One reason why we care so much about who gets admitted "on the merits" is because . . . admission to . . . selective schools . . . pays off handsomely for individuals of all races, from all backgrounds. But it is not individuals alone who gain. Substantial additional benefits accrue to society at large through the leadership and civic participation of the graduates and through the broad contributions that the schools themselves make to the goals of a democratic society. These societal benefits are a major justification for the favored tax treatment that colleges and universities enjoy and for the subsidies provided by public and private donors. The presence of these benefits also explains why these institutions do not allocate scarce places in their entering classes by the simple expedient of auctioning them off to the highest bidders. The limited number of places is an exceedingly valuable resource—valuable both to the students

Reprinted from *The Shape of the River* (Princeton: Princeton University Press, 1998), by permission of the publisher.

admitted and to the society at large—which is why admissions need to be based "on the merits."

Unfortunately, however, to say that considerations of merit should drive the admissions process is to pose questions, not answer them. There are no magical ways of automatically identifying those who merit admission on the basis of intrinsic qualities that distinguish them from all others. Test scores and grades are useful measures of the ability to do good work, but they are no more than that. They are far from infallible indicators of other qualities some might regard as intrinsic, such as a deep love of learning or a capacity for high academic achievement. ... Moreover, such quantitative measures are even less useful in answering other questions relevant to the admissions process, such as predicting which applicants will contribute most in later life to their professions and their communities.[1]

Some critics believe, nevertheless, that applicants with higher grades and test scores are more deserving of admission because they presumably worked harder than those with less auspicious academic records. According to this argument, it is only "fair" to admit the students who have displayed the greatest effort. We disagree on several grounds.

To begin with, it is not clear that students who receive higher grades and test scores have necessarily worked harder in school. Grades and test scores are a reflection not only of effort but of intelligence, which in turn derives from a number of factors, such as inherited ability, family circumstances, and early upbringing, that have nothing to do with how many hours students have labored over their homework. Test scores may also be affected by the quality of teaching that applicants have received or even by knowing the best strategies for taking standardized tests, as coaching schools regularly remind students and their parents. For these reasons, it is quite likely that many applicants with good but not outstanding scores and B+ averages in high school will have worked more diligently than many other applicants with superior academic records.

More generally, selecting a class has much broader purposes than simply rewarding students who are thought to have worked especially hard. The job of the admissions staff is not, in any case, to decide who has earned a "right" to a place in the class, since we do not think that admission to a selective university is a right possessed by anyone. What admissions officers must decide is which set of applicants, *considered individually and collectively*, will take fullest advantage of what the college has to offer, contribute most to the educational process in college, and be most successful in using what they have learned for the benefit of the larger society. Admissions processes should, of course, be "fair," but "fairness" has to be understood to mean only that each individual is to be judged according to a consistent set of criteria that reflect the objectives of the college or university. Fairness should not be misinterpreted to mean that a particular criterion has to apply—that, for example, grades and test scores must always be considered more important than other qualities and characteristics so that no student with a B average can be accepted as long as some students with As are being turned down.

Nor does fairness imply that each candidate should be judged in isolation from all others. It may be perfectly "fair" to reject an applicant because the college has already enrolled many other students very much like him or her. There are numerous analogies. When making a stew, adding an extra carrot rather than one more potato may make excellent sense—and be eminently "fair"—if there are already lots of potatoes in the pot. Similarly, good basketball teams include both excellent shooters and sturdy defenders, both point guards and centers. Diversified investment portfolios usually include some mix of stocks and bonds, and so on.

To admit "on the merits," then, is to admit by following complex rules derived from the institution's own mission and based on its own experiences educating students with different talents and backgrounds. These "rules" should not be thought of as abstract propositions to be deduced through contemplation in a Platonic cave. Nor are they rigid formulas that can be applied in a mechanical fashion. Rather, they should have the status of rough guidelines established in large part through empirical examination of the actual results achieved as a result of long experience. . . .

Above all, merit must be defined in light of what educational institutions are trying to accomplish. In our view, race is relevant in determining which candidates "merit" admission because taking account of race helps institutions achieve three objectives central to their mission—identifying individuals of high potential, permitting students to benefit educationally from diversity on campus, and addressing long-term societal needs.

Identifying Individuals of High Potential

An individual's race may reveal something about how that person arrived at where he or she is today—what barriers were overcome, and what the individual's prospects are for further growth. Not every member of a minority group will have had to surmount substantial obstacles. Moreover, other circumstances besides race can cause "disadvantage." Thus colleges and universities should and do give special consideration to the hardworking son of a family in Appalachia or the daughter of a recent immigrant from Russia who, while obviously bright, is still struggling with the English language. But race is an important factor in its own right, given this nation's history and the evidence presented in many studies of the continuing effects of discrimination and prejudice. Wishing it were otherwise does not make it otherwise. It would seem to us to be ironic indeed—and wrong—if admissions officers were permitted to consider all other factors that help them identify individuals of high potential who have had to overcome obstacles, but were proscribed from looking at an applicant's race.

Benefiting Educationally from Diversity on the Campus

Race almost always affects an individual's life experiences and perspectives, and thus the person's capacity to contribute to the kinds of learning through diversity that occur on campuses. This form of learning will be even more important going forward than it has been in the past. Both the growing diversity of American society and the increasing interaction with other cultures worldwide make it evident that going to school only with "the likes of oneself" will be increasingly anachronistic. The advantages of being able to understand how others think and function, to cope across racial divides, and to lead groups composed of diverse individuals are certain to increase.

To be sure, not all members of a minority group may succeed in expanding the racial understanding of other students, any more than all those who grew up on a farm or came from a remote region of the United States can be expected to convey a special rural perspective. What does seem clear, however, is that a student body containing many different backgrounds, talents, and experiences will be a richer environment in which to develop. In this respect, minority students of all kinds can have something to offer their classmates. The black student with high grades from Andover may challenge the stereotypes of many classmates just as much as the black student from the South Bronx. . . .

Addressing Long-Term Societal Needs

Virtually all colleges and universities seek to educate students who seem likely to become leaders and contributing members of society. Identifying such students is another essential aspect of admitting "on the merits," and here again race is clearly relevant. There is widespread agreement that our country continues to need the help of its colleges and universities in building a society in which access to positions of leadership and responsibility is less limited by an individual's race than it is today. . . .

Fundamental judgments have to be made about societal needs, values, and objectives. When a distinguished black educator visited the Mellon Foundation, he noted, with understandable pride, that his son had done brilliantly in college and was being considered for a prestigious graduate award in neuroscience. "My son," the professor said, "needs no special consideration; he is so talented that he will make it on his own." His conclusion was that we should be indifferent to whether his son or any of the white competitors got the particular fellowship in question. We agreed that, in all likelihood, all of these candidates

179

would benefit from going to the graduate school in question and, in time, become excellent scientists or doctors. Still, one can argue with the conclusion reached by the parent. "Your son will do fine," another person present at the meeting said, "but that isn't the issue. *He may not need us, but we need him!* Why? Because there is only one of him."

That mild exaggeration notwithstanding, the relative scarcity of talented black professionals is all too real. It seemed clear to a number of us that day, and it probably seems clear to many others, that American society needs the high-achieving black graduates who will provide leadership in every walk of life. This is the position of many top officials concerned with filling key positions in government, of CEOs who affirm that they would continue their minority recruitment programs whether or not there were a legal requirement to do so, and of bar associations, medical associations, and other professional organizations that have repeatedly stressed the importance of attracting more minority members into their fields. In view of these needs, we are not indifferent to which student gets the graduate fellowship.

Neither of the authors of this study has any sympathy with quotas or any belief in mandating the proportional representation of groups of people, defined by race or any other criterion, in positions of authority. Nor do we include ourselves among those who support race-sensitive admissions as compensation for a legacy of racial discrimination.[2] We agree emphatically with the sentiment expressed by Mamphela Ramphele, vice chancellor of the University of Cape Town in South Africa, when she said: "Everyone deserves opportunity; no one deserves success." But we remain persuaded that present racial disparities in outcomes are dismayingly disproportionate. At the minimum, this country needs to maintain the progress now being made in educating larger numbers of black professionals and black leaders.

Selective colleges and universities have made impressive contributions at both undergraduate and graduate levels. To take but a single illustration: since starting to admit larger numbers of black students in the late 1960s, the Harvard Law School has numbered among its black graduates more than one hundred partners in law firms, more than ninety black alumni/ae with the title of chief executive officer, vice president, or general counsel of a corporation, more than seventy professors, at least thirty judges, two members of Congress, the mayor of a major American city, the head of the Office of Management and Budget, and an assistant U.S. attorney general. . . . If, at the end of the day, the question is whether the most selective colleges and universities have succeeded in educating sizable numbers of minority students who have already achieved considerable success and seem likely in time to occupy positions of leadership throughout society, we have no problem in answering the question. Absolutely.

We commented earlier on the need to make clear choices. Here is perhaps the clearest choice. Let us suppose that rejecting, on race-neutral grounds, more than half of the black students who otherwise would attend these institutions would raise the probability of acceptance for another white student from 25 percent to, say, 27 percent at the most selective colleges and universities. Would we, as a society, be better off? Considering both the educational benefits of diversity and the need to include far larger numbers of black graduates in the top ranks of the business, professional, governmental, and not-for-profit institutions that shape our society, we do not think so.[3]

How one responds to such questions depends very much, of course, on how important one thinks it is that progress continues to be made in narrowing black-white gaps in earnings and in representation in top-level positions. As the United States grows steadily more diverse, we believe that Nicholas Katzenbach and Burke Marshall are surely right in insisting that the country must continue to make determined efforts to "include blacks in the institutional framework that constitutes America's economic, political, educational and social life." This goal of greater inclusiveness is important for reasons, both moral and practical, that offer all Americans the prospect of living in a society marked by more equality and racial harmony than one might otherwise anticipate.

We recognize that many opponents of race-sensitive admissions will also agree with Katzenbach and Marshall, but will argue that there are better ways of promoting inclusiveness. There is everything to be said, in our view, for addressing the underlying problems in families, neighborhoods, and primary and secondary schools that many have identified so clearly. But this is desperately difficult work, which will, at best, produce results only over a very long period of time. Meanwhile, it is important, in our view, to do what can be done to make a difference at each educational level, including colleges and graduate and professional schools.

The alternative seems to us both stark and unworthy of our country's ideals. Turning aside from efforts to help larger numbers of well-qualified blacks gain the educational advantages they will need to move steadily and confidently into the mainstream of American life could have extremely serious consequences. Here in the United States, as elsewhere in the world, visible efforts by leading educational institutions to make things better will encourage others to press on with the hard work needed to overcome the continuing effects of a legacy of unfair treatment.

Notes

1. Martin Luther King, Jr., now regarded as one of the great orators of this century, scored in the bottom half of all test takers on the verbal GRE.
2. Justice Thurgood Marshall made such an argument in the *Bakke* case in urging his colleagues on the Supreme Court to uphold the racial quotas provided by the University of California Davis School of Medicine; in his view, such programs were simply a way

"to remedy the effects of centuries of unequal treatment. . . . I do not believe that any-one can truly look into America's past and still find that a remedy for the effects of that past is impermissible" (438 U.S. at p. 402). Understandable as this argument may seem against a historical background of slavery and segregation, it did not prevail because the remedy is not precise enough to be entirely just in its application. Not every minor-ity student who is admitted will have suffered from substantial discrimination, and the excluded white and Asian applicants are rarely responsible for the racial injustices of the past and have sometimes had to struggle against considerable handicaps of their own. For these reasons, a majority of justices in the *Bakke* case rejected Marshall's rea-soning, although similar arguments continue to be heard.

3. This emphasis on the consequences of rejecting race-neutral policies will seem mis-placed to some of the most thoughtful critics of affirmative action, who will argue that their objection to race-based policies is an objection in principle: in their view, no one's opportunities should be narrowed, even by an iota, by reference to the individual's race. We respect this line of argument. However, we do not agree, "in principle," that colleges and universities should ignore the practical effects of one set of decisions or another when making difficult decisions about who "merits" a place in the class. The clash here is principle versus principle, not principle versus expediency. As we argued earlier in the chapter, in making admissions decisions, what is right in principle depends on how one defines the mission of the educational institution involved. For us, the missions of colleges and universities have strong educational and public policy aspects and do not consist solely of conferring benefits on particular individuals.

Does Your "Merit" Depend upon Your Race?
A Rejoinder to Bowen and Bok

Stephan Thernstrom and *Abigail Thernstrom*

In his *Reflections of an Affirmative Action Baby*, Stephen Carter tells us that his academic record as an undergraduate at Stanford was strong, but not good enough to win him admission to Harvard Law School. Shortly after he got a rejection letter from Harvard, though, he received a telephone call informing him that there had been a mistake in the review of his application. The admissions committee had somehow failed to notice that Mr. Carter was an African American, and that made all the difference. As an ordinary applicant, Carter did not make the grade. But Harvard Law School had a lower standard for black applicants, so it was eager to have him.

Stephen Carter felt patronized and demeaned by Harvard Law School, and chose to go elsewhere for his law education. He recognized that his race may well have given him a boost at the other schools that admitted him, but he could not be sure how much. Only Harvard made it crystal clear, inadvertently making the racial basis of its judgment completely transparent. He was not being admitted because of his personal achievements; he was not unequivocally outstanding, but merely outstanding compared with other African-American applicants.

Derek Bok, once the dean of Harvard Law School, and William G. Bowen cannot grasp why a Stephen Carter might feel deflated and diminished by such treatment. Although they claim to be making the case for nuanced, holistic, highly individualized admissions decisions, in fact what they defend are crude judgments that reduce applicants to members of racial categories. From their perspective, society needs more black attorneys, and the elite law schools have to do their part. If energetic recruitment efforts do not yield enough minority applicants who would win admission strictly on the basis of their individual qualifications, schools must do their duty by accepting black and Latino applicants with weaker credentials. What's the problem? After all, everyone they admit is qualified. That many whites and Asians whom they reject are *better* qualified doesn't matter, because "society" already has enough white and Asian attorneys.

Bowen and Bok, of course, once headed two of the most distinguished universities in the United States—indeed, in the world. Bowen was president of Princeton University, and Bok was president of Harvard. The shining reputations of Princeton and Harvard derive primarily from the excellence of their faculties and their student bodies, and that excellence has been the result of a commitment to meritocratic selection procedures. They admit the very best students from their applicant pools, and they hire the best scholars they can find to teach them.

It was not always so. Before World War II, both Harvard and Princeton held Jewish applicants to a higher standard than gentiles, and kept the numbers of Jews in the student body severely limited, in order to leave ample room for alumni sons who were more notable for their social graces than for their intelligence. They also were extremely reluctant to hire Jews as faculty members.[1]

Bowen and Bok's effort to relativize the "meaning of merit" drains the concept of any clear meaning and echoes the arguments made by proponents of the Jewish quotas in the bad old days. Test scores and grades are but very limited measures of individual potential, they claim. Such objective measures of academic performance may not identify applicants who have "a deep love of learning" or "a capacity for high academic achievement," much less those who "will contribute most in later life to their professions and their communities," they say. Earlier Ivy League presidents would have added "character" to the list, but the notion of judging who will contribute most to "their professions and their communities" may amount to the same thing.

These are disturbingly subjective criteria, and it is well to recall that in the past they were applied in a manner that few would defend today. Isaac Levine from P.S. 164 in Brooklyn had a straight-A record and 1480 on the SATs, but Yale would have had too many Jews if it took him. Bowen and Bok tell us that "adding an extra carrot rather than one more potato" to the stew "may make excellent sense—and be eminently 'fair'—if there are already lots of potatoes in the pot." This metaphor is profoundly revealing—more revealing than its authors realize. Winthrop Brooks IV of Andover Academy might be the extra carrot that was needed. Despite his mediocre academic qualifications, he would likely "contribute" more to society when he joined his father's investment banking firm after graduation. Doubtless he had a better "character" as well, at least as character was rated by Yale admissions officers. Yale had enough students of Levine's "kind," and needed more of Brooks's kind. A supposedly nuanced judgment of competing individuals, in this instance, would have been made on the basis of gross ethnic and social class stereotypes.

Decisions like these amounted to naked discrimination against Jews, and were indefensible. And yet we wonder what Bowen and Bok would have to say about the matter. Their very long book about admissions to elite schools never mentions this unsavory history, although it seems extremely pertinent. It may seem difficult to deny that Jewish quotas were discriminatory, but that conclusion rests on the assumption that grades and test scores are a reasonable measure of the qualifications of an applicant to college—a reasonable gauge of his or her "merit." Once you relativize and racialize merit, as Bowen and Bok do, it is impossible to say that any unsuccessful candidate has been treated unfairly. "Sure, Levine was a good potato, but we had enough potatoes. We really needed more carrots in the pot."

Fortunately, academic merit as measured by high school grades and test scores matters far more to admissions officers at Harvard, Princeton, and other elite schools than Bowen and Bok would have us believe. Their stew metaphor implies that such institutions don't want too many students with exceptional academic qualifications—a stew with nothing but beef would not be very tasty. Presumably the carrots, potatoes, bay leaf, and thyme are people with weaker grades and lower SATs but other outstanding characteristics. However, a glance at any of the standard guides to colleges and universities will reveal that the average student admitted to such schools has SAT scores in the top 2 to 3 percent and ranks at or very close to the top of his or her high school class. Princeton cannot be accepting significant numbers of applicants whose grades and test scores are merely average or below average because it is convinced they nonetheless have a "deep love for learning," a "special rural perspective," or some other equally fuzzy attribute.

The authors' scorn for standardized tests even leads them to remark in a footnote that "Martin Luther King, Jr., now regarded as one of the great orators of this century, scored in the bottom half of all test-takers" on the verbal portion of the Graduate Record Examination. But of course no one defends SATs and GREs on the grounds that they identify people with Dr. King's remarkable talents. These tests, however, do a good job in predicting academic performance, numerous studies have shown.

All of Bowen and Bok's rhetoric about how "merit" is a multifaceted, relative, many-splendored thing is designed to obscure a simple and regrettable fact. If students were admitted to the most selective colleges and universities strictly on the basis of their academic merit, the number of African Americans and Hispanics who would be successful in the competition would be very small.

Some figures from California illustrate the problem vividly. Admission to a campus of the University of California, the best state university system in the country, is guaranteed to state residents who rank in the top eighth of their high school graduating class. Grades are the primary criterion, but SAT scores are also considered in determining the list of students deemed to have the merit to make them "UC-eligible."

What is the racial mix among the UC-eligibles? The most recent data available are for 1999, and indicate that just 2.8 percent of African-American public high school seniors in the state had strong enough records to be guaranteed a place at the University of California. The proportion was only slightly higher— 3.8 percent—for Latino students. This did not mean, though, that non-Hispanic whites had more than their proportional share of places in the top-eighth group. In fact, 12.4 percent of California's white 12th-graders ranked in the top 12.5 percent. The only group of overachievers was Asian Americans. An astonishing 31.5 percent met the requirements for admission. Asian-American students were 2.5 times more likely than their white classmates to qualify for admission to the University of California—a stunning achievement. At the two most prestigious and competitive schools in the UC system—Berkeley and UCLA—four out of ten students are Asian American. Remarkably, they outnumber whites on both campuses, even though there are four times as many whites as Asians in the population of California as a whole.

These huge racial disparities, it should be noted, cannot be blamed on the allegedly discriminatory nature of the SATs.[2] A 1997 study by the UC administration demolishes that common argument.[3] It found that if grades alone determined who is UC-eligible, the number of Hispanic students admitted would rise slightly—by 5 percent. The proportion of Asians would decline a bit—by 3 percent. The two groups most affected would be blacks and whites, but the effects would be precisely the opposite of what SAT critics maintain. The number of blacks admitted would *decline* by 18 percent if the SAT were eliminated from consideration, and the number of whites would *rise* by 17 percent. The racial mix of the entering class would have looked even less balanced racially than it actually was with SAT scores factored in.

Suppose that we wanted to make the student body of the University of California more representative of the population of the state. Proportional representation is the norm implicit in all proposals for engineering "diversity" by means of racial double standards in admissions. Bowen and Bok, we believe, are being disingenuous when they deny that they advocate proportional representation at elite schools. They may not insist upon going all the way to precise racial and ethnic proportionality, and indeed the pool of "qualified" black and Hispanic applicants, even by their expansive definition, is too small to attain proportionality. But the central theme of their long book is that without racial preferences, not enough non-Asian minorities would attend elite colleges, although it's not clear how they can conclude that a freshman class that is, say, 2 to 3 percent black does not have enough African Americans without some standard of what a sufficient share would be. And what could that standard be except the black share of the total population?

California could make the UC student body match the racial mix of the state's population by taking Bowen and Bok's relativistic conception of merit to its logical conclusion. It could simply declare that the top 12.5 percent of students *from each racial group* are qualified. If merit is relative to social circumstances, why not? That would quadruple black enrollment, triple Latino enrollment, and leave the white share of UC-eligibles completely unchanged.

The only losers would be Asian Americans, whose share would be cut by nearly two-thirds (dropping from 31.5 percent to 12.5 percent). The performance of an Asian-American high school student who hoped to attend the University of California would then be appraised not in comparison to all other students in the state but relative to that of other Asian Americans. People of Asian descent would be rejected even though their academic records were far stronger than those of whites, as well as blacks and Hispanics.[4] What principled objection could Bowen and Bok make to that? For them, after all, "fairness" in admissions does not mean that "grades and test scores must always be considered more important than other qualities and characteristics, so that no student with a B average can be accepted as long as students with As are being turned down.'"

Employing racial double standards in admissions, we have demonstrated in detail, elsewhere, does not have the benign effects Bowen and Bok attribute to them, and has many unintended negative consequences we lack the space to spell out here.[5] Suffice it to say that racial preferences reinforce the dreadful stereotype that blacks just aren't academically talented. And they involve the arbitrary assignment of individuals to racial and ethnic categories, and assume it is legitimate to offer them different opportunities depending upon the group to which they have been assigned. They state that race-neutral admissions are "unworthy of our country's ideals" and seem to believe that the sorting of American citizens along lines of race and ethnicity is what the framers of the Fourteenth Amendment had in mind. It is true that judging citizens by the color of their skin is indeed as American as apple pie. But the civil rights warriors of the 1950s and 1960s did not put their lives on the line to perpetuate such terrible habits of mind, we firmly believe, and their vision of a color-blind society was embodied in the Civil Rights Act of 1964.

In the concluding pages of their book, Bowen and Bok issue a warning. If forced to choose, today's educational leaders will see creating a certain racial mix on campus as more important than maintaining intellectual standards. Here we have a breathtakingly candid statement of the priorities of two of the most distinguished figures in higher education today—priorities that reflect those of the higher education establishment as a whole. Intellectual excellence should be sacrificed on the altar of diversity.

This repugnant trade-off would not be necessary, of course, if we concentrated our efforts on closing the yawning racial gap in educational performance among elementary and secondary school pupils. The massive database compiled by the National Assessment of Educational Progress reveals that the average African-American high school senior today reads at the same level as the average white or Asian in the eighth grade, and Hispanics do little better. Racial differentials are even sharper at the extremes of the distribution. Black and Latino high school graduates with academic records that would qualify them for admission to elite colleges and universities are in pathetically short supply, as the California evidence cited above makes clear.

As long as the average black high school senior reads at the eighth-grade level, efforts to engineer parity in the academy are doomed to failure. For a generation now, racial preferences in higher education have been a pernicious palliative that has deflected our attention from the real problem: the need for much better schooling in the pre-K–12 years. That desperate need is *the* civil rights issue of our time.

Notes

1. The history of Jewish admissions quotas at Harvard, Yale, and Princeton is well told in Marcia Graham Synnott, *The Half-Opened Door: Discrimination and Admissions at Harvard, Yale, and Princeton* (Westport, CT: Greenwood Press, 1979). Synnott's account is too soft on Harvard, though, because key internal Harvard documents were not open to scholars when her research was being conducted. For the full story, based upon much newly available evidence, see Morton Keller and Phyllis Keller, *Making Harvard Modern: The Rise of America's University* (New York: Oxford University Press, 2001), which also includes disturbing evidence of Harvard's reluctance to appoint Jews to the faculty in the 1930s and 1940s.
2. See our critical appraisals of the most popular recent book attacking the SATs, Nicolas Lemann's *The Big Test* (1999): Stephan Thernstrom, "Status Anxiety," *National Review*, December 6, 1999, and Abigail Thernstrom, "Shooting the Messenger," *Times Literary Supplement*, June 9, 2000.
3. University of California, Office of the President, Student Academic Services, *University of California Follow-up Analyses of the 1996 CPEC Eligibility Study* (Berkeley, CA: 1997).
4. If this seems too fanciful, it should be noted that for many years the best public high school in San Francisco, Lowell High, operated a racial quota that worked exactly this way. An examination was used to sift out applicants, and Chinese-American students had to get a higher score than other Asians, with a lower cutoff score for whites and a still lower one for blacks and Hispanics. The San Francisco Unified School District was forced to abandon the system in 1999, after it was sued by Chinese parents complaining that the system deprived their children of the equal protection of the laws guaranteed them by the Fourteenth Amendment.

5. For a detailed and highly critical evaluation of Bowen and Bok's work, see Stephan Thernstrom and Abigail Thernstrom, "Reflections on *The Shape of the River*," *UCLA Law Review* 46, June 1999. A somewhat shorter version of this paper that includes newer evidence is "Racial Preferences in Higher Education: An Assessment of the Evidence," in *One America? Political Leadership, National Identity, and the Dilemmas of Diversity,* ed. Stanley A. Renshon (Washington, D.C.: Georgetown University Press, 2001).

Diversity

George Sher

My topic in this article is the argument that preferential treatment is needed to increase diversity in educational institutions and the workplace. Although this argument has achieved considerable currency, and although it is often thought to sidestep the complications that arise when preferential treatment is viewed as a form of compensation, its normative basis has rarely been made explicit. Thus, one aim of my discussion is simply to explore the different forms that the diversity argument can take. However, a further and more substantive aim is to show that its alleged advantages are illusory—that in every version, the appeal to diversity raises difficult questions whose most plausible answers turn on tacit appeals to past wrongdoing.

I

Justifications of preferential treatment come in two main types. Arguments of one type—often called backward looking—make essential reference to the discrimination and injustice that blacks, women, and members of certain other groups have suffered in the past. These arguments urge that current group members be given preference in employment or admission to educational institutions to make amends for or rectify the effects of such wrongdoing—to put things right or, as far as possible, "make the victims whole."[1] By contrast, the other type of justification—often called forward looking—makes *no* essential

Reprinted from *Philosophy and Public Affairs* 28, no. 2 (1999). Copyright © 1999 by Princeton University Press. Reprinted by permission of Princeton University Press.

reference to past wrongdoing, but instead defends preferential treatment entirely as a means to some desirable future goal.[2] Even when the goal is to eliminate inequalities or disadvantages that *were in fact* caused by past wrongdoing, the reason for eliminating them is not *that* they were caused by past wrongdoing. Rather, their continued existence is said to violate some purely *non*historical principle or ideal—for example, the principle of utility or some ideal of equality.[3]

Of the two types of argument, the forward-looking type is often viewed as more straightforward. Those who look exclusively to the future are spared both the daunting task of documenting the effects of past injustice on specific individuals and the even more difficult task of specifying *how much* better off any given individual would now be in its absence. In a more theoretical vein, they need not answer the troublesome question of whether (and if so why) we must compensate persons who would not even have existed, and so *a fortiori* would not be better off, if historical wrongs such as slavery had not taken place; and neither need they specify how many generations must elapse before claims to compensation lose their force.[4] Perhaps for these reasons, defenders of preferential treatment seem increasingly inclined to eschew the backward-looking approach and to cast their lot with forward-looking arguments.

It seems to me, however, that this strategy is badly misguided for two distinct but related reasons: first, because the forward-looking defenses of preferential treatment are only superficially less problematic than their backward-looking counterparts, and, second, because the most promising way of rectifying their inadequacies is to reintroduce precisely the sorts of reference to the past that their proponents have sought to avoid. Although a full elaboration of these claims is beyond my scope, I can at least illustrate them with a few observations about the utilitarian variant of the forward-looking approach.

For no less than any backward-looking defender of preferential treatment, a utilitarian defender must answer some hard questions of both an empirical and a theoretical nature. On the empirical side, he must explain why it is reasonable to expect the benefits of preferential treatment to outweigh its costs. The costs that are often cited include the losses of efficiency that occur when less-than-best-qualified applicants are chosen, the hostility and suspicion of the bypassed candidates who believe—rightly or wrongly—that their efforts and accomplishments have been ignored, the more subtle effects of preference on those who believe they have received it, and the damaging balkanization of public life that many consider to flow from policies centered on group membership. To show that these costs are less weighty than some equally heterogenous collection of benefits, one would need an integrative argument of a type that no one has even begun to provide. In addition, on the more theoretical side, a utilitarian must explain why, if we are obligated or permitted to discriminate in favor of minorities and women when doing so would maximize utility, we are not similarly obligated or permitted to discriminate *against* the members of these groups when doing *that* would maximize utility. Although a good deal has been written about each topic, I think it is fair to say that the empirical situation remains too complex to assess with any confidence and that the theoretical challenge has not been convincingly met.[5]

These observations suggest that the apparently greater simplicity of at least the utilitarian version of the forward-looking approach is largely illusory. But in addition, they lend credence to two further and even more important points, one concerning the underlying structure of the utilitarian argument, the other concerning the thinking of those who advance it.

The further point about the argument's structure is that anyone who defends preferential treatment on the grounds that it maximizes utility, yet insists that mere utility can never justify outright racial or sexual discrimination, is committed to the view that blacks and women differ from white males in some morally important dimension. Because intrinsic differences do not seem relevant, the crucial difference seems apt to lie in the histories of the respective groups;[6] and the most pertinent historical facts are of course those of discrimination and injustice. Thus, if selecting a less-than-best-qualified applicant is to be an acceptable way of promoting utility when the chosen applicant is black or female but not when that applicant is a white male, the reason is very likely to be that blacks and women, but not white males, were often treated unjustly in the past.

The other further point that needs to be made is simply that this reasoning is very likely to have shaped many people's actual beliefs. When someone rejects all forms of racial and sexual discrimination but defends preferential treatment on utilitarian grounds—and, we may add, when someone rejects racial and sexual discrimination but defends preferential treatment on *egalitarian* grounds—the best explanation of his willingness to set aside his usual merit-based standards is that he takes the exception to be warranted by the pressing need to rectify the continuing effects of past injustice.[7] Also, given both the salience of that injustice and the moral passion with which defenders of preferential treatment often press their case, I suspect that many who defend that practice on utilitarian grounds are moved less by their high degree of confidence in its favorable cost-benefit ratio than by the quite different thought that it is especially important to benefit members of groups whose disadvantages were wrongfully inflicted. And, along similar lines, I strongly suspect that the reason many favor preferential treatment to mitigate inequalities that follow racial and sexual lines, yet are quite willing to tolerate many other inequalities (including the very inequalities of reward that make some positions worth distributing preferentially), is precisely that they view only the former inequalities as having resulted from previous wrongdoing.

My topic here, however, is neither the general contrast between the forward- and backward-looking defenses of preferential treatment nor the prospects for mounting a successful utilitarian or egalitarian defense. Instead, I mention these matters only to frame what I want to say about a different forward-looking defense that has recently come to the fore. This new defense is, of course, the one I mentioned at the outset—the argument that preferential treatment is justified by the need to promote racial, sexual, and ethnic diversity in such crucial sectors of our society as the academy and the workplace. A bit more precisely, it is the argument that preferential treatment is justified when, and because, it moves us closer to a situation in which the holders of every (desirable) type of job and position include representatives of all racial, sexual, and ethnic groups in rough proportion to their overall numbers.

The rhetoric of this new argument is all around us. Its ideal of diversity informs such phrases as "underrepresented group," and is also implicit in President Clinton's call for a cabinet that "looks like America." Yet just because the diversity argument is generally advanced by politicians and others with political agendas—bureaucrats, academic administrators, and the like—it is seldom formulated with much precision or care. Thus, before we can hope to assess its claims, we must get clearer about what these are. That means asking both why diversity should be conceived primarily in racial, sexual, and ethnic terms and why diversity as so conceived is morally important. To these questions, I now turn.

II

Why is racial, sexual, and ethnic diversity morally important? It is a measure of how entrenched this ideal has become that the very question has a heretical sound. However, like many other heresies, this one is all the more worth committing because it challenges a rarely examined orthodoxy.

I can envision four possible ways of arguing that racial, sexual, and ethnic diversity is morally important. To show this, someone might argue that such diversity is either (1) a requirement of justice or (2) intrinsically valuable or (3) conducive to the general welfare or (4) conducive to some value *other* than well-being. However, as we will see, each version of the diversity argument remains vulnerable to essentially the same objection that I advanced against the other forward-looking defenses of preferential treatment—namely, that when we ask why the argument focuses only on certain groups, we are invariably thrown back on the injustice or discrimination that their past members have suffered.

Consider first the claim that diversity is a requirement of justice. To defend this claim, one must first specify the relevant conception of justice and then show why it requires that every desirable job and position be distributed among all racial, sexual, and ethnic groups in rough proportion to their numbers. Although there are obviously many ways of filling in the blanks, I shall consider only two that I think may actually exert some influence. Of these two

proposals, one construes racial, sexual, and ethnic groups as morally fundamental entities with claims of justice of their own, while the other takes these
groups to be only derivatively relevant.

Suppose, first, that racial, sexual, and ethnic groups do themselves have
claims of justice; and suppose, further, that the best theory of justice is egalitarian. In that case, the best theory of justice will require that all racial, sexual, and
ethnic groups be made roughly equally well off. Because such groups are not
organized entities, and so are incapable either of having experiences or of pursuing goals, their well-being cannot reside either in the quality of their subjective states or in their success in achieving their goals. Instead, each group's
well-being must be a function of the well-being of its individual members,
which in turn can be expected to vary with the members' income and social
standing. Because these connections hold, any society that wishes to implement a conception of justice that requires that all racial, sexual, and ethnic
groups be made equally well off may indeed have to distribute all desirable jobs
and positions among all relevant groups in rough proportion to their numbers.

Here, then, is one way of grounding the case for racial, sexual, and ethnic
diversity in a broader conception of justice. But should we accept this argument? Elsewhere, I have contended that racial, sexual, and ethnic groups are in
fact *un*likely to have independent claims of justice;[8] I also doubt that the best
theory of justice is straightforwardly egalitarian. However, in the current discussion, I shall simply grant both premises and focus only on the argument's further assumption that not all groups, but only some subset that includes racial,
sexual, and ethnic groups, have independent claims of justice.

Why, exactly, must the argument make this further assumption? One answer
is simply that if enough other groups *did* have independent claims of justice,
then even distributing every desirable position among all racial, sexual, and
ethnic groups in exact proportion to their numbers would at best eliminate
only a small fraction of a society's unjust inequalities. However, while this
answer is not wrong, it does not go far enough. The more decisive answer is that
if enough other groups also had independent claims of justice, then no increase
in a society's diversity could possibly bring *any* increase in its overall justice.

To see why this is so, consider a simple case. Letting "B1," "B2," etc., designate individual blacks, "W1," "W2," etc., designate individual whites, and "D"
and "U" designate desirable and undesirable positions, suppose the initial distribution of desirable and undesirable positions among blacks and whites
within a society is

B1U, B2U, B3U, B4U
W1D, W2D, W3D, W4D

Suppose, further, that as a result of a campaign to increase racial diversity, this
distribution is changed to

B1D, B2D, B3U, B4U
W1U, W2U, W3D, W4D

After this change, the society may appear to be at least marginally more just, since whatever inequalities remain, at least one significant inequality—the one that initially obtained between blacks and whites—has now been eliminated.

Yet if enough other groups also have moral standing, then the gain in racial diversity will mean *no* overall increase in the society's justice; for the new equality between the groups of blacks and whites will be precisely matched by a new *in*equality between the mixed groups [W1, W2, B3, B4] and [B1, B2, W3, W4]. Before the campaign to increase diversity, the distribution of desirable and undesirable positions between the two mixed groups was

W1D, W2D, B3U, B4U
B1U, B2U, W3D, W4D

Afterwards, it is

W1U, W2U, B3U, B4U
B1D, B2D, W3D, W4D

Because the first mixed group has thus gone from having half of the society's desirable positions to having none while the second has gone from having half to having all, the loss of equality between these groups will exactly offset the gain in equality between blacks and whites. Assuming that all four groups are equally significant, the society's overall level of equality, and so too its degree of justice, will therefore be unaffected by its increased racial diversity. Thus, if anyone wants to argue that racial, sexual, and ethnic diversity *is* a requirement of justice among groups, he must deny that mixed groups such as [W1, W2, B3, B4] and [B1, B2, W3, W4] have the same moral status as natural groups such as [B1, B2, B3, B4] and [W1, W2, W3, W4].

But on what basis could someone deny this? One obvious difference between racial and mixed groups is that skin color and other traits associated with race (and, by extension, sex and ethnicity) are salient in a way that the membership in a mixed group is not. However, this will not yield the desired conclusion because the mere fact that a trait is salient does not endow it with any special moral status. Nor, despite what some have said, can it plausibly be argued that racial, sexual, and ethnic groups are more significant than others because their members identify far more with the fortunes and accomplishments of other group members (and with the fortunes of the group itself) than do the members of most other groups. Here again, the problem is not that this premise is false—it plainly contains much truth—but rather that it does not yield the desired conclusion. For, at least offhand, what really follows from a high degree of mutual identification within a group is not that the group *itself* has any special moral standing, but only that the well-being of each member is connected to the well-being of many other members in a rather distinctive way.[9]

There are, of course, many other possible ways of arguing that mixed groups lack the moral status of racial, sexual, and ethnic groups. Thus, the mere fact that the cited arguments fail is hardly decisive. Still, in the absence of any better argument, the best explanation of the impulse to single out certain racial, sexual, and ethnic groups is again that it reflects a desire to make amends for (or rectify the lingering effects of) the discrimination that their past members have suffered. As Paul Taylor has put it, the guiding thought appears to be that the relevant groups were "as it were, *created* by the original unjust practice[s]" (chap. 4, p. 15). I think, in fact, that this way of formulating the moral importance of past injustice is highly misleading, but I shall not argue that point here. Instead, in keeping with my broader theme, I shall simply observe that if anyone *were* to elaborate the diversity argument in these terms, he would be abandoning all pretense that his argument is purely forward looking.

III

What, next, of the suggestion that racial, sexual, and ethnic diversity is a requirement of justice for individuals? Unlike its predecessor, this suggestion does not presuppose a problematic moral ontology. Yet just because the suggestion does not construe groups as morally fundamental, it raises a difficult new question—namely, why should justice for individuals call for *any* special distribution of positions among groups?

Although this question, too, can be answered in various ways, I shall consider only the single answer that I think proponents of diversity would be most likely to give. Put most briefly, that answer is, first, that the operative principle of justice is one of equality of opportunity, and, second, that a lack of racial, sexual, and ethnic diversity is significant precisely because it shows that opportunities remain *un*equal. Even though legal barriers are a thing of the past, the fact that relatively few blacks, women, and members of other minorities hold well-paying, authoritative positions is often viewed as compelling evidence that the members of these groups have lacked, and continue to lack, equal opportunity. That in turn may be thought to show that using preferential treatment to bring about their representation within desirable professions in proportion to their numbers is justified by the fact that it will make opportunities *more* equal.

But, whatever else is true, the last step of this argument is surely questionable; for if a given group is now "underrepresented" within a profession, then bringing its representation into proportion with its numbers in the general population will require that it be *over*represented in the profession's new hires. For example, if group G comprises 20 percent of the overall population but only 10 percent of profession P, then any attempt to diversify P will require that *more* than 20 percent of P's *new* members be Gs. Thus, assuming that genuine equality of opportunity exists only when each group that comprises n percent of the population wins n percent of the competitions for each type of position—and this, of course, is precisely the assumption that is needed to support the inference that opportunities for Gs have been unequal up to now—the hiring of Gs at a rate greater than 20 percent must entail the denial of equal opportunity to at least some current non-Gs. When preferential treatment is used to promote the proportional representation of all racial, sexual, and ethnic groups, its immediate effect is therefore not to make opportunities more equal, but only to compound any earlier inequalities that may have existed.

This observation does not show that such uses of preferential treatment cannot make opportunities more equal; but it does show that any relevant gains must be long-term rather than immediate. The point must be not that opportunities will be more equal *when* the preferential treatment is used, but rather that they will be more equal *afterwards*. This will be true (the argument must run) because the proportional distribution of desirable positions among all racial, sexual, and ethnic groups will convey to the members of previously excluded groups the message that people like them can successfully acquire and hold such positions, and that in turn will raise the aspirations of many. Because this reasoning appeals to the effects of diversity upon the motivation of future group members, it is, in essence, a variant of the familiar "role model" argument.

But motivation is a dangerous topic for someone who seeks to link diversity to equal opportunity to introduce; for if he is willing to say that the *future* distribution of desirable positions among different groups will be affected by the motivation as well as the skills of their members, then he can hardly deny that the *current* distribution of desirable positions is likely to have been similarly affected. Thus, in particular, he must acknowledge that if a given group is underrepresented within a profession, at least some, and perhaps much, of its underrepresentation is probably traceable to its members' attitudes and choices. This complicates what was initially proffered as a straightforward inference from "some groups are underrepresented in desirable positions" to "the members of those groups have not had equal opportunities to compete"; for a group's underrepresentation within a given field will *not* reflect a lack of equal opportunity if the majority of its members have freely chosen to pursue a different path.

It would, of course, be foolish to suppose either that all preferences have been innocently acquired or that all choices have been freely made. Someone whose low aspirations were determined by a culture forged in oppression has been harmed by that oppression as definitely, if not as directly, as the grandparents who were simply not allowed to work or learn. Thus, if the choices that led to a group's underrepresentation within a profession were expressions of such attitudes, it may be true both that the group's underrepresentation is largely a reflection of its members' choices *and* that the members who made the choices were denied equal opportunity.

But, once again, it is precisely the role of past injustice that makes this suggestion compelling. If the culture that causes the members of a group to acquire counterproductive preferences is itself an effect of past wrongdoing—if, for instance, that culture is an adaptive response to generations of slavery, discrimination, and Jim Crow laws—then we will quite naturally classify those preferences among the mechanisms through which the opportunities of the current group members are kept unequal. But if, instead, the preferences responsible for a group's underrepresentation are manifestations of an innate disposition of the kind that the maternal urge is sometimes said to exemplify—if, as some have claimed, female biology is (statistical) destiny—then the claim that the group's members lack equal opportunity will have no force. Thus, in this context, too, what at first looks like a purely forward-looking defense of preferential treatment turns out, on closer examination, to have an important backward-looking component.

If all preferences and attitudes were either innate or else the results of past wrongdoing, we could end this part of our discussion here. However, in fact, these alternatives are not exhaustive. Many people have acquired their current attitudes from cultures that did *not* evolve in response to wrongdoing or oppression; and such attitudes, too, can lead the relevant groups to be underrepresented within professions. It may be, for example, that the reason relatively few members of a given group have pursued careers that require academic success or extended training is simply that the group's culture, which was shaped by its earlier agrarian lifestyle, does not attach much value to education. If internalizing this attitude also counts as being denied equal opportunity, and if increasing the group's presence within various professions would help eventually to dispel the attitude, then using preferential treatment to promote such diversity may indeed be justified on purely forward-looking grounds.

How significant is this challenge to my thesis that every ostensibly forward-looking defense of diversity has a backward-looking core? That depends, I think, on the answers to several further questions. It depends, most obviously, on whether equal opportunity *does* require that no one be brought up in a culture that instills attitudes unconducive to success in the modern world; but it depends, as well, on whether equal opportunity trumps respect for ancestral cultures; whether increasing diversity would effectively diminish the transmission of counterproductive attitudes; and whether, even if it would, we can more effectively alter these attitudes in some other way (or can simply wait until they are transformed in the American melting pot as were the attitudes of previous generations of immigrants). I suspect that a careful investigation of these questions would at least mitigate if not eliminate the challenge to my thesis; but I cannot undertake that investigation here. Thus, pending further discussion, this issue must simply remain unresolved.

IV

So far, I have discussed only the first of the four possible arguments for racial, sexual, and ethnic diversity. That argument, which construes such diversity as a requirement of justice, predictably raised a variety of complications. By contrast, the second and third arguments—that diversity is intrinsically valuable and that it is conducive to the general welfare—raise fewer new issues and so can be dealt with much more quickly.

The challenge to someone who holds that racial, sexual, and ethnic diversity is *intrinsically* valuable is to provide some justification of this claim that goes beyond the bare fact that he believes it. He cannot simply assert that the claim is self-evident because such assertions are equally available to his opponents; yet once we ask what else can be said, we almost immediately run out of argument. I say "almost immediately" because many of the metaphors that are commonly used in this connection—for example, descriptions of a diverse society as a tapestry or a "gorgeous mosaic"—can themselves be viewed as arguments that the relevant intrinsic values are familiar aesthetic ones. However, I hope it goes without saying that the aesthetic appeal of a given pattern of distribution is not a proper basis for any decision about social policy.

Because the appeal to intrinsic value is essentially a nonargument, I cannot pinpoint the exact place at which it goes historical. Yet just because that appeal has so little to recommend it, the best explanation of whatever influence it has—and, though I cannot prove it, I think it does have some influence—is again that it provides cover for a policy whose real aim is to benefit members of unjustly disadvantaged groups.

The third possible argument for diversity—that it is conductive to the general welfare—is very different; for unlike the appeal to intrinsic value, this argument can be developed in various ways. One obvious possibility is to exploit our earlier observation that the members of many racial, sexual, and ethnic groups identify strongly with the fortunes and accomplishments of other group members; for given this mutual identification, increasing diversity will benefit not only those group members who actually gain prestigious, well-paying positions, but also the many others who take pride and pleasure in their success. Alternatively or in addition, it can be argued that working closely with members of unfamiliar groups breaks down barriers and disrupts stereotypes, and that increasing racial, sexual, and ethnic diversity will therefore increase overall well-being by fostering understanding and harmony.

Because diversity yields these and other benefits, there is an obvious case for the use of preferential treatment to promote it. However, when the issue is framed in these terms, the diversity argument is no longer an alternative to a utilitarian defense of preferential treatment, but rather is itself such a defense. Despite its interposition of diversity, its essential message is precisely that preferential treatment is justified by its beneficial consequences. Thus, if my conjecture about the other utilitiarian defenses was correct—if the disparity between the difficulties they confront and the confidence with which they are advanced suggests that their proponents' real impulse is compensatory—then that conjecture must apply here too.

V

That leaves only the fourth argument for diversity's importance—the argument that it promotes some value *other* than well-being. Although there are many non-welfarist values to which appeal might theoretically be made, the only live version of this argument is one that appeals to the intellectual values of the academy.

That increasing racial, sexual, and ethnic diversity will advance the academic enterprise is an article of faith among many academics. Neil Rudenstine, the president of Harvard, expressed the conventional wisdom this way: "A diverse educational environment challenges [students] to explore ideas and arguments at a deeper level—to see issues from various sides, to rethink their own premises, to achieve the kind of understanding that comes only from testing their own hypotheses against those of people with other views."[10] Although these claims obviously do not support all forms of preferential treatment—they are, for example, irrelevant both to nonacademic hiring and to contractual "set-asides"—they do purport to justify, through an appeal to values internal to the academy's own mission, both preferential admission to many educational institutions and preferential hiring across the curricular spectrum.

Like many of the other arguments we have considered, this one can itself be fleshed out in various ways. Some of its proponents, including Rudenstine himself, stress the value *to students* of exposure to different perspectives, while others stress the value of diversity in research. Of those who focus on research, some argue that including hitherto excluded groups will open up new areas of investigation, while others emphasize the value of diverse challenges to all hypotheses, including, or especially, hypotheses in traditional, well-worked areas. Of those who emphasize challenges to hypotheses, some stress the importance of confronting all hypotheses with the broadest possible range of potentially falsifying tests, while others focus on exposing the hidden biases of investigators.[11] Because the appeal to diversity's contribution to intellectual inquiry is so protean, I cannot work systematically through its variants, but will pose only a single question that applies to each. That question, predictably enough, is why we should single out the contributions of any small set of groups such as those on the official affirmative action list.

For even if diversity yields every one of the intellectual benefits that are claimed for it, why should we benefit most when the scholarly community contains substantial numbers of blacks, women, Hispanics, (American) Indians,

Aleuts, and Chinese Americans? Why not focus instead, or in addition, on Americans of Eastern European, Arabic, or (Asian) Indian extraction? For that matter, can't we achieve even greater benefit by extending preference to *native* Africans, Asians, Arabs, and Europeans? And why understand diversity only in terms of gender, ethnicity, and national origin? Why should a population that is diverse in this dimension provide any more educational or scholarly benefit than one that is ethnically homogeneous but includes suitable numbers of gays, religious fundamentalists, the young, the old, the handicapped, ex-military officers, conservatives, Marxists, Mormons, and blue-collar workers? These groups, too, have characteristic concerns, types of experience, and outlooks on the world. Thus, why not also monitor the degree to which *they* are represented in academic circles? Why not also give *them* preference when they are not represented in proportion to their numbers?[12] And why, to realize the benefits of the female perspective, must we further increase the number of women when the academy already contains far more women than members of many other groups with distinct perspectives?

The most salient features of the groups on the official list is of course the discrimination they have suffered. This may not entirely explain why just these groups are included—that may in part be traceable to the play of political forces—but it does explain the prominence of such core groups as blacks and women. This strongly suggests that the current argument is also covertly backward looking. However, before we can draw this conclusion, we must consider an important alternative—namely, that the real reason for concentrating on previously oppressed groups is not that their members alone are owed compensation, but rather that beliefs and attitudes shaped by oppression are better suited than others to advance educational or scholarly aims.

For although we obviously cannot assume that all the members of any group think alike, a history of discrimination may indeed affect the way many of a group's members tend to view the world. In addition to the already-noted high degree of collective identification, the perspective of the oppressed is often said to include a keen awareness of the motives, prejudices, and hidden agendas of others, a heightened sense of the oppressive effects of even seemingly benign social structures, and a strong commitment to social change. As a corollary, that perspective may include a degree of antagonism toward received opinion and a certain impatience with abstraction. Thus, the question that remains to be addressed is whether, and if so how, any of these beliefs, attitudes, or traits might make a special contribution to education or research.

Here it is important to distinguish between the educational or scholarly value of *learning about* the perspective of the oppressed and the educational or scholarly value of *actually taking* that perspective. This distinction is important because some who urge wide exposure to the relevant beliefs, attitudes, etc., do appear to believe that what matters is simply learning about them. That, at any rate, is one natural interpretation of the common claim that diversity is important because it acquaints nonminority students with the hardships and obstacles that many members of minority groups confront daily, and because it teaches nonminority students that many members of these groups consider themselves disenfranchised and do not trust social institutions whose necessity and justice others take for granted. Yet while such knowledge may contribute significantly to mutual understanding and social harmony, the beliefs, attitudes, traits, and experiences that are characteristic of oppressed groups are in the end only one class of facts among innumerable others. Considered simply as objects of study—and that is how we must consider them if the current argument is not to be yet another tributary of the great utilitarian river[13]—the beliefs, attitudes, traits, and experiences of the oppressed are no more important than those of the nonoppressed, which in turn are no more important than indefinitely many other possible objects of inquiry.

Thus, to give their variant of the argument a fighting chance, those who attach special educational and scholarly value to the perspective of the oppressed must take the other path. They must locate its special educational or scholarly value not in anyone's *coming to know* that oppressed groups hold certain beliefs, attitudes, etc., but rather in the contribution of those beliefs and attitudes to the acquisition of *other* knowledge. Their argument must be that this perspective uniquely enhances our collective ability to pose or resolve questions across much of the intellectual spectrum. To show that the perspective of the oppressed generates new lines of inquiry, friends of diversity often cite the tendency of women to pursue scientific research with humanitarian rather than militaristic applications and the contributions that various minorities have made to history and other fields by studying their own past and present. To show that this perspective contributes to the investigation of established topics, they point out that black and female investigators tend to be specially attuned to the inclusion of blacks and women in experimental control groups, that black students bring to the study of law a well-founded mistrust of the police, and that enhanced sensitivity to power relations has opened up fruitful new ways of interpreting literary texts.

We certainly must agree that the beliefs, attitudes, and traits of oppressed groups have made important contributions to the way academic questions are now formulated and addressed. However, what friends of diversity must show is not merely that these beliefs, attitudes, and traits make *some* significant contribution to effective inquiry, but that they are *more* conducive to it, all things considered, than any of the alternative mixtures that would emerge if there were no affirmative action or if preference were given to other sorts of groups. To see what is wrong with this stronger conclusion, we need only revisit the argument's two main claims, that the members of oppressed groups are likely to pose novel questions and that they are likely to bring novel perspectives to familiar ones.

For, first, oppressed groups are hardly the only ones whose concerns and interests can be expected to channel research in some directions rather than others. Just as the recent influx of blacks, Hispanics, and women has led to a variety of new scientific, historical, and literary projects, and to various new interpretive strategies, so would any comparable influx of (say) Baptists, Muslims, Marxists, or vegetarians. More subtly, any admissions policy that self-consciously sought out persons with certain traits of intellect or character would also greatly influence what people study and how they study it. The academic agenda would evolve in one way if students and faculty were selected primarily for (say) altruism, in another if they were selected for intellectual honesty, and in yet others if they were selected for dogged persistence, intellectual playfulness, or literary imagination and a flair for language. Indeed, even without any such attempt to depart from traditional merit-based selection criteria, the endless play of human creativity can be expected to ensure continuing novelty in the projects and approaches that find adherents. The history of intellectual inquiry prior to affirmative action is hardly a chronicle of stagnation.

Nor, second, are the beliefs, attitudes, and traits of the oppressed any more likely to be helpful in *answering* intellectual questions than any number of others. There are, to be sure, many contexts in which antagonism toward received opinion, impatience with useless abstraction, and a desire to unearth or vindicate the contributions of a particular group do make important contributions to the solution of a problem—but in many other contexts, these traits and attitudes are distracting and counterproductive. They are, for example, more likely to be a hindrance than a help if one is trying to construct a mathematical proof, evaluate the properties of a new chemical compound, understand how neurotransmitters work, or write a computer program. Where such tasks are concerned, the biases of others are irrelevant unless they issue in bad inferences or dishonesty in handling data—flaws which the standard techniques of review and replication seem well suited to discover. Neither skepticism about others' motives nor a deep commitment to social change seems likely to generate many potentially falsifying hypotheses.

My own view is that we will make the most progress if we simply stock the academy with persons who display the traditional academic excellences to the highest degree. The students and faculty members who are most likely to help us progress toward true beliefs, powerful explanations, deep understanding, and a synoptic worldview are just the ones with the greatest analytical ability, the most imagination, the best memory, and the strongest desire to pursue the truth wherever it leads. However, while these are things that I deeply believe, my argument does not require any premise this strong. Instead, it requires only the much weaker premise that indefinitely many traits of intellect or character are sometimes useful in advancing cognitive or pedagogical aims, and that we have no reason to expect the beliefs and attitudes of the oppressed to be preeminent among these.

This reasoning of course presupposes that the aims of the academy are to be understood in terms of truth, understanding, explanation, and the rest. If they are not—if, for example, the basic aim is instead to promote social change—then the case for favoring the beliefs and attitudes of the oppressed may well be stronger. However, if someone does take the basic aim to be social change, and if he urges the hiring and admission of more members of oppressed groups to expedite the desired changes, then he will no longer be appealing to the very academic values that even his opponents share. He will, instead, be mounting an appeal to some further conception of social justice—one whose evaluation must await its more precise articulation. Thus, pending further discussion, my main thesis—that every major defense of diversity is either incomplete or backward looking—remains intact.

VI

This completes my discussion of the attempt to justify preferential treatment on the grounds that it promotes diversity. The account that has emerged is partly analytical and partly diagnostic. It is analytical in that I have sought to provide clear statements of the most promising arguments for diversity; but it is diagnostic in that I have repeatedly tried to explain why diversity is favored in terms that its proponents themselves would not accept. Although the preferred explanation of why someone believes something is always one that matches (even if it elaborates) his professed reasons, I think my speculations about what really motivates proponents of diversity are justified by the manifest inadequacy of their professed reasons.

The motivation I have stressed—a desire to rationalize the use of preferential treatment to benefit members of previously wronged groups—is a complex mixture of the admirable and the base. It is admirable because it reflects a high-minded conception of what justice requires, base because it substitutes the use of half-truths, half-arguments, and persuasive slogans for a frank willingness to acknowledge what is really at stake. In fact, compensatory justice *is* immensely problematic, and the moral status of preferential treatment is immensely problematic too. We do not advance the cause of justice, but only degrade public discourse, if we blur these difficulties instead of seeking to overcome them.

Notes

I am grateful to Alan Wertheimer, Emily Fox Gordon, and the editors of *Philosophy and Public Affairs* for their helpful comments on an earlier draft of this article.
   1. For two versions of the backward-looking approach, see Judith Jarvis Thomson, chapter 9 of this volume, and my own "Justifying Reverse Discrimination in Employment," chapter 11.

2. For two important early versions of the forward-looking approach, see Ronald Dworkin, *Taking Rights Seriously* (Cambridge, MA: Harvard University Press, 1977), and Thomas Nagel, "Equal Treatment and Compensatory Discrimination," *Philosophy and Public Affairs* 2, no. 4 (summer 1973): 348–63. For an influential recent version, see William G. Bowen and Derek Bok, *The Shape of the River: Long-Term Consequences of Considering Race in College and University Admissions* (Princeton, NJ: Princeton University Press, 1998).

3. As one of the editors of *Philosophy and Public Affairs* has pointed out, there is also another way in which someone might invoke past injustices such as slavery to make the case for preferential treatment. Instead of taking those injustices to show that compensation is owed to black Americans, someone might view them as evidence for "a certain grim view about the country," and hence as singling out certain effects of preferential treatment—in particular, the emergence of a black middle class—as especially important because they show that despite appearances, "the country is not founded on racial exclusion." Although this argument assigns a key evidential role to past injustice, it is said not to be backward looking in my sense because its normative principles make no reference to the past. I shall not comment on the argument except to remark that more needs to be said about what the nation's history of injustice is supposed to be evidence *for*. We hardly need historical evidence to assess either the justice of our current arrangements or the degree to which racism persists now; yet if what the historical evidence suggests (that the nation is "founded on racial exclusion") is itself a claim about the past, then any normative argument in which that claim figures is indeed likely to be backward looking in my sense.

4. For discussion of the first question, see my article "Ancient Wrongs and Modern Rights," *Philosophy and Public Affairs* 10, no. 1 (winter 1981): 3–17; for discussion of the second, see my "Compensation and Transworld Personal Identity," *The Monist* 62, no. 3 (July 1979): 378–91. Both articles are reprinted in my *Approximate Justice: Studies in Non-Ideal Theory* (Lanham, MD: Rowman and Littlefield, 1998), pp. 15–27 and 29–43.

5. For further discussion, see my "Preferential Treatment, the Future, and the Past," *Approximate Justice*, pp. 79–95.

6. It might be suggested that the crucial difference is instead that our society contains far more bias against blacks and women than it does prejudice against white males. However, while racist and sexist attitudes are indeed relevant to the question of which policies *would* maximize utility, they are far less obviously relevant to the question of why it is *legitimate* to maximize utility by discriminating against some groups but not others.

7. The idea of merit-based standards is of course elastic, in that different academic disciplines draw upon very different skills and abilities. It is also true that many who oppose racial and sexual discrimination in university admissions are not similarly opposed to the relaxing of admissions standards for athletes and legacies. Still, even when both points are conceded, it remains clear that the standard objection to such racial and sexual discrimination is precisely that the members of the discriminated-against groups are excluded for reasons independent of their academic promise.

8. The argument appears in "Groups and Justice," *Ethics* 87, no. 1 (October 1977): 81–87; reprinted in *Approximate Justice*, pp. 55–64.

9. Another possible way of arguing that racial and ethnic groups have a status that mixed groups lack is to contend that the members of racial and ethnic groups, but not of mixed groups, share a common culture whose value is distinct from the value of any individual group member's well-being. However, even if shared cultures do have independent value—and this itself is highly controversial—it will remain unclear why their value should support either the conclusion that the well-being of

the groups that share them is also valuable or the conclusion that those groups have special claims of justice. Indeed, these inferences are especially troublesome in the current context because the relevant cultures are ones that developed partly in *response* to poverty and oppression. Also, of course, the current proposal would imply that sexual groups do *not* have special status, since there is no single culture that is common to either men or women.

10. Neil L. Rudenstine, "Why a Diverse Student Body Is So Important," *Chronicle of Higher Education,* April 19, 1996, p. B1.
11. For discussion that touches on both positions, see Elizabeth Anderson, "The Democratic University: The Role of Justice in the Production of Knowledge," *Social Philosophy and Policy* 12, no. 2 (summer 1995): 186–219.
12. For related discussion, see Robert Simon, "Affirmative Action in the University," in *Affirmative Action and the University,* ed. Steven M. Cahn (Philadelphia: Temple University Press, 1993), pp. 74–82.
13. This, in effect, is what the argument would be if someone were to defend its exclusive emphasis on oppressed groups on the grounds that the members of these groups are especially likely to take dissenting positions on the most divisive questions we face, and that it is especially valuable for our society's future leaders to be exposed to forceful statements of such positions.

Preference or Impartiality?

In Favor of Affirmative Action

Tom L. Beauchamp

Affirmative action policies have had their strongest appeal when discrimination that barred groups from desirable institutions persisted although forbidden by law. Policies that establish target goals, timetables, and quotas were initiated to ensure more equitable opportunities by counterbalancing apparently intractable prejudice and systemic favoritism. The policies that were initiated with such lofty ambitions are now commonly criticized on grounds that they establish quotas that unjustifiably elevate the opportunities of members of targeted groups, discriminate against equally qualified or even more qualified members of majorities, and perpetuate racial and sexual paternalism.

Affirmative action policies favoring *groups* have been controversial since President Lyndon Johnson's 1965 executive order that required federal contractors to develop affirmative action policies.[1] Everyone now agrees that *individuals* who have been injured by past discrimination should be made whole for the injury, but it remains controversial whether and how past discrimination against groups justifies preferential treatment for the group's *current* members. Critics of group preferential policies hold that compensating individuals for unfair discrimination can alone be justified, but it is controversial whether individuals can be harmed merely by virtue of a group membership.[2]

Those who support affirmative action and those who oppose it both seek the best means to the same end, a color-blind, sex-blind society. Their goals do not differ. Nor do they entirely disagree over the means. If a color-blind, sex-blind society can be achieved and maintained by legal guarantees of equal

Reprinted from *Journal of Ethics* 2 (1998) by permission of the publisher.

opportunities to all, both parties agree that social policies should be restricted to this means. Here agreement ends. Those who support affirmative action do not believe such guarantees can be fairly and efficiently achieved other than by affirmative action policies. Those who seek an end to affirmative action believe that the goals can be achieved in other ways and that affirmative action policies themselves unjustifiably discriminate. I will be supporting affirmative action policies against this counterposition.

Two Pivotal Concepts

Like virtually all problems in practical ethics, the meaning of a few central terms can powerfully affect one's moral viewpoint. The terms "affirmative action" and "quotas" have proved particularly troublesome, because they have been defined in both minimal and maximal ways. The original meaning of "affirmative action" was minimalist. It referred to plans to safeguard equal opportunity, to protect against discrimination, to advertise positions openly, and to create scholarship programs to ensure recruitment from specific groups.[3] Few now oppose open advertisement and the like, and if this were all that were meant by "affirmative action," few would oppose it. However, "affirmative action" has assumed new and expanded meanings. Today it is typically associated with quotas and preferential policies that target specific groups, especially women or minority members.

I will not favor either the minimalist or the maximalist sense of "affirmative action." I will use the term to refer to positive steps taken to hire persons from groups previously and presently discriminated against, leaving open what will count as a "positive step" to remove discrimination. I thus adopt a broad meaning.

A number of controversies have also centered on the language of *quotas*.[4] A "quota," as I use the term, does not mean that fixed numbers of a group must be admitted, hired, or promoted—even to the point of including less-qualified persons if they are the only available members of a targeted group. Quotas are target numbers or percentages that an employer, admissions office, recruitment committee, and the like sincerely attempt to meet. Less-qualified persons are occasionally hired or promoted under a policy that incorporates quotas; but it is no part of affirmative action or the meaning of "quotas" to hire persons who lack basic qualifications. Quotas are numerically expressible goals pursued in good faith and with due diligence.

The language of "quotas" can be toned down by speaking of hopes, objectives, and guidelines; but cosmetic changes of wording only thinly obscure a policy established to recruit from groups in which the goals are made explicit by numbers. Thus when John Sununu—presumably a strong opponent of quotas—told Secretary of Defense Richard Cheney that he, Sununu, "wanted

30 percent of the remaining 42 top jobs in the Defense Department to be filled by women and minorities,"[5] he was using a quota. Likewise, universities sometimes use quotas when the subtleties of faculty and staff hiring and promotion and student admission make no mention of them. For example, if the chair of a department says the department should hire two to three women in the next five available positions, the formula constitutes a quota, or at least a numerical target.

Reasons typically offered in defense of targeted affirmative action, with or without quotas, are the following: "We have many women students who need and do not have an ample number of role models and mentors." "The provost has offered a group of special fellowships to bring more minorities to the university." "More diversity is much needed in this department." "The goals and mission of this university strongly suggest a need for increased representation of women and minorities." In pursuing these objectives, members of departments and committees commonly act in ways that suggest they willingly endorse what either is or has a strong family resemblance to a specific target.

The Prevalence of Discrimination as the Rationale for Affirmative Action

The moral problem of affirmative action is primarily whether specific targets, including quotas in the broad sense, can legitimately be used. To support affirmative action as a weapon against discrimination is not necessarily to endorse it in all institutions. Racial, sexual, and religious forms of discrimination affecting admission, hiring, and promotion have been substantially reduced in various sectors of American society, and perhaps even completely eliminated in some. The problem is that in other social sectors it is common to encounter discrimination in favor of a favored group or discrimination against disliked, distrusted, unattractive, or neglected groups. The pervasive attitudes underlying these phenomena are the most important background conditions of the debate over affirmative action, and we need to understand these pockets of discrimination in order to appreciate the attractions of affirmative action.

Statistics. Statistics constituting at least prima facie evidence of discrimination in society are readily available. These data indicate that in sizable parts of American society white males continue to receive the highest entry-level salaries when compared to all other social groups; that women with similar credentials and experience to those of men are commonly hired at lower positions or earn lower starting salaries than men and are promoted at one-half the rate of their male counterparts, with the consequence that the gap between salaries and promotion rates is still growing at an increasing rate; that 70 percent or more of white-collar positions are held by women, although they hold only about 10 percent of management positions; that three out of seven U.S. employees occupy white-collar positions, whereas the ratio is but one of seven for African Americans; and, finally, that a significant racial gap in unemployment statistics is a consistent pattern in the United States, with the gap now greatest for college-educated, African-American males.[6] Whether these statistics demonstrate invidious discrimination is controversial, but additional data drawn from empirical studies reinforce the judgment that racial and sexual discrimination are reasons for and perhaps the best explanation of these statistics.

Housing. For example, studies of real estate rentals, housing sales, and home mortgage lending show a disparity in rejection rates—for example, loan rejection rates between white applicants and minority applicants. Wide disparities exist even after statistics are adjusted for economic differences; minority applicants are over 50 percent more likely to be denied a loan than white applicants of equivalent economic status. Other studies indicate that discrimination in sales of houses is prevalent in the United States. Race appears to be as important as socioeconomic status in failing to secure both houses and loans, and studies also show that the approval rate for African Americans increases in lending institutions with an increase in the proportion of minority employees in that institution.[7]

Jobs. A similar pattern is found in employment. In 1985 the Grier Partnership and the Urban League produced independent studies that reveal striking disparities in the employment levels of college-trained African Americans and whites in Washington, D.C., one of the best markets for African Americans. Both studies found that college-trained African Americans have much more difficulty than their white counterparts in securing employment. Both cite discrimination as the major underlying factor.[8]

In a 1991 study by the Urban Institute, employment practices in Washington, D.C., and Chicago were examined. Equally qualified, identically dressed white and African-American applicants for jobs were used to test for bias in the job market, as presented by newspaper-advertised positions. Whites and African Americans were matched identically for speech patterns, age, work experience, personal characteristics, and physical build. Investigators found repeated discrimination against African-American male applicants. The higher the position, the higher the level of discrimination. The white men received job offers three times more often than the equally qualified African Americans who interviewed for the same position. The authors of the study concluded that discrimination against African-American men is "widespread and entrenched."[9]

These statistics and empirical studies help frame racial discrimination in the United States. Anyone who believes that only a narrow slice of surface discrimination exists will be unlikely to agree with what I have been and will be arguing, at least if my proposals entail strong affirmative action measures. By contrast, one who believes that discrimination is securely and almost invisibly entrenched in many sectors of society will be more likely to endorse or at least tolerate resolute affirmative action policies.

Although racism and sexism are commonly envisioned as intentional forms of favoritism and exclusion, intent to discriminate is not a necessary condition of discrimination. Institutional networks can unintentionally hold back or exclude persons. Hiring by personal friendships and word of mouth are common instances, as are seniority systems. Numerical targets are important remedies for these camouflaged areas, where it is particularly difficult to shatter patterns of discrimination and reconfigure the environment.[10]

The U.S. Supreme Court has rightly upheld affirmative action programs with numerically expressed hiring formulas when intended to quash the effects of both intentional and unintentional discrimination.[11] The Court has also maintained that such formulas have sometimes been structured so that they unjustifiably exceed proper limits.[12] The particulars of the cases will determine how we are to balance different interests and considerations.

The Justification of Affirmative Action

This balancing strategy is warranted. Numerical goals or quotas are justified if and only if they are necessary to overcome the discriminatory effects that could not otherwise be eliminated with reasonable efficiency. It is the intractable and often deeply hurtful character of racism and sexism that justifies aggressive policies to remove their damaging effects. The history of affirmative action, though short, is an impressive history of fulfilling once-failed promises, displacing disillusion, and protecting the most vulnerable members of society against demeaning abuse. It has delivered our country from what was little more than a caste system and a companion of apartheid.

We have learned in the process that numerical formulas are sometimes essential tools, sometimes excessive tools, and sometimes permissible but optional tools—depending on the subtleties of the case. We can expect each case to be different, and for this reason we should be cautious about general pronouncements regarding the justifiability of numerical formulas—as well as the merit of merit-based systems and blind systems. The better perspective is that until the facts of particular cases have been carefully assessed, we are not positioned to support or oppose any particular affirmative action policy or its abandonment.

The Supreme Court has allowed these numerical formulas in plans that are intended to combat a manifest imbalance in traditionally segregated job categories (even if the particular workers drawn from minorities were not victims of past discrimination). In *Local 28 v. Equal Employment Opportunity Commission*, a minority hiring goal of 29.23 percent had been established. The Court held that such specific numbers are justified when dealing with persistent or egregious discrimination. The Court found that the history of Local 28 was one of complete "foot-dragging resistance" to the idea of hiring without discrimination in its apprenticeship training programs from minority groups. The Court argued that "affirmative race-conscious relief" may be the only reasonable means to the end of assuring equality of employment opportunities and to eliminate deeply ingrained discriminatory practices.[13]

In a 1989 opinion, by contrast, the Supreme Court held in *City of Richmond v. J. A. Croson* that Richmond, Virginia, officials could not require contractors to set aside 30 percent of their budget for subcontractors who owned "minority business enterprises." This particular plan was not written to remedy the effects of prior or present discrimination. The Court found that *this way* of fixing a percentage based on race, in the absence of evidence of identified discrimination, denied citizens an equal opportunity to compete for subcontracts. Parts of the reasoning in this case were reaffirmed in the 1995 case of *Adarand Constructors Inc. v. Pena.*

Some writers have interpreted *Croson, Adarand,* and the 1997 decision of a three-judge panel of the 9th U.S. Circuit Court of Appeals to the effect that California's voter-approved ban on affirmative action (Proposition 209) is constitutional as the dismantling of affirmative action plans that use numerical goals. Perhaps this prediction will turn out to be correct, but the U.S. Supreme Court has consistently adhered to a balancing strategy that I believe captures the fitting way to frame issues of affirmative action.[14] It allows us to use race and sex as relevant bases of policies if and only if it is essential to do so in order to achieve a larger and justified social purpose.

These reasons for using race and sex in policies are far distant from the role of these properties in invidious discrimination. Racial discrimination and sexual discrimination typically spring from feelings of superiority and a sense that other groups deserve lower social status. Affirmative action entails no such attitude or intent. Its purpose is to restore to persons a status they have been unjustifiably denied, to help them escape stigmatization, and to foster relationships of interconnectedness in society.[15]

Affirmative action in pockets of the most vicious and visceral racism will likely be needed for another generation, after which we should have reached our goals of fair opportunity and equal consideration. Once these goals are achieved, affirmative action will no longer be justified and should be abandoned. The goal to be reached at that point is not proportional representation, which has occasionally been used as a basis for fixing target numbers in affirmative action policies, but as such is merely a means to the end of discrimination, not an end to be pursued for its own sake. The goal is simply fair opportunity and equal consideration.

Voluntary Affirmative Action Plans

Many affirmative action policies are voluntary plans, and these plans have often been more successful than government-mandated policies.[16] Numerous American institutions have learned that discrimination causes the institution to lose opportunities to make contact with the full range of qualified persons who might be contacted. Their competitive position is thereby weakened, just as a state university would be weakened if it hired faculty entirely from its own state. These institutions have found that promoting diversity in the work-force is correlated with high-quality employees, reductions in the costs of discrimination claims, a lowering of absenteeism, less turnover, and increased customer satisfaction.[17]

If we were now to abolish these established forms of affirmative action hiring, we would open old wounds in many institutions that have been developing plans through consent decree processes with courts as well as direct negotiations with minority groups and unions. Many corporations report that they have invested heavily in eliminating managerial biases and stereotypes while training managers to hire appropriately. They are concerned that without the pressure of an affirmative action plan, which they draft internally, managers will fail to recognize their own biases and stereotypes.[18]

Tolerating Reverse Discrimination

It has often been said that reverse discrimination is caused by affirmative action policies and that this discrimination is no better than the racial or sexual discrimination that affirmative action allegedly frustrates.[19] Some instances of such discriminatory exclusion do occur, of course, and compensation or rectification for an injured party is sometimes the appropriate response. However, some of these setbacks to the interests of those excluded by a policy may be no more objectionable than various burdens produced by social policies that advantage some members of society and disadvantage others. Inheritance laws, for example, favor certain members of society over others, whereas policies of eminent domain disadvantage persons who wish to retain what is legitimately their property in order to advance the public good. Such laws and outcomes are warranted by a larger public benefit and by justice-based considerations that conflict with the interests of the disadvantaged parties. The point is that disadvantages to majorities produced by affirmative action may be warranted by the promotion of social ideals of equal treatment for groups that were severely mistreated in the past.

In assessing the disadvantages that might be caused to members of majorities (primarily white males), we should remember that there are disadvantages to other parties that operate in the current system, many of which will not be affected by affirmative action or by its absence. For example, just as young white males may now be paying a penalty for wrongs committed by older white males (who will likely never be penalized), so the older members of minority groups and older women who have been most disadvantaged in the past are the least likely to gain an advantage from affirmative action policies. Paradoxically, the younger minority members and women who have suffered least from discrimination now stand to gain the most from affirmative action. Despite these unfairnesses, there is no clear way to remedy them.

Policies of affirmative action may have many other shortcomings as well. For example, they confer economic advantages upon some who do not deserve them and generate court battles, jockeying for favored position by a multiple array of minorities, a lowering of admission and work standards in some institutions, heightened racial hostility, and continued suspicion that well-placed women and minority group members received their positions purely on the basis of quotas, thereby damaging their self-respect and the respect of their colleagues. Affirmative action is not a perfect social tool, but it is the best tool yet created as a way of preventing a recurrence of the far worse imperfections of our past policies of segregation and exclusion.

Judging the Past and the Present

Looking back at this deplorable history and at the unprecedented development of affirmative action policies over the past thirty years, what moral judgments can we reach about persons who either initiated these policies or those who failed to initiate such programs? Can we say that anyone has engaged in moral wrongdoing in implementing these policies, or exhibited moral failure in not implementing them? Addressing these questions should help us better judge the present in light of the past.

I will examine these questions through the classic AT&T affirmative action agreement in the 1970s. The salient facts of this case are as follows: The U.S. Equal Employment Opportunity Commission (EEOC) had investigated AT&T in the 1960s on grounds of alleged discriminatory practices in hiring and promotion. In 1970 the EEOC stated that the firm engaged in "pervasive, system-wide, and blatantly unlawful discrimination in employment against women, African-Americans, Spanish-surnamed Americans, and other minorities."[20] The EEOC argued that the employment practices of AT&T violated several civil rights laws and had excluded women from all job classifications except low-paying clerical and operator positions.

AT&T denied all charges and produced a massive array of statistics about women and minorities in the workforce. However, these statistics tended to undermine the corporation's own case. They showed that half the company's 700,000 employees were female, but that the women were all either secretaries or operators. It became apparent that the company categorized virtually all of its jobs in terms of men's work and women's work. The federal government was determined to obliterate this aspect of corporate culture in the belief that no other strategy would break the grip of this form of sexism. Eventually AT&T threw in the towel and entered a consent decree, which was accepted by a court in Philadelphia in 1973. This agreement resulted in payments of $15 million in back wages to 13,000 women and 2,000 minority-group men and $23 million in raises to 36,000 employees who had been harmed by previous policies.

Out of this settlement came a companywide "model affirmative action plan" that radically changed the character of AT&T hiring and its promotion practices. The company agreed to create an "employee profile" in its job classifications to be achieved faster than would normally occur. It established racial and gender goals and intermediate targets in fifteen job categories to be met in quarterly increments. The goals were determined by statistics regarding representative numbers of workers in the relevant labor market. The decree required that under conditions of a target failure, a less-qualified (but qualified) person could take precedence over a more-qualified person with greater seniority. This condition applied only to promotions, not to layoffs and rehiring, where seniority continued to prevail.

As was inevitable under this arrangement, reverse discrimination cases emerged. The well-known McAleer case came before Judge Gerhard A. Gesell, who held in 1976 that McAleer was a faultless employee who became an innocent victim through an unfortunate but justifiable use of the affirmative action process.[21] Gesell ruled that McAleer was entitled to monetary compensation (as damages), but not entitled to the promotion to which he thought he was entitled because the discrimination the consent decree had been designed to eliminate might be perpetuated if a qualified woman were not given the promotion.[22]

This AT&T case history, like many affirmative action cases, is a story of changed expectations and changing moral viewpoints. At the core of any framework for the evaluation of such cases is a distinction between *wrongdoing* and *culpability*, which derives from the need to evaluate the moral quality of actions by contrast to agents. For example, we might want to say that AT&T hiring practices were wrong and that many employees were wronged by them, without judging anyone culpable for the wrongs done.

Virtually everyone is now agreed, including AT&T officials, that AT&T's hiring and promotion practices did involve unjustified discrimination and serious wrongdoing. Even basic moral principles were violated—for example, that one ought to treat persons with equal consideration and respect, that racial and sexual discrimination are impermissible, and the like. Less clear is whether the agents involved should be blamed. Several factors place limits on our ability to make judgments about the blameworthiness of agents—or at least the fairness of doing so. These factors include culturally induced moral ignorance, a changing circumstance in the specification of moral principles, and indeterminacy in an organization's division of labor and designation of responsibility. All were present to some degree in the AT&T case.

Judgments of exculpation depend, at least to some extent, on whether proper moral standards were acknowledged in the culture in which the events transpired—for example, in the professional ethics of the period. If we had possessed clear standards regarding the justice of hiring and promotion in the 1950s and 1960s, it would be easier to find AT&T officials culpable. The absence of such standards is a factor in our reflections about culpability and exculpation, but need not be part of our reflection on the wronging that occurred.

The fact of culturally induced moral ignorance does not by itself entail exculpation or a lack of accountability for states of ignorance. The issue is the degree to which persons are accountable for holding and even perpetuating or disseminating the beliefs that they hold when an opportunity to remedy or modify the beliefs exists. If such opportunities are unavailable, a person may have a valid excuse; but the greater the opportunity to eliminate ignorance, the less is exculpation appropriate. Persons who permit their culturally induced moral ignorance to persist through a series of opportunities to correct the beliefs thereby increase their culpability.

The more persons are obstinate in not facing issues, and the more they fail to perceive the plight of other persons who may be negatively affected by their failure to act, the more likely are we to find their actions or inactions inexcusable. No doubt culturally induced moral ignorance was a mitigating factor in the 1960s and early 1970s, but I believe history also shows that it was mixed with a resolute failure to face moral problems when it was widely appreciated that they were serious problems and were being faced by other institutions.

The central issue for my purposes is not whether discriminatory attitudes should be judged harshly in the pre–affirmative action situation at AT&T, but whether the affirmative action policy that was adopted itself involved wrongdoing or constituted, then or now, an activity for which we would blame persons who establish such policies. I do not see how agents could be blamed for maintaining and enforcing this program, despite its toughness. Given AT&T's history as well as the desperate situation of discrimination in American society, under what conditions could agents be culpable even if McAleer-type cases of reverse discrimination occasionally resulted? Even if we assume that McAleer and others were wronged in the implementation of the policy, it does not follow that the agents were culpable for their support of the policy.

Today, many corporate programs similar to the AT&T policy are in place. We can and should ask both whether persons are wronged by these policies and whether those who use the policies are culpable. The answer seems to me the same in the 1990s as it was in the 1970s: As long as there is persistent, intractable discrimination in society, the policies will be justified and the agents nonculpable, even if some persons are harmed and even wronged by the policies. To say that we should right wrongs done by the policies is not to say that we should abandon the policies themselves.

Indeed, I defend a stronger view: Affirmative action was a noble struggle against a crippling social ill in the 1960s and 1970s, and those who took part in the struggle deserve acknowledgment for their courage and foresight. Those who failed to seize the opportunity to enact affirmative action policies or some functional equivalent such as companywide enforcement of equal opportunity are culpable for what, in many cases, were truly serious moral failures.

There is no reason to believe that, in this respect, the situation is changed today from the 1970s. Today persons in corporations, universities, and government agencies who are aware or should be aware that a high level of racism or sexism exists are culpable if they fail to move to counteract its invidious effects by affirmative policies or similarly serious interventions such as meaningful enforcement of fair opportunity. To say that we should judge the officers of these institutions culpable for their moral failures is not to say that there are no mitigating conditions for their failures, such as the mixed messages they have received over the past fifteen years from federal officials and the general cultural climate of moral indifference to the problem. At the same time, the mitigating conditions are weaker today than in the 1970s because the excuse of culturally induced moral ignorance is weaker. In general, there are now fewer excuses available for not taking an aggressive posture to combat discrimination than ever before.

All of this is not to say that we are never culpable for the way we formulate or implement affirmative action policies. One aspect of these policies for which we likely will be harshly judged in the future is a failure of truthfulness in publicly disclosing and advertising the commitments of the policies—for example, in advertising for new positions.[23] Once it has been determined that a woman or a minority group member will most likely be hired, institutions now typically place advertisements that include lines such as the following:

> Women and minority-group candidates are especially encouraged to apply. The University of X is an equal opportunity, affirmative action employer.

Advertisements and public statements rarely contain more information about an institution's affirmative action objectives, although often more information might be disclosed that would be of material relevance to applicants. The following are examples of facts or objectives that might be disclosed: A department may have reserved its position for a woman or minority; the chances may be overwhelming that only a minority group member will be hired; the interview team may have decided in advance that only women will be interviewed; the advertised position may be the result of a university policy that offers an explicit incentive (perhaps a new position) to a department if a minority representative is appointed, etc. Incompleteness in disclosure and advertising sometimes stems from fear of legal liability, but more often from fear of departmental embarrassment and harm either to reputation or to future recruiting efforts.

The greater moral embarrassment, however, is our ambivalence and weak conceptions of what we are doing. Many, including academics, fear making public what they believe to be morally commendable in their recruiting efforts. There is something deeply unsatisfactory about a reluctance to disclose one's real position. This situation is striking, because the justification for the position is presumably that it is a morally praiseworthy endeavor. Here we have a circumstance in which the actions taken may not be wrong, but the agents are culpable for a failure to clearly articulate the basis of their actions and to allow those bases to be openly debated so that their true merits can be assessed by all affected parties.

Conclusion

During the course of the last thirty years, the widespread acceptance of racial segregation and sexual dominance in America has surrendered to a more polite culture that accepts racial integration and sexual equality. This discernible change of attitude and institutional policy has led to an imposing public opposition to preferential treatment on the basis of race and sex in general. In this climate what should happen to affirmative action?

As long as our choices are formulated in terms of the false dilemma of either special preference for groups or individual merit, affirmative action is virtually certain to be overthrown. Americans are now wary and weary of all forms of group preference, other than the liberty to choose one's preferred groups. I would be pleased to witness the defeat of affirmative action were the choice the simple one of group preference or individual merit. But it is not. Despite the vast changes of attitude in thirty years of American culture, the underlying realities are naggingly familiar. Perhaps in another thirty years we can rid ourselves of the perils of affirmative action. But at present the public good and our sense of ourselves as a nation will be well served by retaining what would in other circumstances be odious policies. They merit preservation as long as we can say that, on balance, they serve us better than they disserve us.

Notes

1. Executive Order 11246. C.F.R. 339 (1964–65).
2. See J. Angelo Corlett, "Racism and Affirmative Action," *Journal of Social Philosophy* 24 (1993): 163–75; and Cass R. Sunstein, "The Limits of Compensatory Justice," *Nomos XXXIII: Compensatory Justice,* ed. John Chapman (New York: New York University Press, 1991): 281–310.
3. See Thomas Nagel, "A Defense of Affirmative Action," testimony before the Subcommittee on the Constitution of the Senate Judiciary Committee, June 18, 1981; and Louis Pojman, "The Moral Status of Affirmative Action," *Public Affairs Quarterly* 6 (1992): 181–206.
4. See the analyses in Gertrude Ezorsky, *Racism and Justice* (Ithaca, NY: Cornell University Press, 1991); and Robert Fullinwider, *The Reverse Discrimination Controversy* (Totowa, NJ: Rowman and Allanheld, 1980).
5. Bob Woodward, *The Commanders* (New York: Simon and Schuster, 1991), p. 72.
6. Bron Taylor, *Affirmative Action at Work: Law, Politics, and Ethics* (Pittsburgh: University of Pittsburgh Press, 1991); Morley Gunderson, "Male-Female Wage Differentials and Policy Responses," *Journal of Economic Literature* 27 (March 1989), and Morley Gunderson, "Pay and Employment Equity in the United States and Canada," *International Journal of Manpower* 15 (1994): 26–43; Patricia Gaynor and Garey Durden, "Measuring the Extent of Earnings Discrimination: An Update," *Applied Economics* 27 (August 1995): 669–76; Marjorie L. Baldwin and William G. Johnson, "The Employment Effects of Wage Discrimination Against Black Men," *Industrial & Labor Relations Review* 49 (1996): 302–16; Franklin D. Wilson, Marta Tienda, and Lawrence Wu, "Race and Unemployment: Labor Market Experiences of Black and White Men, 1968–1988," *Work & Occupations* 22 (1995): 245–70; National Center for Education Statistics, *Faculty in Higher Education Institutions, 1988, Contractor Survey Report,* compiled by Susan H. Russell et al. (Washington, DC: U.S. Dept. of Education, March 1990), pp. 5–13; Betty M. Vetter, ed., *Professional Women and Minorities: A Manpower Data Resource Service,* 8th ed. (Washington, DC: Commission on Science and Technology, 1989); (anonymous) "Less Discrimination for Women but Poorer Prospects at Work than Men," *Management Services* 40 (1996): 6; Cynthia D. Anderson and Donald Tomaskovic-Devey, "Patriarchal Pressures: An Exploration of Organizational Processes that Exacerbate and Erode Gender Earnings Inequality," *Work & Occupations* 22 (1995): 328–56; Thomas J. Bergman and G. E. Martin, "Tests for Compliance with Phased Plans to Equalize Discriminate Wages," *Journal of Applied Business Research* 11 (1994/1995): 136–43.
7. Brent W. Ambrose, William T. Hughes, Jr., and Patrick Simmons, "Policy Issues Concerning Racial and Ethnic Differences in Home Loan Rejection Rates," *Journal of Housing Research* 6 (1995): 115–35; Gerald D. Jaynes and Robin M. Williams, Jr., eds., *A Common Destiny: Blacks and American Society,* Committee on the Status of Black Americans, Commission on Behavioral and Social Sciences and Education, National Research Council (Washington, DC: NAS Press, 1989), pp. 12–13, 138–48; Sunwoong Kim, Gregory D. Squires, "Lender Characteristics and Racial Disparities in Mortgage Lending," *Journal of Housing Research* 6 (1995): 99–113; Glenn B. Canner and Wayne Passmore, "Home Purchase Lending in Low-Income Neighborhoods and to Low-Income Borrowers," *Federal Reserve Bulletin* 81 (February 1995): 71–103; Constance L. Hays, "Study Says Prejudice in Suburbs Is Aimed Mostly at Blacks," *New York Times,* November 23, 1988, p. A16; John R. Walter, "The Fair Lending Laws and Their Enforcement," *Economic Quarterly* 81 (fall 1995): 61–77; Stanley D. Longhofer, "Discrimination in Mortgage Lending: What Have We Learned?" *Economic Commentary* [Federal Reserve Bank of Cleveland], August 15, 1996: 1–4.

8. As reported by Rudolf A. Pyatt, Jr., "Significant Job Studies," *Washington Post*, April 30, 1985, pp. D1–D2. See also Paul Burstein, *Discrimination, Jobs, and Politics* (Chicago: University of Chicago Press, 1985); Bureau of Labor Statistics, *Employment and Earnings* (Washington, DC: U.S. Dept. of Labor, Jan. 1989); Jaynes and Williams, *A Common Destiny*, pp. 16–18, 84–88.

9. See Margery Austin Turner, Michael Fix, and Raymond Struyk, *Opportunities Denied, Opportunities Diminished: Discrimination in Hiring* (Washington, DC: Urban Institute, 1991).

10. See Laura Purdy, "Why Do We Need Affirmative Action?" *Journal of Social Philosophy* 25 (1994): 133–43; Farrell Bloch, *Antidiscrimination Law and Minority Employment: Recruitment Practices and Regulatory Constraints* (Chicago: University of Chicago Press, 1994); Joseph Sartorelli, "Gay Rights and Affirmative Action" in *Gay Ethics*, ed. Timothy F. Murphy (New York: Haworth Press, 1994); Taylor, *Affirmative Action at Work*.

11. *Fullilove v. Klutznick*, 448 U.S. 448 (1980); *United Steelworkers v. Weber*, 443 U.S. 193 (1979); *United States v. Paradise*, 480 U.S. 149 (1987); *Johnson v. Transportation Agency*, 480 U.S. 616 (1987); *Alexander v. Choate*, 469 U.S. 287, at 295.

12. *Firefighters v. Stotts*, 467 U.S. 561 (1984); *City of Richmond v. J. A. Croson Co.*, 109 S.Ct. 706 (1989); *Adarand Constructors Inc. v. Federico Pena*, 63 LW 4523 (1995); *Wygant v. Jackson Board of Education*, 476 U.S. 267 (1986); *Wards Cove Packing v. Atonio*, 490 U.S. 642.

13. In 1964 the New York Commission for Human Rights investigated the union and concluded that it excluded nonwhites through an impenetrable barrier of hiring by discriminatory selection. The state Supreme Court concurred and issued a "cease and desist" order. The union ignored it. Eventually, in a 1975 trial, the U.S. District Court found a record "replete with instances of bad faith" and ordered a "remedial racial goal of 29% nonwhite membership" (based on the percentage of nonwhites in the local labor pool). Another court then found that the union had "consistently and egregiously violated" the law of the land (Title 7, in particular). In 1982 and 1983 court fines and civil contempt proceedings were issued. In the early 1980s virtually nothing had been done to modify the discriminatory hiring practices after 22 years of struggle.

14. For a very different view, stressing inconsistency, see Yong S. Lee, "Affirmative Action and Judicial Standards of Review: A Search for the Elusive Consensus," *Review of Public Personnel Administration* 12 (1991): 47–69.

15. See Robert Ladenson, "Ethics in the American Workplace," *Business and Professional Ethics Journal* 14 (1995): 17–31; Gertrude Ezorsky, *Racism and Justice: The Case for Affirmative Action*; Thomas E. Hill, Jr., "The Message of Affirmative Action," *Social Philosophy and Policy* 8 (1991): 108–29; Jorge L. Garcia, "The Heart of Racism," *Journal of Social Philosophy* 27 (1996): 5–46.

16. For an interesting example in academia, see Penni Stewart and Janice Drakich, "Factors Related to Organizational Change and Equity for Women Faculty in Ontario Universities," *Canadian Public Policy* 21 (1995): 429–48.

17. Jerry T. Ferguson and Wallace R. Johnston, "Managing Diversity," *Mortgage Banking* 55 (1995): 32–36L; Joseph Semien, "Opening the Utility Door for Women and Minorities," *Public Utilities Fortnightly*, July 5, 1990, pp. 29–31; Walter Kiechel, "Living with Human Resources," *Fortune*, August 18, 1986, esp. p. 100; Irene Pave, "A Woman's Place Is at GE, Federal Express, P&G . . . " *Business Week*, June 23, 1986, p. 76; Peter Perl, "Rulings Provide Hiring Direction: Employers Welcome Move," *Washington Post*, July 3, 1986, pp. A1, A11.

18. See Jeanne C. Poole and E. Theodore Kautz, "An EEO/AA Program that Exceeds Quotas—It Targets Biases," *Personnel Journal* 66 (January 1987), pp. 103–105; Mary

Thornton, "Justice Dept. Stance on Hiring Goals Resisted," *Washington Post*, May 25, 1985, p. A2; Pyatt, "The Basis of Job Bias," p. D2; Linda Williams, "Minorities Find Pacts with Corporations Are Hard to Come By and Enforce," *Wall Street Journal*, August 23, 1985, p. 13.

19. See Robert Fullinwider, *The Reverse Discrimination Controversy*; Nicholas Capaldi, *Out of Order* (Buffalo, NY: Prometheus Books, 1985); F. R. Lynch, *Invisible Victims: White Males and the Crisis of Affirmative Action* (Westport, CT: Greenwood Press, 1989); Barry R. Gross, ed., *Reverse Discrimination* (Buffalo, NY: Prometheus Books, 1977).

20. U.S. Equal Employment Opportunity Commission, "Petition to Intervene," Federal Communications Commission Hearings on AT& T Revised Tariff Schedule, December 10, 1970, p. 1.

21. *McAleer v. American Telephone and Telegraph Company*, 416 F. Supp. 435 (1976); "AT&T Denies Job Discrimination Charges, Claims Firm Is Equal Employment Leader," *Wall Street Journal*, December 14, 1970, p. 6; Richard M. Hodgetts, "AT& T versus the Equal Employment Opportunity Commission," in *The Business Enterprise: Social Challenge, Social Response* (Philadelphia: W. B. Saunders, 1977), pp. 176–82.

22. According to a representative of the legal staff in AT&T's Washington, DC, office (phone conversation on March 10, 1982).

23. See Steven M. Cahn, "Colleges Should Be Explicit about Who Will Be Considered for Jobs," *Chronicle of Higher Education*, April 5, 1989, p. B3.

Reverse Discrimination

Sidney Hook

The phrase *reverse discrimination* has come into recent English usage in consequence of efforts to eliminate the unjust discrimination against human beings
on the basis of race, color, sex, religion, or national origin. The conscience of
the American community has caught up with the immoral practices of its past
history. The Civil Rights Act of 1964 and the presidential executive orders
which it inspired have made the absence of open or hidden discrimination of
the kind described a required condition of government contracts. An equal
opportunity employer is one who pledges himself to a program of affirmative
action in order to ensure that the invidious discriminations of the past are not
perpetuated in masked or subtle form.

An appropriate affirmative action program requires that an intensive and
extensive recruitment search be undertaken in good faith, sometimes supplemented by remedial educational measures, in order to equalize opportunities
for employment or study. Such programs presuppose that once the recruitment
search is over, once the remedial training is completed, the actual selection of
the candidates for the post will be determined by one set of equitable standards
applied to all. If the standards or tests are not equitable, if they are not related
to or relevant to the actual posts that are to be filled, then the standards or tests
must be modified until they are deemed satisfactory. In no case must a double
standard be employed which enables one group to benefit at the expense of any
other. Customarily this adhesion to one set of standards designed to test merit

Reprinted from *Philosophy and Public Policy* (Carbondale and Edwardsville: Southern
Illinois University Press, 1980).

or to determine who of all contending candidates is the best qualified for the post has been known as the civil service principle. It is the only way by which incompetence, corruption, and invidious discrimination can be eliminated. Preferential hiring on the basis of sex, race, color, religion, or national origin clearly violates the civil service principle and the programs of affirmative action that seek to enlarge the areas of equal opportunity.

Why, then, is the demand made for reverse discrimination under various semantic disguises? If all invidious or unfair discrimination is wrong, how can reverse discrimination be justified? The answer sometimes made is that reverse discrimination is not unfair, for it seeks to undo the injustice of the past and the effects of that injustice in the present, by compensating the victims of past injustice at the expense of those responsible for their plight. Were this the case with respect to any particular individual who has suffered from discriminatory practice there would be no moral objection to compensating him or her for the loss and depriving or punishing those responsible for the past act of discrimination. This would be a simple matter of justice, redressing the grievance of the past, and in no sense an act of discrimination—direct or reverse.

It is an altogether different situation, however, when we discriminate against members of any group today in favor of members of another group, not because the individuals of the first group have been guilty of past or present oppression or discrimination against members of the second group, but because the ancestors of the latter have been victimized in previous times. Yet this is precisely what is being done today when preferential hiring practices on the basis of race or sex are followed or when numerical goals or quotas are used as guidelines instead of criteria of merit or qualification.

All such practices which stem from the distortions or misreading of the Civil Rights Act of 1964 and the presidential executive orders are attempts to undo the injustices of the past against members of minority groups and women by perpetrating injustices against members of nonminority groups and men in the present. Can such practices be defended on moral grounds? Let us consider a few historic cases to get our moral bearings:

It is commonly acknowledged that the Chinese laborers who were employed during the last century in building the transcontinental railroad were abominably treated, underpaid, overworked, wretchedly housed, and subjected to all sorts of humiliating discriminations. Is anyone prepared to argue that their descendants today or other Chinese should therefore be paid more than non-Chinese or given preference over non-Chinese with respect to employment regardless of merit or specific qualifications?

Until the Nineteenth Amendment of the U.S. Constitution was adopted in 1920, American women, who were citizens of the country and subject to all its laws, were denied the right to vote. Would it be reasonable to contend that women should have been compensated for past discrimination against their maternal forebears by being given an extra vote or two at the expense of their male fellow citizens? Would it have been just to deprive the male descendants of prejudiced white men of the past of their vote in order to even the score?

Take a more relevant case. For many years blacks were shamelessly and unfairly barred from professional sports until Jackie Robinson broke the color bar. Would it not be manifestly absurd to urge therefore today that in compensation for the long history of deprivation of blacks there should be discrimination against whites in professional athletics? Would any sensible or fair person try to determine what the proportion of whites and blacks should be on our basketball or football or baseball teams in relation to racial availability or utilizability? What could be fairer than the quest for the best players for the open positions regardless of the percentage distribution in relation to the general population or the pool of candidates trying out? What would be the relevance of numerical goals or quotas here? Why should it be any different in any situation in which we are looking for the best-qualified person to fill a post? If we oppose, as we should, all invidious discrimination, why not drop all color, sex, religious, and national bars in an honest quest for the best qualified—regardless of what the numerical distribution turns out to be. Of course, the quest must be public and not only be fair but must be seen to be fair.

Whenever we judge a person primarily on the basis of membership in a group, except where membership in a group bears on the task to be performed (soprano voices, wet nurses, clergymen of the same denomination), an injustice is done to individuals. This is the point of my final illustration. When I graduated from the City College of New York in the early 1920s, many of my classmates who had taken the premedical course applied to American medical schools. Most of them were rejected because at the time a thinly disguised quota system existed limiting the number of Jewish applicants. This was a great blow to those affected. A few went abroad. Some entered the Post Office system and prepared for other vocations. Now consider the position of their grandchildren who apply to medical schools that have admission practices based on numerical goals or quotas designed to counteract the discriminatory practices of the past against women and minorities. These candidates do not request preferential treatment but only that they be evaluated by equitable standards applicable to all. Is it fair to them to select those who are less qualified under professionally relevant standards? Can they or their forebears be taxed with responsibility for the unjust discriminatory practices of the past which victimized them as well as others? And cannot students of Italian, Polish, Slovak, Armenian, Irish, and Ukrainian origin ask the same questions?

There are certain questionable assumptions in the rationale behind the practices of reverse discrimination. The first is that preferential hiring (or promotion) on the basis of race or sex to correct past bias is like school desegregation rulings to correct the admittedly immoral segregation practices of the past. This overlooks the key difference. In correcting the immorality of past segregation we are not discriminating *against* white students. They are not being injured or deprived of anything by the color of their classmates' skin. All students may profit in virtue of desegregation. But the situation with respect to the allocation of jobs is different. If X and Y are competing for a post, my decision to hire X is in the nature of the case a decision not to hire Y. And if my decision is based on X's sex or race, and not on merit, then it is a case of racial or sexual discrimination *against* Y, which is morally wrong. All invidious discrimination *in favor* of anyone is invidious discrimination *against* someone else.

A second assumption is that one can tell by statistical distribution alone whether objectionable discrimination exists that calls for corrective action. This is absurd on its face. Unless there is specific evidence of individual discrimination, at most only a suspicion of discrimination can be drawn warranting further inquiry. Only when we are dealing with random selection where no criteria of merit are involved, as in jury rolls or in registration procedures or voting behavior, are statistical disproportions at variance with population distribution prima facie evidence of bias in the process of selection. My favorite example of nondiscriminatory statistical disproportion is that in the past the overwhelming majority of the captains of the tugboats in New York Harbor were of Swedish origin but this constituted no evidence of the presence of anti-Semitism or prejudice against blacks. The disproportion of black teachers in black college faculties is certainly not evidence of a policy of discrimination against whites.

A third related assumption is a particularly mischievous one. It holds that where there is no overt or covert discrimination, and equal opportunities are offered, the various minorities within the community will be represented in all disciplines, professions, and areas of work in roughly numerical proportionality to their distribution in the total pool of the population or in the community pool or in the pool of the potentially utilizable. There is not a shred of evidence for this assumption. Human beings do not constitute a homogenized mass in which interests, ambitions, historical and social traditions are equally shared. Potentially all groups may be capable of acquiring or developing any cultural interest just as at birth any normal child is equipped with the capacity to speak any language. But in actual practice family, national, regional traditions, and allegiances as well as the accidents of history incline some groups toward some occupational activities rather than others even where there are no legal obstacles to the pursuit of any. For historical reasons, Polish immigrants and their descendants did not go into sheepherding or fishing while Basques and Portuguese did. Whenever anyone maintains, in the absence of discriminatory practices, that minority persons or women are "underrepresented" or "underutilized," the assumption is unconsciously being made that there is a "natural" or "proper" or "correct" norm or level of their representation. Who determines what is the "natural" representation of women among firefighters, of Irish among policemen and politicans, of Italians among opera singers, of blacks among actors, of Jews among pants pressers, diamond cutters, and mathematical physicists? In time there will undoubtedly be *some* representation from all groups in all fields but only political absolutisms will impose fixed quotas.

A fourth assumption is that with respect to minorities and women, even if all present forms of discrimination against them were completely eliminated, this would still not enable them to compete on an equal basis with others because of the continuing debilitating effects of past generations of discrimination against them. It is sometimes said in emphasizing this point, "If you handicap a runner at the outset by burdening him with heavy weights and let him run half the race, you cannot make it a fair race by removing the weights when the race has been half run. He will still suffer unfairly from the effects of that handicap." This is perfectly true for that individual runner in that race and possibly in other races he engages in. He is certainly entitled to special consideration to overcome his handicap on the same principle that any specific individual who has been discriminated against in the past is entitled to compensatory treatment. But surely this does not entitle a descendant of this person who is running against others in a subsequent race to a privilege or handicap over them. Who knows but that the ancestors of the others were also handicapped in past races?

This entire analogy breaks down because it really assumes the inheritance of acquired characteristics. Women in Elizabethan times were barred from acting in the theater and from certain industrial pursuits in the nineteenth century. Did this have a continuing debilitating effect upon their capacities in the twentieth century? If past discrimination has a continuing debilitating effect, how can we explain the tens of thousands of cases of members of minorities who have made good in their professions and vocations without benefit of preferential treatment or reverse discrimination?

Another conscience-appeasing justification for the manifestly immoral violations of the principle of equal treatment under just law is the claim that measures adopted to implement reverse discrimination are "merely temporary" or "transitional," until such time as the necessity for them disappears, and race and sex can be disregarded in hiring and promotion practices. This is the position, among others, of the American Civil Liberties Union. It is obviously question-begging. When will the necessity for reverse discrimination disappear? When all minorities and women are represented in all avenues of work in proportion to their numbers in the populations? The American Civil Liberties Union would be outraged at the proposal "to suspend temporarily" a person's right to a fair trial until the crime wave subsides. Why should any morally principled clear-headed opponent of all forms of discrimination temporarily suspend the protection of equal rights under the law?

We know from other situations that nothing is so permanent as the temporary, especially when vested interest develops in its perpetuation. Once numerical goals or quotas are introduced as "temporary expedients" to overcome the alleged discriminations of the past, psychologically any subsequent effort to abandon or even to modify the goals or quotas is likely to be interpreted as a rebirth of invidious discrimination. On the other hand, the mandatory application of goals or quotas in the hiring and promotion of members of minorities and women is certain to generate resentment among members of nonminorities and men who will regard racial and sexual criteria of appointment as arbitrary, motivated by political considerations for which they pay the costs. They will visit this resentment even on those minority persons and women who have obtained advancement purely on the basis of their own merit. The collegiality among workers will be shattered, and existing racial and sexual antagonisms that may abate in time when fair standards of merit are strictly enforced will instead be intensified.

Another dubious assumption is that once careers are truly opened to talents, members of minorities and women will never make it on their own without the crutch of reverse discrimination in their favor. This either gratuitously takes for granted that the practices of invidious discrimination of the past will continue, despite the laws against them, or it is an expression of racism and sexism. The absence of members of minorities and women in many areas today is not a consequence of their failure to perform satisfactorily in them but to social attitudes, stereotyped expectations of what roles men and women are fit for, which happily are now changing but which in the past discouraged them from trying out. There is no cogent reason to doubt that just as members of ethnic immigrant groups who suffered from the prejudiced judgments of native Americans have overcome the obstacles thrown up in their path, so the blacks and Chicanos will in time also succeed. The main reason why today larger numbers of these minorities are not found in the professions and specialized academic pursuits is not invidious discrimination against them but rather the absence of qualified applicants in consequence of educational and economic disadvantages. Here is where vigorous remedial action must be undertaken not only by public agencies but by private organizations along the lines of the Reverend Jesse Jackson's "Push Towards Excellence."

Special educational measures must be adopted to improve the quality of schooling on the elementary and secondary school levels and to encourage career choices oriented toward professional and academic life. It cannot be too strongly emphasized that despite the social disadvantages from which minority groups suffer, and which the community as a whole has the responsibility to mitigate and ultimately remove, the minorities themselves are not merely passive recipients of what befalls them, helpless wards of the state whose future is shaped by what others decide for them. They can do, and often have done, much to reshape the educational opportunities, to rekindle the pride and strengthen the drive to succeed in a world that requires more skills and more knowledge, and more schooling to acquire them, than in the past. Studies of the adjustments of immigrant groups to the hardships and environmental deprivation they initially encountered have shown that the family atmosphere, the presence or absence of strong parental guidance, has been more decisive in determining the willingness to avail oneself of educational opportunities than the legislative action itself that prolonged the age of mandatory schooling.

Our educational system must be geared not only to meet the educational needs of the superior students but of ordinary students and even of those who are not scholastically gifted. A vast range of talents is found among all peoples and races. The focus must be on each individual student, regardless of sex or color, in order to determine what his or her educational needs are. Provision must be made therefore for various types of educational institutions, beyond the elementary and secondary level, for students of varying capacities and interests, and for continuing adult education in the liberal and vocational arts to accommodate both personal development and social change. There is a uniqueness about every student which the spirit and practice of a democratic education must respect. This respect is perfectly compatible with the application of a single and relevant standard of achievement or reward for all in any given institution, according to which some pass and some fail. We may and should guarantee the basic needs of food, shelter, health, and education of all citizens but we cannot guarantee anyone against educational failure. Further, everyone in a democratic welfare society such as ours has a right to employment (or to some kind of unemployment insurance) but no one regardless of merit and experience can claim a right to any specific job.

It is apparent that this analysis is based on the belief that it is the individual person who is the carrier of human rights and not the ethnic, national, sexual, or racial group. Once we disregard this universalistic approach which is blind to color, deaf to religious dogma, indifferent to national origin or sex where merit should count, we practically ensure the presence of endemic conflicts in which invidious discriminations are rife. This has been the sad story of the past which we are or should be trying to get away from. Some progress has been made and much more is possible. Reverse discrimination, however, threatens that progress. It increases the existing tensions among different groups and converts our pluralistic society into a more polarized society. The evidence that this is already happening is at hand whenever the admirable, original purposes of affirmative action programs have been misconstrued by arbitrary bureaucratic fiat, and guidelines promulgated that mandate numerical goals or quotas.

Successive polls have shown that the overwhelming majority of the population has endorsed equality of opportunity but at the same time has strongly disapproved of numerical goals, quotas, or preferential hiring. A majority may be wrong but with respect to the theory and practice of reverse discrimination, the logic and ethics of the argument support the condemnation. The reasons that lead us morally to disapprove of discrimination in the past are the same as those that justify disapproval of reverse discrimination in the present and future.

About the Authors

Steven M. Cahn is Professor of Philosophy at the Graduate Center of the City University of New York.

James W. Nickel is Professor of Philosophy at the University of Colorado.

J. L. Cowan is Professor Emeritus of Philosophy at the University of Arizona.

Michael D. Bayles (1941–1990) was Professor of Philosophy at Florida State University.

Paul W. Taylor is Professor Emeritus of Philosophy at Brooklyn College of the City University of New York.

William A. Nunn III practices law in Virginia.

Alan H. Goldman is Professor of Philosophy at the University of Miami.

Paul Woodruff is Professor of Philosophy at the University of Texas at Austin.

Judith Jarvis Thomson is Professor of Philosophy at the Massachusetts Institute of Technology.

Robert Simon is Professor of Philosophy at Hamilton College.

George Sher is Professor of Philosophy at Rice University.

Robert K. Fullinwider is Senior Research Scholar at the Institute for Philosophy and Public Policy at the University of Maryland, College Park.

Robert Amdur is Adjunct Assistant Professor of Political Science at Columbia University.

Carl Cohen is Professor of Philosophy at the University of Michigan at Ann Arbor.

Ronald Dworkin is University Professor of Jurisprudence at Oxford University and Professor of Law at New York University.

Barbara R. Bergmann is Professor Emerita of Economics at American University.

Anita L. Allen is Professor of Law at Georgetown University.

Celia Wolf-Devine is Associate Professor of Philosophy at Stonehill College.

William G. Bowen is President of the Andrew W. Mellon Foundation and former president of Princeton University.

Derek Bok is Professor at the John F. Kennedy School of Government and former president of Harvard University.

Stephan Thernstrom is Professor of History at Harvard University.

Abigail Thernstrom is Senior Fellow at Manhattan Institute and a member of the Massachusetts State Board of Education.

Tom L. Beauchamp is Professor of Philosophy at Georgetown University.

Sidney Hook (1902–1989) was Professor of Philosophy at New York University.

Bibliographical Note

In several cases, authors whose essays are reprinted in this volume subsequently published more fully developed statements of their positions. For James W. Nickel, see "Preferential Policies in Hiring and Admissions: A Jurisprudential Approach," *Columbia Law Review* 75[3] (1975). For Alan H. Goldman, see *Justice and Reverse Discrimination* (Princeton, NJ: Princeton University Press, 1979). For George Sher, see "Preferential Hiring" in *Just Business: Essays in Business Ethics*, ed. Tom Regan (New York: Random House, 1984). For Robert K. Fullinwider, see *The Reverse Discrimination Controversy: A Moral and Legal Analysis* (Totowa, NJ: Rowman and Allenheld, 1980). For Carl Cohen, See *Naked Racial Preference: The Case against Affirmative Action* (Lanham, MD: Madison Books, 1995). For Celia Wolf-Devine, see *Diversity and Community in the Academy: Affirmative Action in Faculty Appointments* (Lanham, MD: Rowman and Littlefield, 1997). For the editor, Steven M. Cahn, see "Two Concepts of Affirmative Action," *Academe* 83 (1997).